IARIA

DATA ANALYTICS 2022

The Eleventh International Conference on Data Analytics

November 13 - 17, 2022

Valencia, Spain

DATA ANALYTICS 2022 Editors

Ivana Semanjski, Ghent University, Belgium

Printed from e-media with permission by:

Curran Associates, Inc.
57 Morehouse Lane
Red Hook, NY 12571

Some format issues inherent in the e-media version may also appear in this print version.

Printed with permission by Curran Associates, Inc. (2023)

International Academy, Research, and Industry Association (IARIA)
412 Derby Way
Wilmington, DE 19810

Phone: (408) 893-6407
Fax: (408) 527-6351

petre@iaria.org

Additional copies of this publication are available from:

Curran Associates, Inc.
57 Morehouse Lane
Red Hook, NY 12571 USA
Phone: 845-758-0400
Fax: 845-758-2633
Email: curran@proceedings.com
Web: www.proceedings.com

Table of Contents

DATA ANALYTICS 2022

Forward

The Eleventh International Conference on Data Analytics (DATA ANALYTICS 2022), held between November 13 and November 17, 2022, continued the series on fundamentals in supporting data analytics, special mechanisms and features of applying principles of data analytics, application-oriented analytics, and target-area analytics.

Processing of terabytes to petabytes of data, or incorporating non-structural data and multi-structured data sources and types require advanced analytics and data science mechanisms for both raw and partially-processed information. Despite considerable advancements on high performance, large storage, and high computation power, there are challenges in identifying, clustering, classifying, and interpreting of a large spectrum of information.

The conference had the following tracks:

- Application-oriented analytics
- Big Data
- Sentiment/opinion analysis
- Data Analytics in Profiling and Service Design
- Fundamentals
- Mechanisms and features
- Predictive Data Analytics
- Transport and Traffic Analytics in Smart Cities

We take here the opportunity to warmly thank all the members of the DATA ANALYTICS 2022 technical program committee, as well as all the reviewers. The creation of such a high quality conference program would not have been possible without their involvement. We also kindly thank all the authors that dedicated much of their time and effort to contribute to DATA ANALYTICS 2022. We truly believe that, thanks to all these efforts, the final conference program consisted of top quality contributions.

We also gratefully thank the members of the DATA ANALYTICS 2022 organizing committee for their help in handling the logistics and for their work that made this professional meeting a success.

We hope that DATA ANALYTICS 2022 was a successful international forum for the exchange of ideas and results between academia and industry and to promote further progress in the field of data analytics. We hope that Valencia provided a pleasant environment during the conference and everyone saved some time to enjoy the charm of the city.

DATA ANALYTICS 2022 Steering Committee

Sandjai Bhulai, Vrije Universiteit Amsterdam, the Netherlands
Ivana Semanjski, Ghent University, Belgium
Les Sztandera, Thomas Jefferson University, USA
Kerstin Lemke-Rust, Hochschule Bonn-Rhein-Sieg, Germany
Wolfram Wöß, Institute for Application Oriented Knowledge Processing | Johannes Kepler University,

Linz, Austria
George Tambouratzis, Institute for Language and Speech Processing, Athena R.C., Greece

DATA ANALYTICS 2022 Publicity Chair

Mar Parra, Universitat Politecnica de Valencia, Spain
Sandra Viciano Tudela, Universitat Politecnica de Valencia, Spain

DATA ANALYTICS 2022

COMMITTEE

DATA ANALYTICS 2022 Steering Committee

Wolfram Wöß, Institute for Application Oriented Knowledge Processing | Johannes Kepler University, Linz, Austria
George Tambouratzis, Institute for Language and Speech Processing, Athena R.C., Greece
Ivana Semanjski, Ghent University, Belgium
Kerstin Lemke-Rust, Hochschule Bonn-Rhein-Sieg, Germany
Les Sztandera, Thomas Jefferson University, USA
Sandjai Bhulai, Vrije Universiteit Amsterdam, The Netherlands

DATA ANALYTICS 2022 Publicity Chair

Mar Parra, Universitat Politecnica de Valencia, Spain
Sandra Viciano Tudela, Universitat Politecnica de Valencia, Spain

DATA ANALYTICS 2022 Technical Program Committee

Arianna Agosto, University of Pavia, Italy
Irfan Ahmed, Virginia Commonwealth University, USA
Raed Ibrahim Alharbi, University of Florida, USA
Madyan Alsenwi, Kyung Hee University, Global Campus, South Korea
Katie Antypas, Lawrence Berkeley National Laboratory, USA
Najet Arous, University of Tunis Manar, Tunisia
Abderazek Ben Abdallah, The University of Aizu, Japan
Flavio Bertini, University of Parma, Italy
Nik Bessis, Edge Hill University, UK
Sandjai Bhulai, Vrije Universiteit Amsterdam, Netherlands
Jean-Yves Blaise, UMR CNRS/MC 3495 MAP, Marseille, France
Jan Bohacik, University of Zilina, Slovakia
Ozgu Can, Ege University, Turkey
Julio Cesar Duarte, Instituto Militar de Engenharia, Rio de Janeiro, Brazil
Richard Chbeir, Université de Pau et des Pays de l'Adour (UPPA), France
Daniel B.-W. Chen, Monash University, Australia
Yujing Chen, VMware, USA
Giovanni Costa, ICAR-CNR, Italy
Mirela Danubianu, University "Stefan cel Mare" Suceava, Romania
Monica De Martino, National Research Council - Institute for Applied Mathematics and Information Technologies (CNR-IMATI), Italy
Corné de Ruijt, Vrije Universiteit Amsterdam, Netherlands
Konstantinos Demertzis, Democritus University of Thrace, Greece
Paolino Di Felice, University of L'Aquila, Italy
Marianna Di Gregorio, University of Salerno, Italy
Dongsheng Ding, University of Southern California, USA

Ivanna Dronyuk, Lviv Polytechnic National University, Ukraine
Magdalini Eirinaki, San Jose State University, USA
Nadia Essoussi, University of Tunis - LARODEC Laboratory, Tunisia
Tobias Feigl, Friedrich-Alexander-University Erlangen-Nuremberg (FAU), Germany
Panorea Gaitanou, Greek Ministry of Justice, Athens, Greece
Fausto Pedro García Márquez, Castilla-La Mancha University, Spain
Mohamed Ghalwash, IBM Research, USA / Ain Shams University, Egypt
Raji Ghawi, Technical University of Munich, Germany
Boris Goldengorin, Moscow Institute of Physics and Technology, Russia
Ana González-Marcos, Universidad de La Rioja, Spain
Geraldine Gray, Technological University Dublin, Ireland
Luca Grilli, Università degli Studi di Foggia, Italy
Qingguang Guan, Temple University, USA
Riccardo Guidotti, ISTI - CNR, Italy
Samuel Gustavo Huamán Bustamante, Instituto Nacional de Investigación y Capacitación en Telecomunicaciones – Universidad Nacional de Ingenieria (INICTEL-UNI), Peru
Tiziana Guzzo, National Research Council/Institute for Research on Population and Social Policies, Rome, Italy
Rihan Hai. Delft University of Technology, Netherlands
Jeff Hajewski, University of Iowa, USA
Qiwei Han, Nova SBE, Portugal
Felix Heine, Hochschule Hannover, Germany
Mohd Helmy Abd Wahab, Universiti Tun Hussein Onn Malaysia, Malaysia
Jean Hennebert, iCoSys Institute | University of Applied Sciences HES-SO, Fribourg, Switzerland
Béat Hirsbrunner, University of Fribourg, Switzerland
Tzung-Pei Hong, National University of Kaohsiung, Taiwan
LiGuo Huang, Southern Methodist University, USA
Sergio Ilarri, University of Zaragoza, Spain
Jam Jahanzeb Khan Behan, Université Libre de Bruxelles (ULB), Belgium / Universidad Politécnica de Cataluña (UPC), Spain
Zahra Jandaghi, University of Georgia, USA
Wolfgang Jentner, University of Konstanz, Germany
Taoran Ji, Moody's Analytics, USA
Wenjun Jiang, Samsung Research America, USA
Antonio Jiménez Martín, Universidad Politécnica de Madrid, Spain
Dimitrios Karapiperis, International Hellenic University, Greece
Ashutosh Karna, HP Inc. / Universitat Politecnica de Catalunya, Barcelona, Spain
Christine Kirkpatrick, San Diego Supercomputer Center - UC San Diego / CODATA, USA
Alina Lazar, Youngstown State University, USA
Kyung Il Lee, Reinhardt University, USA
Kerstin Lemke-Rust, Hochschule Bonn-Rhein-Sieg, Germany
Clement Leung, Chinese University of Hong Kong, Shenzhen, China
Yuening Li, Texas A&M University, USA
Ninghao Liu, Texas A&M University, USA
Weimo Liu, Google, USA
Fenglong Ma, Pennsylvania State University, USA
Ruizhe Ma, University of Massachusetts Lowell, USA
Massimo Marchiori, University of Padua, Italy / European Institute for Science, Media and Democracy,

Belgium
Mamoun Mardini, College of Medicine | University of Florida, USA
Miguel A. Martínez-Prieto, University of Valladolid, Spain
Alfonso Mateos Caballero, Universidad Politécnica de Madrid, Spain
Archil Maysuradze, Lomonosov Moscow State University, Russia
Abbas Mazloumi, University of California, Riverside, USA
Gideon Mbiydzenyuy, Borås University, Sweden
Ryan McGinnis, Thomas Jefferson University, USA
Letizia Milli, University of Pisa, Italy
Yasser Mohammad, NEC | AIST | RIKEN, Japan / Assiut University, Egypt
Thomas Morgenstern, University of Applied Sciences in Karlsruhe (H-KA), Germany
Lorenzo Musarella,University Mediterranea of Reggio Calabria, Italy
Azad Naik, Microsoft, USA
Roberto Nardone, University Mediterranea of Reggio Calabria, Italy
Alberto Nogales, Universidad Francisco de Victoria | CEIEC research center, Spain
Panagiotis Oikonomou, University of Thessaly, Greece
Ana Oliveira Alves, Polytechnic Institute of Coimbra & Centre of Informatics and Systems of the University of Coimbra, Portugal
Riccardo Ortale, Institute for High Performance Computing and Networking (ICAR) - National Research Council of Italy (CNR), Italy
Moein Owhadi-Kareshk, University of Alberta, Canada
Massimiliano Petri, University of Pisa, Italy
Hai Phan, New Jersey Institute of Technology, USA
Gianvito Pio, University of Bari Aldo Moro, Italy
Antonio Pratelli, University of Pisa, Italy
Michela Quadrini, University of Camerino, Italy
Christoph Raab, FHWS - University of Applied Science Würzburg-Schweinfurt, Germany
Víctor Rampérez, Universidad Politécnica de Madrid (UPM), Spain
Andrew Rau-Chaplin, Dalhousie University, Canada
Ivan Rodero, Rutgers University, USA
Sebastian Rojas Gonzalez, Hasselt University / Ghent University, Belgium
Antonia Russo,University Mediterranea of Reggio Calabria, Italy
Gunter Saake, Otto-von-Guericke University, Germany
Bilal Abu Salih, Curtin University, Australia
Burcu Sayin, University of Trento, Italy
Andreas Schmidt, Karlsruher Institut für Technologie (KIT), Germany
Ivana Semanjski, Ghent University, Belgium
Sina Sheikholeslami, EECS School | KTH Royal Institute of Technology, Sweden
Patrick Siarry, Université Paris-Est Créteil, France
Angelo Sifaleras, University of Macedonia, Greece
Josep Silva Galiana, Universitat Politècnica de València, Spain
Alex Sim, Lawrence Berkeley National Laboratory, USA
Malika Smaïl-Tabbone, LORIA | Université de Lorraine, France
Christos Spandonidis, Prisma Electronics R&D, Greece
Les Sztandera, Thomas Jefferson University, USA
George Tambouratzis, Institute for Language and Speech Processing, Athena R.C., Greece
Tatiana Tambouratzis, University of Piraeus, Greece
Chunxu Tang, Twitter, USA

Horia-Nicolai Teodorescu, "Gheorghe Asachi" Technical University of Iasi | Romanian Academy, Romania
Mike Teodorescu, University of Washington Seattle, USA
Ioannis G. Tollis, University of Crete, Greece / Tom Sawyer Software Inc., USA
Juan-Manuel Torres, LIA/UAPV, France
Chrisa Tsinaraki, EU Joint Research Center - Ispra, Italy
Torsten Ullrich, Fraunhofer Austria Research GmbH, Graz, Austria
Inneke Van Nieuwenhuyse, Universiteit Hasselt, Belgium
Ravi Vatrapu, Ted Rogers School of Management, Ryerson University, Denmark
T. Velmurugan, D.G.Vaishnav College, India
Juan Vicente Capella Hernández, Universitat Politècnica de València, Spain
Sirje Virkus, Tallinn University, Estonia
Marco Viviani, University of Milano-Bicocca, Italy
Maria Vlasiou, University of Twente / Eindhoven University of Technology, Netherlands
Zbigniew W. Ras, University of North Carolina, Charlotte, USA / Warsaw University of Technology, Poland / Polish-Japanese Academy of IT, Poland
Haoyu Wang, Yale University, USA
Pengyue Wang, University of Minnesota - Twin Cities, USA
Shaohua Wang, New Jersey Institute of Technology, USA
Juanying Xie, Shaanxi Normal University, China
Shibo Yao, New Jersey Institute of Technology, USA
Feng "George" Yu, Youngstown State University, USA
Ming Zeng, Facebook, USA
Xiang Zhang, University of New South Wales, Australia
Yichuan Zhao, Georgia State University, USA
Qiang Zhu, University of Michigan - Dearborn, USA
Marc Zöller, USU Software AG / University of Stuttgart, Germany

Copyright Information

Overview of European Union Guidelines and Regulatory Framework for Drones in Aviation in the Context of the Introduction of Automatic and Autonomous Flight Operations in Urban Air Mobility

Elham Fakhraian
Industrial Systems Engineering and Product Design
Ghent University
Industrial Systems Engineering (ISyE), Flanders Make
Ghent, Belgium
elham.fakhraian@ugent.be

El-Houssaine Aghezzaf
Industrial Systems Engineering and Product Design
Ghent University
Industrial Systems Engineering (ISyE), Flanders Make
Ghent, Belgium
elhoussaine.aghezzaf@ugent.be

Silvio Semanjski
SEAL Aeronautica S.L.
Barcelona, Spain
silvio.semanjski@sealaero.com

Ivana Semanjski
Industrial Systems Engineering and Product Design
Ghent University
Industrial Systems Engineering (ISyE), Flanders Make
Ghent, Belgium
ivana.semanjski@ugent.be

Abstract—**Over the past years, Unmanned Aircraft Systems (UAS) operations surged exponentially. Due to new air mobility concepts, industries tend to use more advanced technology to build the UASs. So, it is essential to develop regulations in the new and rapidly evolving contexts in which these new technologies are imposed. The European Union drone regulation is in the transition period, in which the existing regulations in individual European member states are replaced with a unified regulation framework across the European Union. However, this European regulatory framework is very young and will be subject to further development. In this sense, efforts must be made in the scientific literature focusing on the regulatory framework of Europe. This paper provides a solid understanding of the drone's legal framework in the European Union.**

Keywords- Unmanned Aircraft Systems (UAS), Drones, Urban Air Mobility (UAM), EU regulation, Regulatory framework.

I. Introduction

Unmanned Aircraft Systems (UAS) are becoming popular. In recent years, drones have been used in various sectors such as agriculture, inspection, media, and entertainment. It is imaginable that remotely piloted aircraft will enter the area of commercial flights, in the near future [1]. Over the last years, new operational concepts based on innovative technologies, such as UAS and Vertical Take-Off and Landing (VTOL) aircrafts, have led to creating new air mobility concepts [2]. Although UAS's operational and technological capabilities have matured to the point where UASs are expected to gain greater freedom, most civil operations of UAS are conducted in low-level uncontrolled areas or in segregated controlled airspace due to safety concerns [1].

A wide range of literature is published around the world, trying to answer the research question of how to adapt UAS with Urban Air Mobility (UAM) and regulations. Clarke [3] investigated the impacts of civilian drones' regulation on behavioral privacy. He also presented the impacts of the civilian drones' regulation on public safety [4]. Thomasen [5] considered the robots (including drones) and robot regulation impact on public spaces. This paper highlights the importance to regulate robotic systems that operate in public spaces. She also presented a feminist perspective on drone privacy regulation. This article contributes to drone privacy literature to examine the technology's impacts on women's privacy and related regulations [6]. Li and Kim [7] examined the dynamics of local drone policy adoption in the largest registered drone population in the United States, California. West et al. [8] reviewed the public's opinions about drone policy, and its fluctuation over time. In the work done by Merkert, Beck, and Bushell [9], they adopt the theoretical road pricing framework to investigate the willingness of drone operators to pay for Low-Altitude Airspace Management (LAAM). Winkler, Zeadally, and Evans [10] highlighted the concerns and needs of privacy and operation of civilian drone regulations. Nelson and Gorichanaz [11] analyzed the emergence of drones and the evolving regulation in 20 cities in southern California, and they suggested trust as an ethical value in emerging technology governance.

While the aviation industry is subjected to an international framework, it is fair to state that efforts must be made to achieve the same framework for civil drones [12]. In the available literature and the official aviation organizations and regulatory authorities' documents in Europe and worldwide, there is no agreed and consolidated definition of the notion of UAM. However, European Union Aviation Safety Agency

(EASA) recently introduced the UAM concept for the purpose of standardizing communication in the European Union, and for future requirement developments: " The safe, secure and sustainable air mobility of passengers and cargo enabled by new generation technologies integrated into a multimodal transportation system conducted in to, within or out of urban environments" [2]. There is also a need to establish a comprehensive regulatory framework addressing the safety, security and environmental aspects of this new form of mobility of people and cargo by air in order to ensure its adequate acceptance and adoption by European citizens. Some elements of this regulatory framework have already been established with the adoption of Commission Implementing Regulation (EU) 2019/947, Commission Delegated Regulation (EU) 2019/945, and Commission Implementing Regulation (EU) 2021/664 of 22 April 2021 on a regulatory framework for the U-space [2].

It is fair to state that there are no efforts in the scientific literature focusing specifically on the regulatory framework of Europe, so far. One of the reasons is that the drone European Union (EU) regulatory framework is currently under transition, and it was fragmented before 2020. So, this paper provides a comprehensive overview of the developed UAS regulation in the European Union considering the regulations provided by the European Aviation Safety Agency (EASA) to develop a reliable basis for future studies of drones' EU regulatory framework. The structure of the paper is as follows: Section II introduces the existing and upcoming European regulatory framework for UASs. Section III defines the UAS operational categories developed by the EASA. Section IV briefly discusses the existing and upcoming European regulatory framework and standards regarding Artificial Intelligence (AI) and autonomous flights. Section V explains how the regulations apply to drones according to the risk assessments. Section VI discusses the potentials and challenges before presenting the conclusion in Section VII.

II. European Union regulatory framework transition

Before 2020, the drone EU regulatory framework was fragmented. The member states regulated civil drones with less than 150 kg operating mass, while the EASA regulated civil drones with over 150 kg operating mass. The difference in extent, content, and level of detail of national regulations led to unreached conditions for mutual recognition of operational authorization between the EU Member States [2].

Since 2020, the European Union drones' legal framework officially subjected to a uniform regulation by European Union Aviation Safety Agency (EASA) under the Regulation 2019/947 and 2019/945. Regulation 2019/947 was expected to be implemented on 1 July 2020; however, due to the COVID-19 crisis, it was delayed to 31 December 2020 [13]. Aircraft airworthiness concerns the safety standards in all construction aspects such as structural strength, safeguard provisions, and design requirements relating to aerodynamics, performance, electrical and hydraulic systems [14].

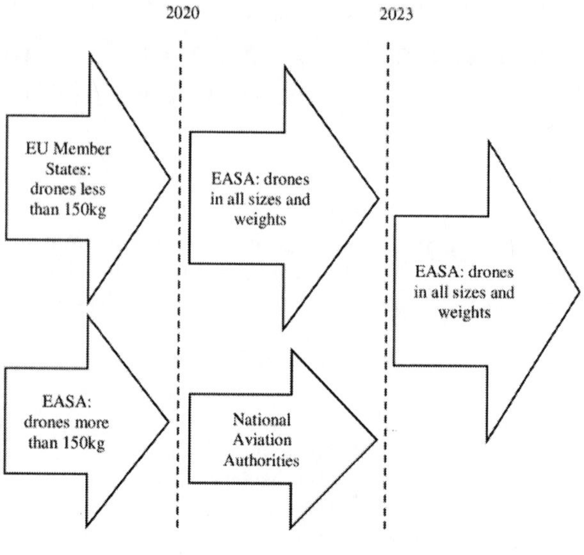

Figure 1. European Union regulatory framework transition

Easy Access Rules for Airworthiness and Environmental Certification (Regulation (EU) No 748/2012) contains the applicable rules for Airworthiness and Environmental Certification of aircraft and related products, parts, and appliances, as well as for the certification of design and production organizations [15]. In general, international and national regulations are focused on safety. Nevertheless, small drones avoid many of these requirements, as they pose fewer risks to people [12]. Figure 1 presents an overview of European Union regulatory framework transition.

III. Civil drone operations categories in the European Union regulatory framework

Civil drones' operational framework in the European Union (EU) is Regulations 2019/947 and 2019/945. These regulations conduct a risk-based approach considering the weight, the specifications, and the intended operation of the civil drone. Regulation 2019/947 defines three categories for civil drone operations: the open, the specific, and the certified category [16], as shown in Figure 2.

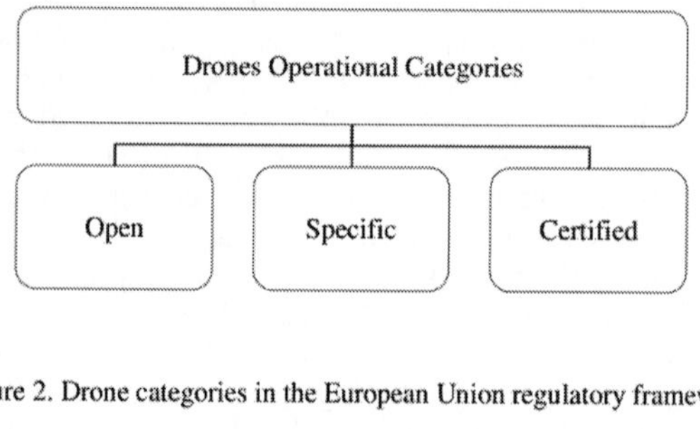

Figure 2. Drone categories in the European Union regulatory framework

A. The open category (low risk)

Drones in low-risk operations (e.g., leisure drone activities and low-risk commercial activities) are categorized as the open category. This category has three sub-categories:

- A1: fly over people but not over assemblies of people
- A2: fly close to people
- A3: fly far from people

Each sub-category comes with its own requirements, depending on the drone's weight. The maximum operational weight in this category is 25 kg [17].

B. The specific category (medium risk)

Riskier drone operations, which fall out of the open category's scope, are in the specific category. Based on the risk assessment outcome conducted under Article 11 of Regulation (EU) 2019/947, operational authorization (issued by the competent authority of registration) is required in this category, unless the operation is covered by a Standard Scenario (STS) that is a predefined operation described in the appendix of EU regulation 2019/947 [18].

C. The certified category (high risk)

The highest level of risk in drone operations and future drones onboard passenger flights (e.g., air taxis) are covered in the certified category. Based on the outcome of risk assessment conducted under Article 11 of Regulation (EU) 2019/947, drones can also be classified in the certified category. These aircraft will always need to be certified. The UAS operator will need an air operator approval issued by the competent authority, and the remote pilot is required to hold a pilot license. In the longer term, drone automation development is expected to reach a level to have fully autonomous drones without remote pilot intervention. The approach used to ensure the safety of these flights will be very similar to the one used for manned aviation, and almost all the aviation regulations will need to be amended. So this will be a major task, and EASA is decided to conduct this activity in multiple phases [19].

Overall, if drone operations contain any of the below conductions, they are certainly classified in the certified category:

- The UAS has a dimension of 3 m or more in the operation involves flying over assemblies of people (flying over assemblies of people with a UAS that has a dimension less than 3 m may be in the specific category unless the risk assessment concludes that it is in the certified category)
- The operation involved transport of people
- The operation involved transport of dangerous goods if the payload is not in a crash-protected container [20].

IV. AUTONOMOUS AND AUTOMATIC UAS

With the advancement of technology, autonomous and automatic UASs are expected to conduct safe operations in

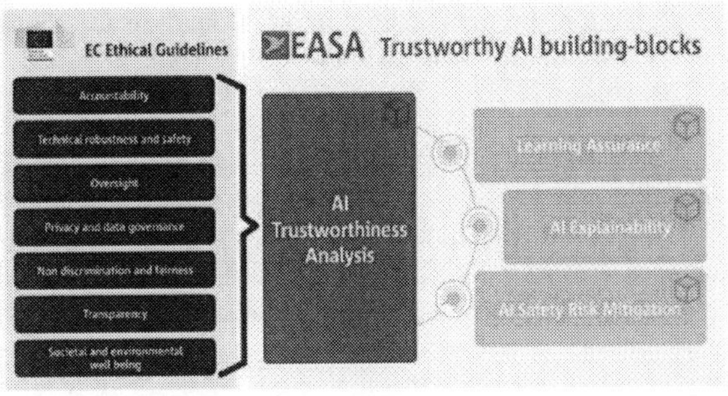

Figure 3. EASA trustworthy AI building-blocks: : AI trustworthiness analysis, learning assurance, AI explainability, and AI safety risk mitigation [21]

Urban Air Mobility (UAM); major differences are between autonomous and automatic concepts. With the help of artificial intelligence, autonomous UAS must cope with unforeseen conditions and unpredictable emergencies to conduct a safe flight without the pilot's intervention. However, the automatic UAS flies on pre-determined routes, and the remote pilot intervenes in case of unforeseen events not programmed in pre-determined operation. While automatic drones are allowed in all categories, autonomous drones are not allowed in the open category. Instead, they can operate in the specific category and the certified category, where the Regulation includes more flexible tools to verify requirements and level of robustness. [22].

The key research question is how autonomy can be safely used in UAM [23]. In 2020, EASA published the first guidance, EASA AI roadmap, for the safe use of artificial intelligence in aviation [21] in several domains such as aircraft design and operation, aircraft production and maintenance, drones, open-air mobility, safety risk management, and cybersecurity [24]. Figure 3 presents the definition of the trustworthy AI building block, which is one of the important contributions of this document [21]. The schedule presented in the EASA AI roadmap document foresees the first approvals of AI starting in 2025 [24].

V. OPERATIONAL RISK ASSESSMENT FOR DRONES IN SPECIFIC CATEGORY

The volume and scope of drone operations have increased in Europe. To ensure safety, particularly in operations conducted in populated areas, the design verification of the drone by EASA is needed depending on the operation's level of risk [25]:

- In drone operations classified as high risk operations (i.e., Specific Assurance and Integrity Level (SAIL) V and VI according to Specific Operation Risk Assessment (SORA)), EASA will issue a type certificate according to Part 21 (Regulation (EU) 748/2012) [15].
- In drones operation classified as medium risk operations (i.e., SAIL III and IV according to SORA),

a more proportionate approach, leading to a design verification report, will be applied [25].

The work in [20] describes the operational risk assessment for drones in detailed steps, and this paper presents an overview of these steps. Overall, there are three categories in the operational risk assessment. The first lower risk category is the operations in Standard Scenarios (STS), and the second category is Predefined Risk Assessment (PDRA). This category also tends to cover some deviations from STS. When the operation is not subject to STS or PDRA, it will be categorized as Specific Operation Risk Assessment (SORA), the last category.

A. *Standard scenario (STS)*

Due to the lower risks in UAS operations when complying with STSs listed in TABLE I, a declaration may be submitted.

B. *Predefined risk assessment (PDRA)*

EASA intends to publish several PDRAs considering the most common operations in Europe. Instead of conducting a full risk assessment, a request for authorization may be submitted based on the mitigations and provisions described in the PDRA when the UAS operation meets the operational characterization described in TABLE II.

While STSs are described in a detailed way, PDRAs are described in a rather generic way to provide flexibility. Two types of PDRAs are provided: the first category is derived from STSs, which allow the UAS operator to conduct similar operations without the UAS class label that is mandated by the STS; and the other category is the more generic PDRAs. The codification of a PDRA includes the letter 'G' (used for generic PDRAs) or 'S' (used for PDRAs that are derived from an STS) [20].

TABLE I. LIST OF THE STANDARD SCENARIOS (STS) PUBLISHED [20]

STS#	**Edition/date**	**UAS characteristics**	**BVLOS/ VLOS****	**Overflown area**	**Maximum range from remote pilot**	**Maximum height**	**Airspace**
STS-01	June 2020	Bearing a C5 class marking (maximum characteristic dimension of up to 3 m and MTOM* of up to 25 kg)	VLOS	Controlled ground area that might be located in a populated area	VLOS	120 m	Controlled or uncontrolled, with low risk of encounter with manned aircraft
STS-02	June 2020	Bearing a C6 class marking (maximum characteristic dimension of up to 3 m and MTOM of up to 25 kg)	BVLOS	Controlled ground area that is entirely located in a sparsely populated area	2 km with an AO*** 1 km, if no AO	120 m	Controlled or uncontrolled, with low risk of encounter with manned aircraft

* Maximum TakeOff Mass
** Beyond Visual Line of Sight / Visual Line of Sight
*** Airspace Observer

TABLE II. LIST OF THE PREDEFINED RISK ASSESSMENTS (PDRA) PUBLISHED [20]

PDRA#	**Edition/date**	**UAS characteristics**	**BVLOS/ VLOS**	**Overflown area**	**Maximum range from remote pilot**	**Maximum height**	**Airspace**	**AMC#* to Article 11**
PDRA-S01	1.0/July 2020	Maximum characteristic dimension of up to 3 m and MTOM of up to 25 kg	VLOS	Controlled ground area that might be located in a populated area	VLOS	120 m	Controlled or uncontrolled, with low risk of encounter with manned aircraft	AMC4
PDRA-S02	1.0/July 2020	Maximum characteristic dimension of up to 3 m and MTOM of up to 25 kg	BVLOS	Controlled ground area that is entirely located in a sparsely populated area	2 km with an AO 1 km, if no AO	120 m	Controlled or uncontrolled, with low risk of encounter with manned aircraft	AMC5
PDRA-G01	1.1/July 2020	Maximum characteristic dimension of up to 3 m and typical kinetic energy of up to 34 kJ	BVLOS	Sparsely populated area	If no AO, up to 1 km	150 m (operational volume)	Uncontrolled, with low risk of encounter with manned aircraft	AMC2
PDRA-G02	1.0/July 2020	Maximum characteristic dimension of up to 3 m and typical kinetic energy of up to 34 kJ	BVLOS	Sparsely populated area	N/a	As established for the reserved airspace	As reserved for the operation	AMC3

* Acceptable Means of Compliance

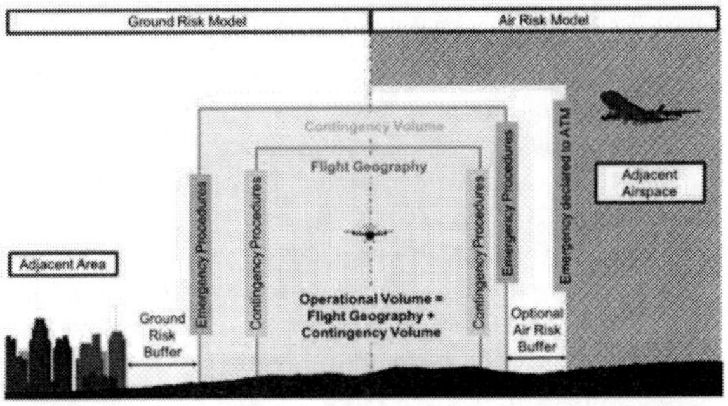

Figure 4. Graphical representation of the SORA semantic model [20]

C. *Specific operation risk assessment (SORA)*

SORA evaluates the safety risks in the UAS operation considering any UAS class and size, or type of operation [20]. Figure 4 provides a visual reference to the SORA methodology. Robustness is one of the concepts to account for when conducting SORA. SORA presents three robustness levels: low, medium, and high. Risk mitigations and Operational Safety Objectives (OSO) can be demonstrated at different robustness levels. Risk is another key concept. Many works of literature exist to define risk. SORA defines risk as: 'the combination of the frequency (probability) of an occurrence and its associated level of severity'. SORA focuses on the assessment of air and ground risks. Figure 5 outlines the needed ten steps to support the SORA methodology. If UAS operates in different environments, some steps may need to be repeated [20].

Before starting the SORA process, it is important to verify the operational feasibility. If the operation is not categorized as the open category or the certified category, not covered by a standard scenario or by a predefined risk assessment, and not subjected to a specific NO-GO from the competent authority, the SORA can be applied [20].

VI. DISCUSSION

One of the distinctive features of the future cities in science fiction movies and novels is flying cars and transport systems. This is one of the basic concepts accepted by society when imagining the future. The technological advances make us wonder if we are a few steps away from having safe automatic and autonomous air transport systems for urban areas in the near future. UAS are becoming popular and it is only a matter of time before they will enter UAM as a way of transporting goods and even individuals. For this vision to become feasible, it is essential to develop a regulatory framework accepted by society. As presented in Figure 1, the European Union regulatory framework for UASs was fragmented before 2020 and each EU Member states were in charge of drones with a Maximum Take-Off Mass (MTOM) of less than 150 Kg and EASA was responsible for drones with MTOM of more than 150 Kg. In 2020, the regulation transition started and EASA has become responsible for drones of all sizes and weights. This young regulatory framework is still under further development. So, the national aviation authority of each country will help this regulation to

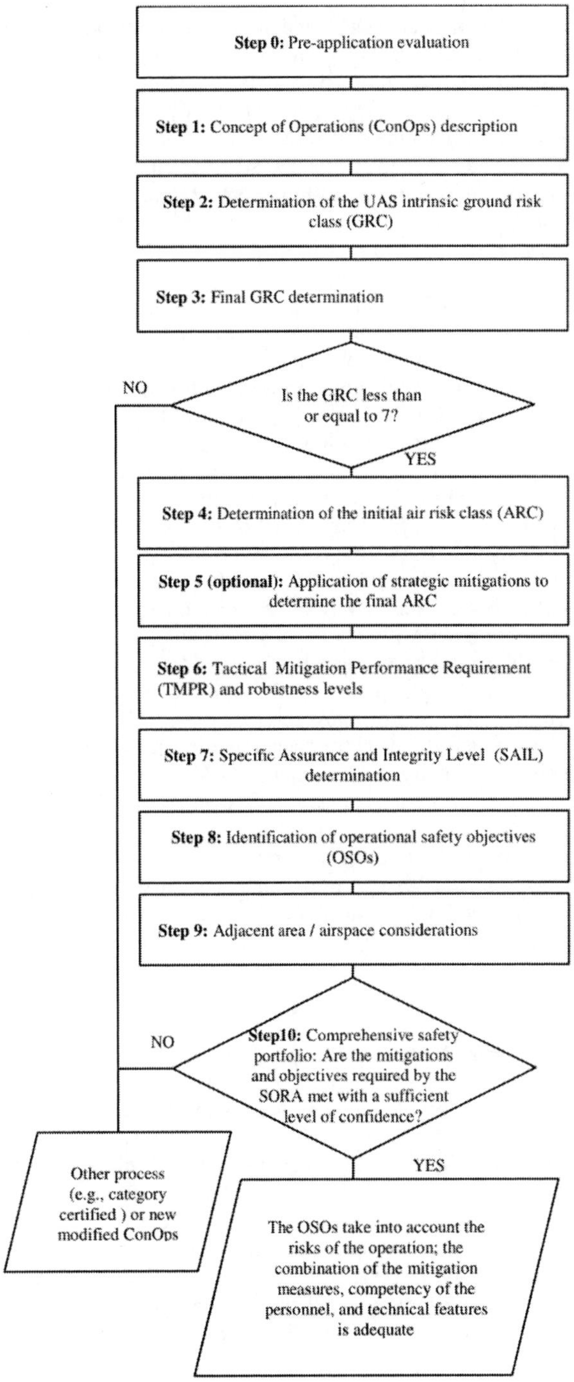

Figure 5. Determination of robustness level [20]

fill its gaps until the year 2023 when this regulatory framework becomes fully developed.

Autonomous and automatic UASs are expected to conduct safe operations in UAM. With the help of artificial intelligence, the autonomous UAS conducts a safe flight without the pilot's intervention, while the automatic UAS flies on pre-determined routes, and the remote pilot can intervene in unforeseen events. With a quick comparison between autonomous and automatic flights, it can be concluded that there is no human safety net in case of unforeseen events when conducting an autonomous flight. So, precise regulations have to be developed in the context of artificial intelligence to make sure of conducting a safe autonomous flight. In 2020, EASA also published the first guidance, the EASA AI roadmap, for the safe use of artificial intelligence in aviation in several domains. However, it is still a long way for the dream of having Science fiction flying transport systems to come true as the schedule presented in the EASA AI roadmap document foresees the first approvals of AI in 2025.

A wide range of literature is published around the world, trying to answer the research question of how to adapt UAS with UAM and regulations. However, there is not much literature effort in the context of the drone EU regulatory framework since this regulatory framework is currently under transition, and it was fragmented before 2020. As mentioned, the concept of drone regulation in the context of the European Union regulation and UAM adaptation to carry cargo and individuals is young. While the devoted regulations for this type of operation, mainly the certified category, are still in the development phase, even in the specific category, lots of factors and parameters need to be considered for the determination of robustness level, as presented in Figure 4, to ensure a safe flight without any complications. For instance, preparing ConOps and calculating the GRC and ARC requires operating conditions data. Moreover, UAS autonomous flights are not currently conducted in most European countries due to safety reasons and uncompleted regulation development. When a new concept is arising, the lack of literature and documents is inevitable in the early stages. So, the first and most important challenge at this moment is to keep track of the developments and changes of the regulation.

VII. Conclusion

The popularity of UAS operations increased over the past years and new air mobility concepts have been created. It is essential to develop regulations in this new technological context. The European Union drone regulation is in the transition period and this young regulatory framework will be subject to further development. This causes a scientific literature gap of no efforts focusing on the regulatory framework of Europe. In this paper, we provide a comprehensive overview of the developed UAS regulation in the European Union to fill this gap and to provide a solid understanding of the drone's legal framework in the European Union for future studies.

Acknowledgment

This project has received funding from the European Union's Horizon 2020 research and innovation programme (H2020-MG-3-6-2020 Research and Innovation Action "Towards sustainable urban air mobility") under Grant Agreement No. 101007134.

References

[1] Z. Liu, K. Cai, and Y. Zhu, "Civil unmanned aircraft system operation in national airspace: A survey from Air Navigation Service Provider perspective," *Chinese Journal of Aeronautics*, vol. 34, no. 3, pp. 200–224, Mar. 2021, doi: 10.1016/J.CJA.2020.08.033.

[2] European Union Aviation Safety Agency (EASA), "EASA publishes world's first rules for operation of air taxis in cities." https://www.easa.europa.eu/newsroom-and-events/press-releases/easa-publishes-worlds-first-rules-operation-air-taxis-cities (accessed Oct. 20, 2022).

[3] R. Clarke, "The regulation of civilian drones' impacts on behavioural privacy," *Computer Law & Security Review*, vol. 30, no. 3, pp. 286–305, Jun. 2014, doi: 10.1016/J.CLSR.2014.03.005.

[4] R. Clarke and L. Bennett Moses, "The regulation of civilian drones' impacts on public safety," *Computer Law & Security Review*, vol. 30, no. 3, pp. 263–285, Jun. 2014, doi: 10.1016/J.CLSR.2014.03.007.

[5] K. Thomasen, "Robots, Regulation, and the Changing Nature of Public Space," *Ottawa Law Review* , vol. 51, no. 2, pp. 275–312, 2020.

[6] K. Thomasen, "Beyond Airspace Safety: A Feminist Perspective on Drone Privacy Regulation," *Canadian Journal of Law and Technology*, vol. 16, no. 2, pp. 307–338, 2016.

[7] X. Li and J. H. Kim, "Managing disruptive technologies: Exploring the patterns of local drone policy adoption in California," *Cities*, vol. 126, p. 103736, Jul. 2022, doi: 10.1016/J.CITIES.2022.103736.

[8] J. P. West, C. A. Klofstad, J. E. Uscinski, and J. M. Connolly, "Citizen support for domestic drone use and regulation," *American Politics Research* , vol. 47, no. 1, pp. 119–151, 2019.

[9] R. Merkert, M. J. Beck, and J. Bushell, "Will It Fly? Adoption of the road pricing framework to manage drone use of airspace," *Transp Res Part A Policy Pract*, vol. 150, pp. 156–170, Aug. 2021, doi: 10.1016/J.TRA.2021.06.001.

[10] S. Winkler, S. Zeadally, and K. Evans, "Privacy and civilian drone use: The need for further regulation," *IEEE Secur Priv*, vol. 16, no. 5, pp. 72–80, 2018.

[11] J. Nelson and T. Gorichanaz, "Trust as an ethical value in emerging technology governance: The case of drone regulation," *Technol Soc*, vol. 59, p. 101131, Nov. 2019, doi: 10.1016/J.TECHSOC.2019.04.007.

[12] M. de Miguel Molina and V. Santamarina-Campos, *Ethics and civil drones: European policies and proposals for the industry*. Springer Nature, 2018.

[13] European Union Aviation Safety Agency (EASA), "EASA provisions: the applicability dates under EU regulation 2019/947 and 2019/945." https://www.easa.europa.eu/the-agency/faqs/drones-uas (accessed Oct. 20, 2022).

[14] T. H.G. Megson, *Aircraft structures for engineering students*, 5th ed., no. 1. Butterworth-Heinemann, 2012.

[15] European Union Aviation Safety Agency (EASA), "Easy Access Rules for Airworthiness and Environmental Certification (Regulation (EU) No 748/2012)."

https://www.easa.europa.eu/document-library/general-publications/easy-access-rules-initial-airworthiness (accessed Oct. 20, 2022).

[16] European Union Aviation Safety Agency (EASA), "Civil drones (unmanned aircraft)." https://www.easa.europa.eu/domains/civil-drones (accessed Oct. 20, 2022).

[17] European Union Aviation Safety Agency (EASA), "open category of civil drones." https://www.easa.europa.eu/domains/civil-drones/drones-regulatory-framework-background/open-category-civil-drones (accessed Oct. 20, 2022).

[18] European Union Aviation Safety Agency (EASA), "Specific Category of Civil Drones." https://www.easa.europa.eu/domains/civil-drones/drones-regulatory-framework-background/specific-category-civil-drones (accessed Oct. 20, 2022).

[19] European Union Aviation Safety Agency (EASA), "Certified Category of Civil Drones." https://www.easa.europa.eu/domains/civil-drones/drones-regulatory-framework-background/certified-category-civil-drones (accessed Oct. 20, 2022).

[20] European Union Aviation Safety Agency (EASA), "Easy Access Rules for Unmanned Aircraft Systems (Regulation (EU) 2019/947 and Regulation (EU) 2019/945)." https://www.easa.europa.eu/document-library/easy-access-rules/easy-access-rules-unmanned-aircraft-systems-regulation-eu (accessed: Oct. 20, 2022)

[21] European Union Aviation Safety Agency (EASA), "EASA Artificial Intelligence Roadmap - A human centric approach to AI in aviation," https://www.easa.europa.eu/newsroom-and-events/news/easa-artificial-intelligence-roadmap-10-published (accessed: Oct. 20, 2022)

[22] European Union Aviation Safety Agency (EASA), "The difference between autonomous and automatic drones." https://www.easa.europa.eu/the-agency/faqs/regulations-uas-drone-explained (accessed Oct. 20, 2022).

[23] C. Torens, F. Jünger, S. Schirmer, S. Schopferer, T. Maienschein, and J. C. Dauer, "Machine Learning Verification and Safety for Unmanned Aircraft-A Literature Study," *AIAA Scitech 2022 Forum*, 2022.

[24] C. Torens, U. Durak, and J. C. Dauer, "Guidelines and Regulatory Framework for Machine Learning in Aviation," *AIAA Scitech 2022 Forum*, 2022.

[25] European Union Aviation Safety Agency (EASA), "EASA issues guidelines for the design verification of drones operated in the specific category." https://www.easa.europa.eu/newsroom-and-events/press-releases/easa-issues-guidelines-design-verification-drones-operated (accessed Oct. 20, 2022).

Aircraft Path Planning for UAM Applications

Silvio Semanjski
SEAL Aeronautica S.L.
Barcelona, Spain
Email: silvio.semanjski@sealaero.com

Ignacio Querol Puchal
SEAL Aeronautica S.L.
Barcelona, Spain
Email: IgnacioQuerolPuchal@sealaero.com

Ronald Ponguillo-Intriago
Dept. of Industrial Systems Engineering and Product Design, Ghent University
Industrial Systems Engineering (ISyE), Flanders Make
Ghent, Belgium
Facultad de Ingenieria en Electricidad y Computacion
Escuela Superior Politecnica del Litoral, ESPOL
Guayaquil, Ecuador
Email: RonaldAlberto.PonguilloIntriago@UGent.be

Ivana Semanjski
Dept. of Industrial Systems Engineering and Product Design, Ghent University
Industrial Systems Engineering (ISyE), Flanders Make
Ghent, Belgium
Email: Ivana.Semanjski@ugent.be

Abstract— **Aircraft path planning in urban air mobility context relates to finding of a continuous path/trajectory that will drive the aircraft from a start to an end location knowing the environment map. This map can be a 3D model, including semantic information (no fly zones, aerial corridors) that are constraints for the path planning algorithm. This paper investigates the aircraft path plan dealing with the flight pre-known obstacles in the 3D space, regardless of their static or dynamic characteristics, that syncs with the local path in cases when pre-flight unknown obstacles are detected along the global path by one of the aircraft's sensors to ensure safe flight between flight origin and destination locations. To achieve this, we rely on a combination of A* and Visibility graphs approach.**

Keywords- Unmanned Aircraft Systems (UAS), Drones, Urban Air Mobility (UAM), Aircraft path planning, Path optimisation, A*, Visibility graphs

I. INTRODUCTION

Aircraft path planning, within Urban Air Mobility (UAM) context, relates to finding of a continuous path/trajectory that will drive the aircraft from a start to an end location knowing the environment map, which is stored in the navigator's memory. This map can be a 3D model, including semantic information (no fly zones, aerial corridors) that are constraints for the aircraft planning algorithm. To ensure a failsafe operation, the aircraft also has to build a local semantic map at the same time as it moves to avoid potential hazards or obstacles. The perception abilities are obviously the starting point to develop the path planning algorithms and allowing the aircraft to accomplish its mission. In this paper, we will describe in more details the development of an aircraft path planning algorithm for the purpose of the urban air mobility applications.

The structure of the paper is as follows. Section II introduces the flight path planning building blocks. Section III elaborates on flight path planning methodology while Section IV briefly discusses obstacle clearance construction. Section V elaborates on the 3D path construction. Section VI discusses non-holonomic constraint, which is followed by a brief conclusion in Section VI.

II. AIRCRAFT PATH PLANNING BUILDING BLOCKS

The search space for our path planning problem is an undirected graph in R^3 that is built from the visible vertices of the physical and non-physical objects on the map of the location where the flight task will be deployed. Physical objects refer to buildings, trees, etc. Non-physical objects refer to geometric objects in R^3 defined by the aeronautical authorities within which it is not possible to navigate, and they are flight constraints for our solver (Figure 1). In practice, these objects are defined in Aeronautical Information Exchange Model (AIXM) [1] format and are called Airspace Volume objects.

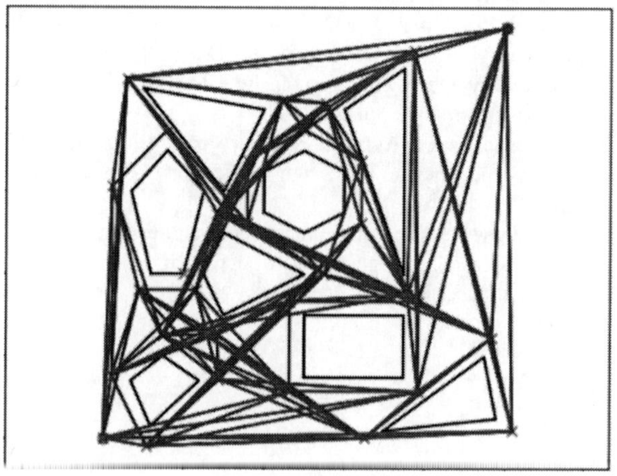

Figure 1. Global path search space example.

In each node of the graph, the geolocation information of the given point in World Geodetic System 84 (WGS84) coordinates and the altitude are placed. The information about the distances for each pair of nodes connected is placed in the corresponding edges.

III. Aircraft Path Planning Method Selection

Due to the nature of the aircraft path planning problem, the number of possible solutions to it is large. A solution can be modelled as an ordered set of points in space conforming a path whose length is minimum with respect to others. To cut back the solution space, some flight path planning methods search some points that are good candidates for belonging to the optimal solution (or optimal path). One of these methods is the Visibility Graph [2], which only considers the origin, destination and the points belonging to the outline of the obstacle. Indeed, this graph consists of a set of inter-visible locations, i.e., pairs of points in the 2D Euclidean plane that can see each other [3]. Each node in the graph represents a point location, and each edge represents a visible connection between them. That is, if the line segment connecting two locations does not intersect any third obstacle, an edge is drawn between them in the graph. One example of a Visibility Graph among a set of polygons is shown in Figure 2. In the case of polygons, just their vertices are considered as nodes of the constructed graph since any intermediate point of any polygon edge would be part of a suboptimal sub-path.

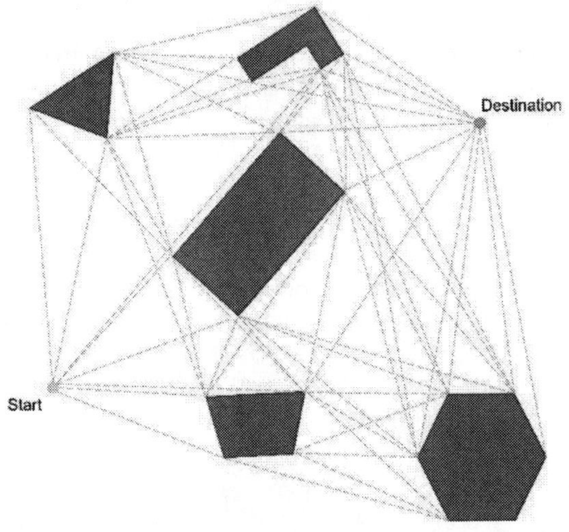

Figure 2. Visibility graph.

The perfect complement for the Visibility Graph is a tree search algorithm, since once the data set is decomposed into a relatively small set of nodes and edges, this type of algorithm can provide a solution in a reasonable amount of time [4]. Among the algorithms that have historically been used for this problem, we find Dijkstra, which is able to compute the optimal solution in O(|E| + |V | log |V |) time complexity (being V the number of vertices and E the number of edges of the graph). However, a generalization of Dijkstra's algorithm has been preferred in this approach. It is called A*, and its main advantage is that it cuts down on the size of the sub-graph that must be explored [5]. It does so by considering a lower bound on the distance to the target, which works well in this case since Euclidean distances are considered. This bound or weight permits us to distinguish promising nodes to explore from nodes that may not be part of the solution. So, with this combination of methods it is possible to exactly solve the problem in 2D and without considering the dynamics of the vehicle.

IV. Obstacles Clearance Construction

One of the most critical parts of the aircraft path planning is the integration of the so-called 'horizontal and vertical clearances' constraints [6]. These have been the first studied constraints after the selection of the path planning method, and due to the nature of this problem, their incorporation was laborious.

In the aircraft plan planning problem, just static objects were considered, that is to say, animals or other vehicles that could intersect the studied vehicle's path during the flight would be avoided locally in an online manner. But, in a first approach, the most efficient but safe route should be computed considering objects which would be (with certain guarantee) in the vehicle's path during the flight. The set of obstacles that we have considered in the aircraft plan planning can be defined in 2D as convex or non-convex regions in space, being the most used representations the circle and the polygon in the UAM framework. In fact, the area enclosing these obstacles should be as close as possible to the original shape of the objects, but it is also pretended to define this area with as few numbers of points as possible. Therefore, being the polygon and the circle the two basic shapes whose combination is able to tightly cover almost all possible figures in 2D space, both have been selected as the main obstacle's representations in this research.

Regarding its provenance, there are two types of obstacles. The first are provided by some aviation institutions like EUROCAE in maps defining the Airspace Class of each region of the atmosphere, named Visual Flight Rules (VFR) [7]. In these maps, the restricted areas or No-Fly Zones of a given region are pointed out. Moreover, in our problem, there is a second type of obstacle which fundamentally consists of the rest of objects against which we do not want the vehicle to collide: buildings, trees, bridges, transmission towers, power lines, etc. Considering both type of obstacles, it is possible to gather a set of forbidden zones in space that the aircraft will have to surround.

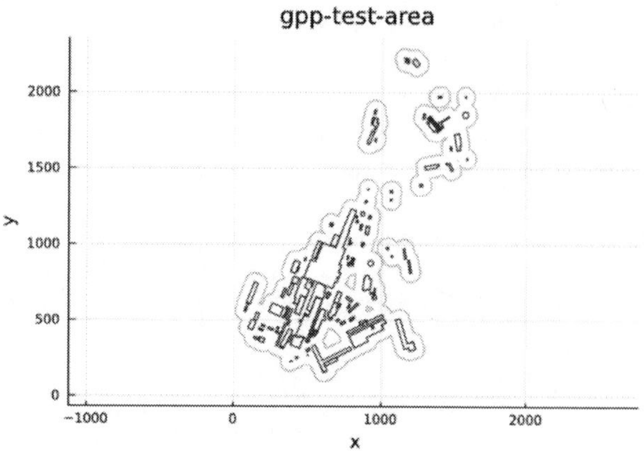

Figure 3. Global path planning test area [8].

By clearance with respect to an obstacle, it is meant to express the distance that the vehicle must respect at all times from each kind of obstacle. There is a distinction between horizontal and vertical clearances in this research, due to the nature of the problem (for example, the aircraft's dynamics). Thus, to guarantee at all times that this constraint is respected, the approach that has been followed is to enlarge the objects, so that the forbidden region is formed by the prism/cylinder volume and the volume which is closer than a given value h_c with respect to the obstacles. In Figure 3 it is possible to see a horizontal projection of these enlarged objects. In blue, a set of buildings that can be encountered in a certain test area for this research are represented. In orange it is possible to see a boundary which is placed at a distance h_c = 60 m from the obstacles, and that contours the forbidden region that must never be trespassed. It is also possible to see that these objects, composed of a set of linear and circular segments, have some holes in their interior.

As commented previously, some difficulties have arisen during the conceiving of this specific part of the algorithm. As the objects represented in 2D can be concave polygons, some exceptions appeared when searching some criterion in order to extract the single contour of this kind of figures. Also, as some objects are adjacent (interior and exterior) with respect to others, some errors were being obtained since these figures were intersecting at several points. By merging these overlapping figures in the first place, it was possible to solve the mentioned problem. Another set of exceptions appeared when integrating the vertical constraint, as it was needed to update the heights of the merged figure and the single ones, so that there was no overlapping among prisms. In this way, it was possible to compute the obstacle clearances at different heights in an efficient manner.

V. 3D Path Construction

In the previous section, the main challenge when integrating the vertical constraint has been stated. As said, this was related to the clearance construction of the objects in the vertical domain. If it was possible to specify the range of heights among which the polygons were extended, then it was possible to compute 2D forbidden area contours (as represented in Figure 4) for several discrete height values. In this manner, it was possible to compute a 3D version of the forbidden areas.

The next step in the pursuance of integrating the third dimension was to update the optimization method. The Visibility Graph together with the A* worked well in 2D but when used within a 3D environment, edges were converted into planes and path must be optimized among these planes. For this reason, the complexity of an integral 3D Visibility Graph algorithm increased a lot. By integral, it is intended to mean a method which computes all the Visibility Graph edges between all the 2D obtained figures even if they belong to different height cuts. In this approach, while a higher degree of freedom is given to the vehicle, certain properties of the problem are not taken into account. These can be found by studying Urban Air Mobility framework, like the height distribution that a vehicle under these conditions would delineate or even the speed distribution [9]. So, by simplifying our model or making some assumptions, it has not only been possible to cut time complexity of the algorithm, but to help it in the resolution of the problem. In Figure 4, it is possible to see some 3D obstacles in blue, the computed obstacle clearances in orange and a path in red which goes under a floating obstacle. The top surfaces of the obstacles and the orange contours are not colored for visualization purposes.

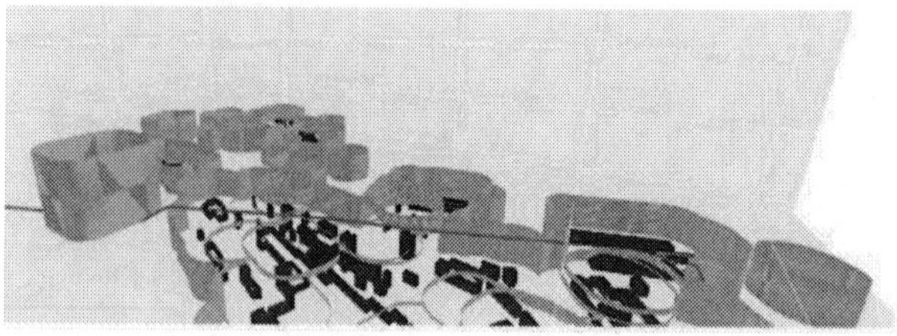
Figure 4. Clearance construction.

VI. Non-Holonomic Constraint

Once the third dimension is added, there is another challenge to face: how to integrate the vehicle's dynamics into the problem. In fact, this constraint prevents some paths or some maneuvers from being valid. Thus, by applying this constraint, it is possible to say that the vehicle follows a non-holonomic system, which in physics and mathematics is a physical system whose state depends on the path taken in order to achieve it. In other words, the vehicle's orientation at a given point depends on the path taken. So, in this way, steep climbs and turns must be eliminated from the solution space.

The approach taken for the purpose of adding this new restriction has been to discretize the flight or the path into some phases. The considered flight phases are the following ones:

- take-off,
- climb,
- cruise,
- approach, and
- landing.

During the cruise phase, the 2D Visibility Graph and A* method is used in order to calculate the optimal path at a constant height. This height is determined a priori based on several criteria: length of the path, safety, time complexity, etc. Like this, it is possible to calculate routes in large datasets including a high number of obstacles. The other flight phases are computed using a heuristic algorithm, tailored to the application. In short, several take-off trajectories are computed considering different azimuths and the ones that are non-valid are removed. Afterwards the transition between the take-off phase and the cruise one is computed. For the landing heuristic, the procedure is almost the same. Like this, steep climbs are removed from the model, while turn radius can be regulated by adjusting the parameter hc, which was the horizontal clearance of the obstacles. In Figure 5, it is possible to see a 3D path which complies with the non-holonomic constraint.

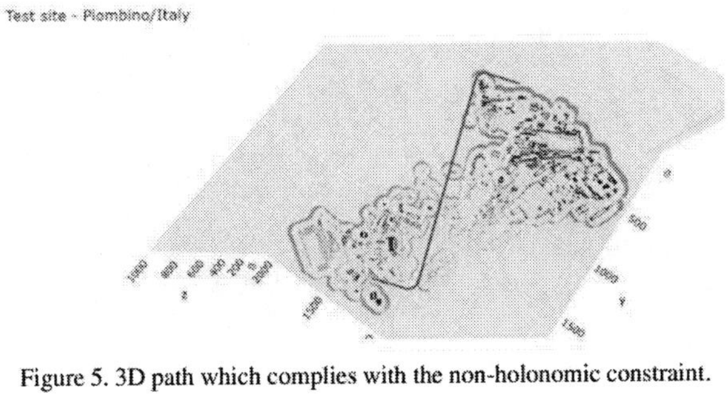

Figure 5. 3D path which complies with the non-holonomic constraint.

VII. CONCLUSION

Challenge of introducing urban air mobility relates to the aircraft path planning and optimization in low airspace area characterized with the presence of multiple obstacles. This requires introduction of adjusted aircraft path planning in 3D environment as well as integration of relevant constrains, including non-holonomic ones, in order to introduce safe operations and reliable flight path plans. This paper briefly introduces one of such approaches based on the visibility graphs method.

ACKNOWLEDGMENT

This project has received funding from the European Union's Horizon 2020 research and innovation programme (H2020-MG-3-6-2020 Research and Innovation Action "Towards sustainable urban air mobility") under Grant Agreement No. 101007134.

REFERENCES

[1] Aeronautical Information Exchange Model," Eurocontrol, [Online]. Available: https://www.aixm.aero/. [Accessed 28 January 2022].

[2] H. Niu, Y. Lu, A. Savvaris and A. Tsourdos, "An energy-efficient path planning algorithm for unmanned surface vehicles," *Ocean Engineering*, vol. 116, pp. 308-321, 2018.

[3] M. de Berg et al., "Visibility graphs," in *Computational geometry.* , Berlin, Heidelberg, Springer, 2000, pp. 307-317.

[4] D. O'Sullivan and A. Turner, "Visibility graphs and landscape visibility analysis," *International journal of geographical information science*, vol. 15, no. 3, pp. 221-237, 2001.

[5] C. Ge, T. Wu and Z. Zhou, "Research on ship meteorological route based on A-star algorithm.," *Mathematical Problems in Engineering*, vol. 2021, 2021.

[6] Y. Gu, "Design and flight testing evaluation of formation control laws," *IEEE Transactions on Control Systems Technology*, vol. 14, no. 6, pp. 1105-1112, 2006.

[7] H. Alturbeh and J. Whidborne, "Visual flight rules-based collision avoidance systems for uav flying in civil aerospace," *Robotics*, vol. 1, no. 8, p. 9, 2020.

[8] S. Semanjski, I. Querol Puchal, I. Semanjski, R. A. Ponguillo Intriago and O. Broca, "Global path planning algorithm," Aurora project, 2022.

[9] AURORA consortium, "AURORA," [Online]. Available: https://aurora-uam.eu/. [Accessed 20th October 2022].

Trusting the Data Analytics Process from the Perspective of Different Stakeholders

Sven Gehrke, Sandra Niemz, Johannes Ruhland
Chair of Business Informatics,
Friedrich-Schiller-University,
Jena, Germany
e-mail: sven.gehrke@uni-jena.de, sandra.niemz@uni-jena.de, johannes.ruhland@uni-jena.de

Abstract—**The paper at hand shows different aspects of the concept of trust. Using the Cross Industry Standard Process for Data Mining (CRISP-DM) phase model, we stress the information asymmetry of the typical stakeholders in a data mining project. Based on the identified influencing factors in relation to trust, problematic aspects of the current approach are verified. We execute various interviews with the stakeholders and the results of the interviews confirm the theoretically identified weak points of the phase model with regard to trust. Based on the finding, we sketch amendments and future research areas.**

Keywords-trust; data mining; CRISP DM; stakeholder management.

I. MOTIVATION

Big data analyses take up an ever-larger part of our lives or influence them indirectly. This can be derived from the number of scientific publications [1], which can be assessed as an indicator of the researchers' interest in the subject. Another indicator is the trend in Internet searches on the subject, e.g., for the term "Data Science" [2], which not only reflects academic interest, but also a broader public interest. In addition to the theoretical interest, the number of mass market products that are essentially based on big data analyses has been increasing for years [3]. The same interest can be seen for the term "social media" [4].

Data mining algorithms are largely based on heuristics, i.e., finding probable solutions with limited knowledge and time. This goes hand in hand with probabilities and trust. While there is an extensive literature canon on trust in general - differences and similarities in trust in general and in specific technology - the interactions between people who request, create, operate and use a specific data mining application with regard to trust and its elements have been little explored [5]. The present paper reports on various studies of the relationship between big data analyses and, in particular, their representation and trust depending on the stakeholders involved. Based on the interviews with major stakeholders of the data mining process, the paper points out open issues and challenges found during the survey.

The rest of the paper is structured as follows. In Section 1, we provide an overview on standard data-mining procedures and, based on a literature review, we examine different concepts on trust depending on the field of study. Both these concepts – data-mining methodology and the components influencing trust are then linked together. In Section 4, we present the interview results from several identified main stakeholders. Since the concepts behind the survey were not equally known by all those involved, mainly semi-structured interviews were chosen. The results were analyzed qualitatively using Mayring's approach [6]. In Section 5, we give a conclusion and list the main findings.

II. LITERATURE REVIEW

A. Big Data Analytics (BDA) / Data Mining (DM)

Big data analyses are not just about the underlying data and the resulting analyses but, as with other information systems, about the organization of the processes and organizational views [7]. This requires the presentation in a holistic end-to-end model that connects and coherently maps the individual elements. Phase models are traditionally used in project management [8] [9], while process models, such as Business Process Model and Notation (BPMN) [10] have established themselves to map the various aspects involved.

Regardless of the learning type or the methods, the Framework Cross Industry Standard Process for Data Mining (CRISP DM) has established itself as the standard procedure in data mining projects [11] [12]. The model describes the basic sequence of individual phases, the relationships between one another (see Figure 1) and the tasks contained therein (see Figure 2).

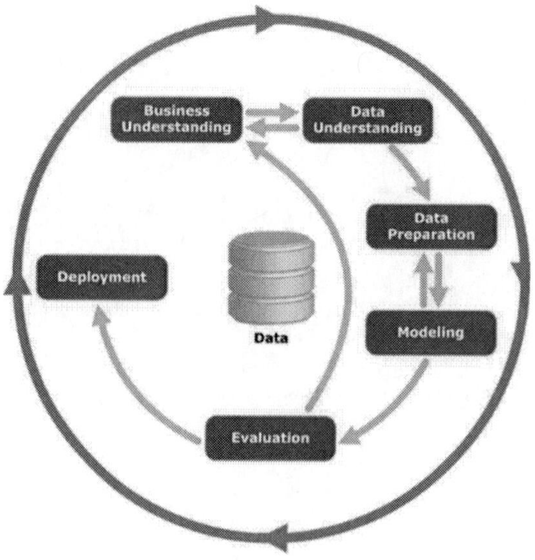

Figure 1. CRISP DM model [12 p. 5].

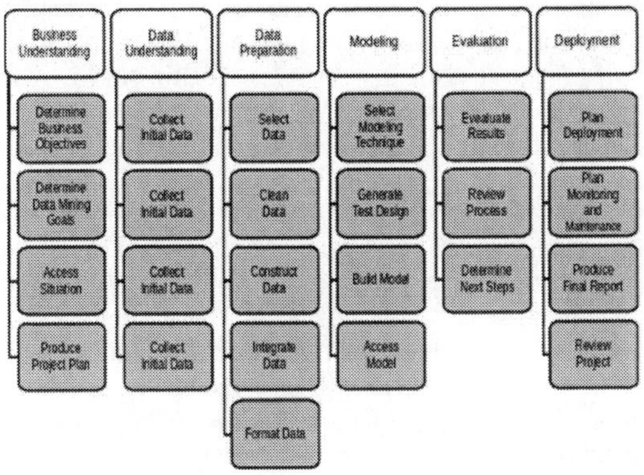

Figure 2. CRISP DM - detailed phases/ tasks [12 p. 6].

The organizational view deals, among other things, with the balancing of interests and information of the stakeholders involved. Only if all those involved find their needs taken into account and respected, they will use the results of the analysis. Obviously, an elementary component like trust has to be treated at every step of the process and cannot be added after the fact. A transfer of trust between different stakeholders is, therefore, necessary in many process steps for trust in the result of the data analysis

Interestingly, typical tasks are listed and described, but no stakeholder identification or explicit role assignment is provided for the tasks in the framework. Accordingly, there is also no consideration of the relationship of trust between the individual stakeholders. As part of this paper, in addition to the standard model, the phases within the framework of a stakeholder analysis, the typical roles involved in a RACI matrix and the information flow were analysed (see also [13] [14]). This is certainly open to discussion in detail, but several things become clear. In the individual phases, there is an information asymmetry to be overcome between the stakeholders and thus a situation of trust in the above sense. Thus, not only is the algorithm itself afflicted with probabilities and thus (trust) risks, the roles involved must also build trust among each other in order to resolve the information asymmetry - and this at different times and in different directions. If data mining is used purely in-house, the business user represents the users or consumers of data mining in the company and can manage the transfer of information and trust. If, however, the consumer of data mining is the general public, it is necessary for the "business user" to put themselves in the most varied of perspectives in the best possible way and to create the basis for the transfer of trust for all stakeholders not directly involved. To make matters worse, the general public is very heterogeneous - both in their personal attitudes and experience, as well as in their institutional environment.

The business user should take the perspective of all major representatives and anticipate and manage their expectations. Looking at the model, (see Figure 1) it becomes clear that this management has to be taken into account both when considering the origin of the data and when communicating the evaluation results / key figures.

TABLE I. ROLE OF STAKEHOLDERS DESCRIBED BY RESPONSIBILITY ASSIGNMENT MATRIX (RACI)

	Project Sponsor (PS)	Business User/ Analyst (BA)	Data Analyst/ Scientist (DA)	Information Ownership/ Flow
Business Understanding	**a**	**r**	c	PS → BA → DA
Data Understanding	**a**	c	**r**	BA/ DA
Data Preparation/ Modeling	**a**	i	**r**	DA
Evaluation	**a**	**r**	c	DA → BA → PS
Deployment	a	r	c	PS

a = accountable; = responsible; c = to consult; i = to inform

B. Acceptance and Trust

Trust is a complex concept that is defined differently in numerous disciplines depending on the specific circumstances. An additional complicating factor is that trust is also used in everyday scenarios, which results in a multitude of meanings without any reference to a concept. In a much-cited 1964 standard by Kaplan, the author goes so far as to recommend that researchers focus on a specific component of trust rather than a generalized view [15]. If, in addition to the use of the term in one language, one also considers the translation into other languages, there is a large number of uses and synonyms with clear deviations in the connotation. Cooperation, confidence and predictability are closely related terms that Mayer et al. used to describe the term in English [16 p. 729]. Trust is the basis for accepting vulnerability from people, technology and, in our case, the use of data analysis results [17].

To measure acceptance of an application or technology in business informatics, the Technology Acceptance Model (TAM) is often used [17] [19].

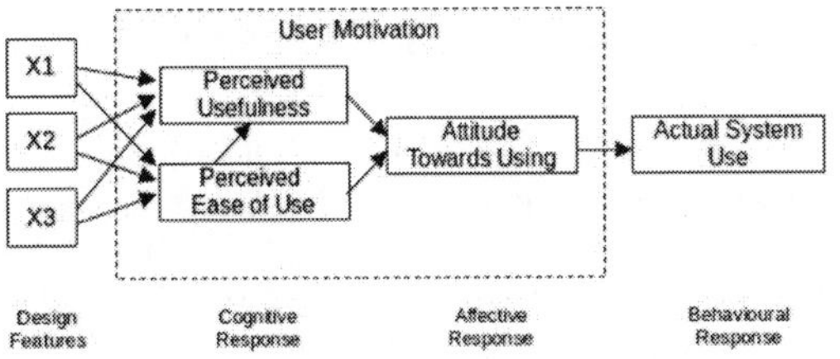

Figure 3. Technology Acceptance Model [41 p. 24].

In Figure 3, the "Attitude Towards Using" is the readiness for use, which is influenced by "Perceived Usefulness" and "Perceived Ease-of-Use". The "Perceived Usefulness" describes the expected benefit, while the "Perceived Ease-of-Use" describes the costs for the user to learn how to use the technology and thus indirectly the costs of building trust. Due to its simplicity, it is easy to use and popular. However, the model focuses on the user and the lack of consideration of the situation / structure is often criticized [20 p. 30]. Furthermore, it does not take time into account and, therefore, a separation of initial trust and continued trust is not explicitly described in the model.

Closely related concepts to trust come from psychology, sociology and social psychology, the latter being understood as a bridge between the former. While psychology focuses on the person-to-person relationship, sociology focuses on the organization-to-organization relationship. What they all have in common is to define trust as "the willingness to take risks" [21 p. 103] or the "intention to accept vulnerability" [22 p. 395]. Basically, Mayer, Davis and Schoorman show that both the personal influence and the organizational or institutional influence of taking risks can be characterized on the basis of competence, benevolence and integrity [16].

After an intensive comparison of the literature, McKnight and Chervany succeeded in bridging the gap between the above-mentioned disciplines and showing the interdependencies [23]. The authors separate between *trusting believes* as the extent to which a target is likely to behave in a way that is "benevolent, competent, honest, predictable in a situation" and the *trusting intentions* as the extent to which a person is willing to make himself vulnerable to another person's actions [23].

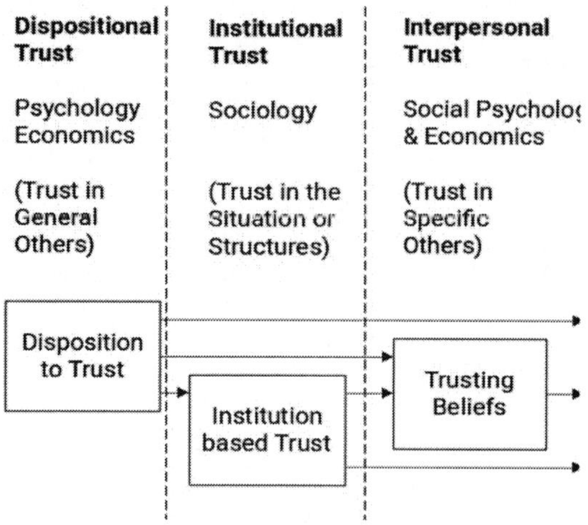

Figure 4. An interdisciplinary Model of High Level Trust Concepts [23]

In a further work, McKnight et al. show that the original characteristics (aka trusting beliefs) of trust in people can be transferred to trust in technologies (functionality, helpfulness, reliability) [5 p. 9]. Thus, the original concept is not limited to natural persons, but can be transferred to people, technologies / objects and even processes [24]. While Figure 4 links different research fields and explains influencing factors from the personal disposition to the trusting intentions, it does not take into account the dimension „time". While continued trust and trusting intentions result from experience and, therefore, the balance of incentives and penalties resulting from trusting, initial trust results from trust transfer - either from person, groups or places [25]–[27].

The microeconomic theory as a further subject area investigates trust in its own branch of research - information theory. It offers a complementary model to the explanatory approaches above. Here, the focus is on trust in goods and the costs of evaluating their properties, less on individual disposition. The underlying assumption is that the information market does not exhibit high degrees of transparency. That is, to evaluate the information, the information must be known, so one has to invest in learning it to evaluate it [28]. In principle, a distinction is made between three types of goods: search goods, experience goods and credence goods. Search goods can be evaluated before purchase or use and, therefore, trusted due to previous experience or easily available product information. Search goods are well known and represent continued trust. Experience goods can be evaluated only after purchase and, therefore, trusted after the purchase and need either a transfer of trust or reduced penalties (e.g., a „refund policy"). Credence goods cannot be evaluated due to prohibitive information retrieval costs or singularity and depend always on external trust transfer [29] [30]. This links the model nicely to the initial model: search goods have a strong linkage towards trust transfer and/ or previous experienced trust, experience goods need initial trust and a positive experience balance for continued usage, and credence goods cannot personally be evaluated over time at all and depend entirely on trust transfer.

From their perspective, all the models presented above are justified and complement each other. The technology acceptance model focuses heavily on the acceptance of a technology without addressing explicitly the wider trust aspect. However, McKnight's model explains the impact of trust in technology and links personal and environmental attitudes, while the microeconomic model deepens insights into how costs affect trust transfer.

C. Linking CRISP DM and Trust

There is only very limited amount of literature about what influences trust in data mining analyses. If one looks at the underlying knowledge and skills of the individual stakeholders in the individual phases of the CRISP DM model (see Figure 1), they will see a strong information asymmetry. To make matters worse, it is noticeable that the responsibility changes in the phases (see Table 1), and external information interests are not explicitly in the focus of the model. This is associated with relatively high costs for obtaining information. Thus, the next step is to evaluate the current practical approaches and problems by interviewing the stakeholders involved.

There are two basic approaches to understand data - compressing the information into key figures/ metrics and visualizing it in graphics. Measures have been around since the dawn of mathematics and are widely used in a wide variety of scientific fields. visualisations of data are just as old as key figures, but have been experiencing increased interest since the 1970s, beginning with Tukey's "Exploratory Data Analysis" [31] and the "Box Plots". Currently, the increased computing power enables complex representations of high-dimensional data and leads to innovative and highly complex forms of representation, e.g., t-distributed Stochastic Neighbor Embedding (t-SNE) [32]. While t-SNE or Uniform Manifold Approximation and Projection (UMAP) help to understand the data directly, graph based visualisation helps to understand hierarchies and dependencies between data or Key Performance Indicators (KPIs) [33]. As an independent specialist discipline, however, visualisation is quite young [34].

Both approaches are to be viewed critically: the key metric α (significance level) used most frequently in statistics and the corresponding p-value (probability) are so often misinterpreted in the scientific literature that the American Statistical Association opposed in 2018 another use of the term "significance" pronounced [35] [36]. On the other hand, visualisations are not problem-free either. A sub-goal of visualisation is to increase the perceived and cognitively processed amount of information and to capture interdependencies in the data structures through aggregation and emphasis. This is intended to support the correctness of decisions and confidence in the decision [37]. Thus, visualisations are not neutral either and depend on the ideas of the creators [38].

Recently, to overcome the aforementioned issues, there is a trend to combine key figures/ metrics with visualisations or allow using interaction in the visualisation. In order to develop a balanced strategy across all critical goals and their respective KPIs, it is particularly important to discover the inherent relationships between all KPIs. In this case, graph-based representations are particularly suitable [39] [40].

D. Identified Research Area

Freedom offered by modern societies, access to loads of sources of information and increased complexities force people to cope with the uncertainty of the global world by themselves. If one considers the factors presented that are important for the trust of the individual stakeholders and if one also considers the CRISP DM phase model, it becomes apparent that the currently leading framework does not explicitly pay attention to the transfer of trust between the stakeholders involved. It should also be clear that trust must be observed from the beginning to the end - interrupting the analysis process would disrupt the transmission of trust. It is important to consistently monitor the level of knowledge of all persons involved. Since the analysis process cannot be explained personally to everyone, it is important to create a framework that passively enables it. A process-oriented, graph-based visual representation as well as additional, generally understandable visualisations should help to show the connections and thus reduce the information asymmetry between the stakeholders. This should be practically substantiated in the following summarized interview with the stakeholders (see Table 2).

III. Practical Survey

As in the theoretical model, trust or the transfer of trust depends on the personal environment ("dispositional trust"), the environment ("institutional trust") and specific influencers ("interpersonal trust"). In order to obtain a representative picture, identified stakeholders were interviewed using different survey methods . In addition to the typical stakeholders already identified (see Table 1), the list was expanded to include "normal consumers" ("consumer A") and "informed consumers" ("consumer B").

In the interviews conducted, the aim was to show which aspects - from the stakeholder's point of view - are necessary in order to develop or transfer trust in data analyses. The questionnaire was based on the identified trust influencing factors during all phases of CRISP DM. Consumer were asked to compare results from data mining analyses with previous expert analyses.

Table 2: Overview of stakeholders and their interviews

Stakeholder	Interview Type	Interview Channel
S1: Data Analyst	semi-structured	face-to-face
S2: Business User	semi-structured	face-to-face
S3: Project Sponsor/ Management	semi-structured	face-to-face
S4A: Normal Consumer	semi-structured / closed	telephone
S4B: Informed Consumer	semi-structured	face-to-face

A. S1 Data Analyst Representative

The data analyst has specialist knowledge of the technical analysis of data, its consistent preparation and the use of appropriate statistical or data mining methods. He needs information about the data used and the business objective of the analysis.

Interview

For the interview, 3 data scientists were asked independently of each other which indicators they believe are relevant in order to trust the data and models. Then they were presented with various business KPIs and visualisations of their department together with the respective business representative and the similarities and differences in understanding were determined.

Main concerns and issues

In the business understanding, it was difficult for the stakeholders involved to interpret the specific KPIs. Concrete examples and the representation of the processes through graphics were essential for understanding.

The interviews showed that the KPIs used to justify the analysis results were rarely understood or misunderstood.

In principle, graphic representations were preferred by the other stakeholders involved. More complex representations were accepted, but required more detailed descriptions, and here again the data analysts often struggled with the business terms. As a compromise for understanding, several simple graphics that build on one another were used.

B. S2 Business Representative

The business analyst represents the business perspective of the departments and has special knowledge of his department. He alone can make sense of the data and explain their origin and meaning and practically validate the results.

Interview

For the interview, 3 representatives were interviewed independently of each other regarding their intentions during the phases in which they are responsible. Then they were presented with various KPIs and visualisations of their department together with the respective data analysts and the similarities and differences in understanding were determined.

Main concerns and issues

The concerns and issues of data analysts reflect the concerns and issues found among business users.

C. S3 Project Sponsor/ Management Perspective

In addition to the roles of data analyst and business user, which are involved operationally, the project sponsor is another relevant role that is more strategically oriented. His trust in the implementation and the results decides initially and finally on the resources used and the use of the results. As a managing role, which is not directly involved but is regularly informed about the analysis and the results, his trust can be seen as the first test of trustworthiness. This role is also responsible to a not inconsiderable extent for the design of the environment, ergo it exerts a great influence on the "institutional trust".

Interview

For the analysis, 10 senior IT managers were asked about their criteria for building trust in a guided interview. The following section summarizes the answers and the underlying intentions.

Main concerns and issues

Looking at the key considerations and underlying intentions, the focus is clearly on promoting institutional trust rather than understanding individual BDA and its metrics. The interviewees emphasized that building a high-quality and transparent data infrastructure is essential for trust in the results. There were different opinions as to whether this should be done step-by-step or with a "big bang". While the majority emphasizes the "step-by-step" approach and thus the step-by-step understanding of the data, a minority fears that too narrow a focus will limit the reference power of the data too much. All project sponsors emphasize that a common understanding is important. To achieve this goal, KPIs, a commonly understood language - which also includes visualisation, are used. For the most part, however, the internal stakeholders are taken into account, but the perspective of the external stakeholders is primarily included through reference to legal data sources.

D. S4 Consumer

When analysing the consumer, a distinction must be made between two stakeholders. The difference lies in the existing experience with analyses. One group are the consumers who have no experience with data mining analysis, data and procedures (see Table 2: "S4A: Normal Consumer"). On the other hand, there are consumers who were not directly involved in the analysis but have personal experience with similar data mining projects (see Table 2: "S4B: Informed Consumer").

Consumers use the results directly for their own purposes, e.g., fitness wearables or evaluations in magazines. However, consumers can also be indirectly affected by the results of the analysis, e.g., as bank customers who are subject to a risk classification when requesting a loan.

E. S4A: Normal Consumer

Interview

In a semi-structured interview, 23 people between the ages of 20 and 60 were asked which factors are relevant for them in different contexts in order to trust data mining analyses.

Main concerns and issues

The results of the data mining were accepted to a very limited extent. Without a well-founded justification for the refusal, it was doubted that the data were representative and reflected the personal circumstances. Although trust was positively influenced by the spread of the BDA (e.g., wearables/ web portals) and by certificates, the results are doubted by 70% - 80% of the respondents and used personally. When it comes to acceptance, the personal opinion of a specialist or friends prevails. If trust has arisen through the transfer of trust from third parties, the trust is not shaken by isolated negative examples or experiences. In principle, the respondents do not see themselves in a position to validate the data bases and functionalities and need support from their environment.

F. S4B: Informed Consumer

Interview

In the interviews, three scientists were questioned in a semi-structured interview. They were not actively involved in the analyses, but they were familiar with the environment.

Main concerns and issues

The expert survey revealed that these people generally trust the analyses, but inform themselves about the data collection, data processing and methods used on a random basis. A renowned environment of the BDA reduces the scope of own validations, but is not sufficient.

IV. CONCLUSION

In principle, the results of the data mining process are accepted by the stakeholders involved in the analysis, but trust in the results correlated strongly with the proximity to the process and the associated costs of information procurement.

In the business and data understanding, the business and data analyst representatives attached great importance to understanding the data and assessing its quality. Less value was placed on a detailed verbal description, the focus was more on use cases and easily understandable key figures.

While the specialists tend to orientate themselves towards the key figures of their specialist area during the evaluation, the other stakeholders involved prefer visual representations in addition to the key figures. Key figures are accepted without understanding their meaning in particular. In order to understand the statements and to trust the results, visual representations prevail. There, too, a trend towards rather simple, well-known representations was discernible. For example, a combination of histogram and box plot was preferred to a violin plot.

The preparation of the analysis process for later users was less of a focus. A fundamental desire was established among all stakeholders to present their findings or interests transparently. However, they often do not realize that the technical terms that describe their special field are not universally understandable. Thus, in data science projects, the focus should be on a more understandable language in advance. In particular, the visualisation seems to have a greater influence on the overall understanding than on specific key figures.

Based on the findings, it would certainly be helpful to add a stakeholder-oriented view to the CRISP DM framework. It should be essential to meet both the information needs of the specialists and to balance the information asymmetry among the stakeholders. In addition to specific, subject-related key figures, this view should be integrated into the CRISP DM process as well as simple visualized representations and generally accessible key figures. This view should also depict the chronological sequence and, so to speak, represent the information transformation nose to tail. In order to do justice to the different levels of knowledge, it should be able to depict different levels of detail.

REFERENCES

[1] Y. Zelenkov and E. Anisichkina, "Trends in data mining research: A two-decade review using topic analysis," *Bus. Inform.*, vol. 15, no. 1, pp. 30–46, Mar. 2021, doi: 10.17323/2587-814X.2021.1.30.46.

[2] "Google Trends 'Data Science,'" *Google Trends*. https://trends.google.de/trends/explore?q=%2Fm%2F0jt3_q3&date=all (accessed Aug. 15, 2022).

[3] "Google Trends 'Fitness App,'" *Google Trends*. https://trends.google.de/trends/explore?date=all&q=%2Fg%2F11cny0zppc (accessed Aug. 15, 2022).

[4] "Google Trends 'Social Media,'" *Google Trends*. https://trends.google.de/trends/explore?date=all&q=social%20media (accessed Aug. 15, 2022).

[5] D. H. Mcknight, M. Carter, J. B. Thatcher, and P. F. Clay, "Trust in a specific technology: An investigation of its components and measures," *ACM Trans. Manag. Inf. Syst.*, vol. 2, no. 2, Art. no. 2, Jun. 2011, doi: 10.1145/1985347.1985353.

[6] P. Mayring, "Qualitative content analysis," *Companion Qual. Res.*, vol. 1, no. 2, pp. 159–176, 2004.

[7] A.-W. Scheer and K. Schneider, "ARIS — Architecture of Integrated Information Systems," in *Handbook on Architectures of Information Systems*, P. Bernus, K. Mertins, and G. Schmidt, Eds. Berlin/Heidelberg: Springer-Verlag, 1998, pp. 605–623. doi: 10.1007/3-540-26661-5_25.

[8] G. Garel, "A history of project management models: From pre-models to the standard models," *Int. J. Proj. Manag.*, vol. 31, no. 5, pp. 663–669, Jul. 2013, doi: 10.1016/j.ijproman.2012.12.011.

[9] P. D. de M. Sánchez, C. G. Gaya, and M. Á. S. Peréz, "Standardized Models for Project Management Processes to Product Design," *Procedia Eng.*, vol. 63, pp. 193–199, 2013, doi: 10.1016/j.proeng.2013.08.176.

[10] M. Chinosi and A. Trombetta, "BPMN: An introduction to the standard," *Comput. Stand. Interfaces*, vol. 34, no. 1, pp. 124–134, Jan. 2012, doi: 10.1016/j.csi.2011.06.002.

[11] P. Chapman *et al.*, "Step-by-step data mining guide," *SPSS*, p. 76, 2000.

[12] R. Wirth and J. Hipp, "CRISP-DM: Towards a standard process model for data mining," in *Proceedings of the 4th international conference on the practical applications of knowledge discovery and data mining*, 2000, vol. 1, pp. 29–39.

[13] C. J. Costa and J. T. Aparicio, "POST-DS: A Methodology to Boost Data Science," in *2020 15th Iberian Conference on Information Systems and Technologies (CISTI)*, Sevilla, Spain, Jun. 2020, pp. 1–6. doi: 10.23919/CISTI49556.2020.9140932.

[14] L. Wehrstein, "CRISP-DM ready for Machine Learning Projects," *Medium*, Dec. 19, 2020. https://towardsdatascience.com/crisp-dm-ready-for-machine-learning-projects-2aad9172056a (accessed Jun. 11, 2021).

[15] A. Kaplan, *The conduct of inquiry: methodology for behavioral science*. Scranton (Pa.): Chandler, 1964.

[16] R. C. Mayer, J. H. Davis, and F. D. Schoorman, "An Integrative Model Of Organizational Trust," *Acad. Manage. Rev.*, vol. 20, no. 3, pp. 709–734, Jul. 1995, doi: 10.5465/amr.1995.9508080335.

[17] B. A. Misztal, "Trust: Acceptance of, Precaution Against and Cause of Vulnerability," *Comp. Sociol.*, vol. 10, no. 3, pp. 358–379, 2011, doi: 10.1163/156913311X578190.

[18] F. D. Davis, "Perceived Usefulness, Perceived Ease of Use, and User Acceptance of Information Technology," *MIS Q.*, vol. 13, no. 3, p. 319, Sep. 1989, doi: 10.2307/249008.

[19] N. Marangunić and A. Granić, "Technology acceptance model: a literature review from 1986 to 2013," *Univers. Access Inf. Soc.*, vol. 14, no. 1, pp. 81–95, Mar. 2015, doi: 10.1007/s10209-014-0348-1.

[20] B. Lunceford, "Reconsidering technology adoption and resistance," *Explor. MEDIA Ecol.*, p. 20, 2009.

[21] N. Luhmann, "Familiarity, Confidence, Trust: Problems and Alternatives," p. 10.

[22] D. M. Rousseau, S. B. Sitkin, R. S. Burt, and C. Camerer, "Not So Different After All: A Cross-Discipline View Of Trust," *Acad. Manage. Rev.*, vol. 23, no. 3, pp. 393–404, Jul. 1998, doi: 10.5465/amr.1998.926617.

[23] D. H. McKnight and N. L. Chervany, "What is Trust? A Conceptual Analysis and an Interdisciplinary Model," *AMCIS 2000 Proc. P382*, p. 8, 2000.

[24] J. B. Thatcher, M. L. Loughry, J. Lim, and D. H. McKnight, "Internet anxiety: An empirical study of the effects of personality, beliefs, and social support," *Inf. Manage.*, vol. 44, no. 4, pp. 353–363, Jun. 2007, doi: 10.1016/j.im.2006.11.007.

[25] D. Belanche, L. V. Casaló, C. Flavián, and J. Schepers, "Trust transfer in the continued usage of public e-services," *Inf. Manage.*, vol. 51, no. 6, pp. 627–640, Sep. 2014, doi: 10.1016/j.im.2014.05.016.

[26] D. Harrison McKnight, V. Choudhury, and C. Kacmar, "The impact of initial consumer trust on intentions to transact with a web site: a trust building model," *J. Strateg. Inf. Syst.*, vol. 11, no. 3, Art. no. 3, Dec. 2002, doi: 10.1016/S0963-8687(02)00020-3.

[27] K. J. Stewart, "Trust Transfer on the World Wide Web," *Organ. Sci.*, vol. 14, no. 1, pp. 5–17, Feb. 2003, doi: 10.1287/orsc.14.1.5.12810.

[28] B. Kahin and H. R. Varian, Eds., *Internet publishing and beyond: the economics of digital information and intellectual property*. Cambridge, Mass: MIT Press, 2000.

[29] S. Fließ, "Qualitätsmanagement bei Vertrauensgütern," *Mark. ZFP*, vol. 26, no. Sonderheft 2004, pp. 33–44, Jan. 2019, doi: 10.15358/0344-1369-2004-Sonderheft-2004-33.

[30] K. Mitra, M. C. Reiss, and L. M. Capella, "An examination of perceived risk, information search and behavioral intentions in search, experience and credence services," *J.*

Serv. Mark., vol. 13, no. 3, pp. 208–228, Jun. 1999, doi: 10.1108/08876049910273763.

[31] J. W. Tukey, *Exploratory data analysis*. Reading, Mass., 1977.

[32] L. Van der Maaten and G. Hinton, "Visualizing data using t-SNE.," *J. Mach. Learn. Res.*, vol. 9, no. 11, 2008.

[33] M. Graham, J. B. Kennedy, and C. Hand, "A comparison of set-based and graph-based visualisations of overlapping classification hierarchies," in *Proceedings of the working conference on Advanced visual interfaces - AVI '00*, Palermo, Italy, 2000, pp. 41–50. doi: 10.1145/345513.345243.

[34] H. Reiterer, T. M. Mann, G. Mussler, and U. Bleimann, "Visualisierung von entscheidungsrelevanten Daten für das Management. In: HMD, Praxis der Wirtschaftsinformatik," vol. 212, 2000, pp. 71–83.

[35] V. Amrhein and S. Greenland, "Remove, rather than redefine, statistical significance," *Nat. Hum. Behav.*, vol. 2, no. 1, pp. 4–4, Jan. 2018, doi: 10.1038/s41562-017-0224-0.

[36] R. L. Wasserstein and N. A. Lazar, "The ASA Statement on *p* -Values: Context, Process, and Purpose," *Am. Stat.*, vol. 70, no. 2, pp. 129–133, Apr. 2016, doi: 10.1080/00031305.2016.1154108.

[37] J.-A. Meyer, *Visualisierung von informationen*. Place of publication not identified: Springer, 1999.

[38] E. Bussemas, "Mehr als Balken und Torten. Eine experimentelle Befragung zur Wahrnehmung von interaktiven Datenvisualisierungen im Journalismus," *Medien Kommun.*, vol. 66, no. 2, pp. 188–216, 2018, doi: 10.5771/1615-634X-2018-2-188.

[39] M. P. Brundage, W. Z. Bernstein, K. C. Morris, and J. A. Horst, "Using Graph-based visualisations to Explore Key Performance Indicator Relationships for Manufacturing Production Systems," *Procedia CIRP*, vol. 61, pp. 451–456, 2017, doi: 10.1016/j.procir.2016.11.176.

[40] N. Elmqvist *et al.*, "Fluid interaction for information visualisation," *Inf. Vis.*, vol. 10, no. 4, pp. 327–340, Oct. 2011, doi: 10.1177/1473871611413180.

[41] F. D. Davis, "A technology acceptance model for empirically testing new end-user information systems: Theory and results (Doctoral dissertation)." Massachusetts Institute of Technology, 1985.

Shapley Values based Regional Feature Importance Measures Driving Error Analysis in Manufacturing

Valentin Göttisheim, Holger Ziekow, Ulf Schreier, Alexander Gerling
Furtwangen University
78120 Furtwangen, Germany
email: {valentin.goettisheim, holger.ziekow, ulf.schreier, alexander.gerling}@hs-furtwangen.de

Abstract – **Data driven manufacturing quality management using machine learning for error detection can leverage predictive models for error analysis. Quality engineer experts evaluate the models input and interpret important features in the context of the specific manufacturing domain. In this paper, we propose three heuristics to determine the importance of features leading to actionable insights for error analysis. All proposed metrics are illustrated on synthetic data and evaluated on a real-world dataset.**

Keywords – manufacturing quality management; error analysis; feature importance; Shapley Values; xAI; machine learning.

I. INTRODUCTION

Quality management in modern manufacturing processes involves extensive testing and collection of detailed measurements along production lines. This provides the basis for data driven error analysis. However, quality managers struggle with finding error causes in large sets of quality data [1]. Artificial Intelligence (AI) methods can help to analyze such data and predict errors [2]. In combination with eXplainable AI (xAI), predictive models can further put quality engineers on the right track for finding causes of production errors. That is, feature importance metrics can reveal features that hint at error causes [3]. However, well known feature importance measures are not tailored to this task. In this paper, we expand our earlier work [4] and introduce new feature importance measures which are designed to reveal features of interest for quality management in manufacturing.

Our work is rooted in a research project with a German manufacturer [5]. Here, we found that combining human expertise with AI-based data analysis is desirable for error analysis in production lines. This is because (a) quality managers seek to understand the error causes and may not blindly trust AI-based results and (b) human experts have background knowledge and a deep understanding of the production process, that the AI does not have access to. Hence, this work explicitly keeps the human experts in the loop and focuses on using AI models for providing input to human analysts.

This work targets typical manufacturing setups, where production lines comprise a sequence of production steps and several test stations along the production line. Test stations perform measurements on each product at different steps of the production. This leads to detailed records of individual product instances that can include hundreds of thousands of measurements per product [6]. However, the high number of different measurements poses challenges for finding causes of errors in the data. Another challenge in error cause analysis is that errors are rare [7]. Modern manufacturing processes are usually highly optimized and quality management is often about driving down rare – but still costly – errors. Yet, existing applications have successfully used such high dimensional and imbalanced data to build AI models for predicting production errors [6][8]. The aim of such models is to take measurements from test stations early in the production sequence and predict errors that occur downstream in the production line. If errors can be predicted early with sufficient reliability, products can be removed early in the process and costs for downstream production steps can be avoided [2].

Furthermore, such AI models can be analyzed to hint at the cause of errors. We leverage this to provide insights to human experts in quality management. Existing works use feature importance measures to identify quality measurements that are relevant in predicting and explaining errors. For example, if a heat measurement of an oven is important in predicting errors, then errors may be avoided by adjusting the temperature setting. Identifying such interesting measurements amongst the thousands of data points can help quality managers to find error causes and improve production [9]. However, existing importance measures are not tailored to find features that are interesting for inspection in error cause analysis. Instead, they take a global view and capture how much a model relies on a given feature on average. As we show in this paper, such a global view is often not useful when it comes to spotting rare but strong relations that lead to actionable insight in error analysis.

In contrast to global importance measures, xAI methods like Shapley Additive Explanations (SHAP) [10] and LIME [12] provide local explanations for the impact of features on a prediction. That is, the impact of features can be estimated for individual data instances. However, analyzing a data instance in isolation is of little use for quality management in manufacturing. That is, a single data instance is not enough to draw conclusions for actionable insights.

With this work, we provide feature importance measures that are conceptually in between global and local feature importance. We refer to this as regional feature importance. With this concept we setup on and expand our earlier work [4]. That is, we analyze sets of local feature importance values for interesting effects. The result of this analysis is captured in new importance measures that capture different interesting aspects. In this paper, we mathematically define our applied notion of interestingness. Intuitively, we consider a feature interesting if it hints at actionable insight for quality managers. Such an action could be setting a threshold in a quality check or adjusting the process to avoid certain value ranges. Intuitively, drastic changes in error rates and high error rates in well-defined parts of a value range make features interesting. In this paper, we provide importance measures that formally capture such notions of interestingness and map them to an importance score. In summary, we make the following key contributions:

1) We introduce and formally define novel feature importance measures that are tailored to find relevant features in manufacturing quality management.

2) We test and illustrate the benefits of our proposed measures with synthetic data.

3) We evaluate the proposed measures on real-world data and compare them with established importance measures.

With these contributions, we help human experts in quality management better leverage results from AI models for driving their analysis.

The remainder of this paper is structured as follows. In Section II, we briefly summarize the corresponding background. In Section III, approaches to derive the regional feature importance are proposed which then are evaluated in a real-world dataset in Section IV. In Section V, we discuss related work and conclude in Section VI.

II. BACKGROUND

When using Machine Learning (ML) support for error analysis in quality management processes, feature importance metrics can become a tool to rank and identify features that are suitable to guide Quality Engineers (QE) in finding error causes in production. Such a process inspired the present work is carried out in the production of an industry partner in the research project [4]. ML-driven quality management processes here focus on QEs as primary actors. Using ML support, QEs are intended to analyze production and take corrective maintenance steps in production. However, the development and deployment of models for the ML support system are embedded in automated pipelines and maintained by data scientists. The automated ML pipeline includes several steps like data preprocessing, i.e., feature selection or evaluation of model performances through cost-sensitive metrics [2]. As such, the system is designed to enable QEs to use ML support for error causes analysis, but not to be engaged with the technical depth of the ML system.

A reference process focusing on QEs intended to investigate errors in production is laid out in [1]. Key steps include the selection of production data for the automated ML pipeline. Later steps involve error identification and correction in production using ML support. To identify error causes the QE is intended to use feature importance to find features that suits as explanations for error causes.

SHAP is one of the more recent advancements in the field of xAI, focusing on the interpretability of ML models. SHAP targets instance-based as opposed to global model explanation. By aggregating explanations of instances, it is possible to evaluate the importance of features incorporating aspects of interest to guide QEs in error cause analysis [3]. SHAP evaluates the marginal contribution a feature has on its model output. The contribution $\phi_f \in \mathbb{R}$ for a feature f with model m is attributed using Shapley Values from game theory:

$$\phi_f = \sum_{S \subseteq N \setminus \{f\}} \frac{|S|!\,(M - |S| - 1)!}{M!} [m_x(S \cup \{f\}) - m_x(S)],$$

where M is the number of all features, S is the set of input values, and |S| is the magnitude of S (for example, $S = x_1, x_2, \dots, x_{f-1}, x_{f+1}, x_n$ and $|S| = n - 1$). To compute the feature contribution usually the explanation model $e(z') = \phi_0 + \sum_{f=1}^{M} \phi_f z'_f$ where $z' \in \{0,1\}^M$ is used. This is the weighted average over all feature contributions. The explanation model is computed using the mapping $m_x(S) = m(e_x(z'))$ which maps all input values S to whether the feature is being used ($z' = 1$) or not known ($z' = 0$).

In an earlier work [4], we already picked up the idea of Shapley Value based heuristics to determine importance measures leading to helpful insights for quality engineering. For completeness, the main ideas are briefly summarized below.

Max-SHAP: The Max-SHAP heuristic focuses on the maximal SHAP values and ranks the features according to their maximum SHAP value. The intuition behind this metric is that a feature showing a high SHAP value for an error instance is a good explanation. Formally, Max-SHAP is defined as:

$$Max\ SHAP_f(m,S) = \max\{\phi_f(m,x) | x \in S\}$$

Max-Main: This metric focuses similarly to the Max-SHAP on maximal values but in contrast, the maximum of the SHAP main effects is assessed. The intuition is that a feature with high main effects is considered a good explanation. SHAP main effects do not include interactions between features and therefore are the single most simple explanation for an error case. The Max-Main metric is defined as:

$$Max\ Main\ Effect_f(m,S) = \max\{\phi_f(m,x) - \sum_{j \neq f} \phi_{f,j}(m,x) | \, | x \in S\}$$

Range-SHAP: Considering a change in SHAP values over the feature value range, the feature with a bigger change is considered more interesting. The intuition is that features with varying contributions are more likely to indicate error cases. The Range-SHAP metric is defined as:

$$Range\ SHAP_f(m,S) = \max\{\phi_f(m,x) | x \in S\} - \min\{\phi_f(m,x) | x \in S\}$$

III. AGGREGATIONS OF SHAP VALUES TO ASSESS REGIONAL FEATURE IMPORTANCE

We aim to identify features that are helpful in finding error causes in production. Production errors are rare events because of the optimized production process. Many error occurrences are of random nature. However, some have a clear cause which is captured in the data. Features that reflect these error events are hints to causes and therefore should be rewarded with high importance scores. The fundamental idea is a scoring-function g: g(f, X, ...)→ ℝ that aggregates SHAP values and scores „interesting" features high. Here, we refer to f as the target feature used in the analysis with the dataset X, and ... represents the use of additional parameters which are unique to each approach later proposed. We further refer to $\phi_f(x)$ as SHAP values of the feature f computed on the data instance $x \in X$ and define $\bar{\phi}_f(X) = \frac{1}{|X|}\sum_{x \in X} \phi(x)$ as the SHAP value mean.

In the following, three approaches to assess the importance score g are proposed. For each approach first, the basic concept is described and then the idea is illustrated using synthetic sample data where the ground truth is known. In all illustrations, the error cause can be attributed to features A, B or random occurrences affecting 1% of the data. We then train an XGBoost classifier [12] for error prediction on the 110,000 data points and compare the importance metrics g with the classic state-of-the-art importance measures implemented in the XGBoost library (v1.3.3). All illustration results are listed in Tables 1 to 3 and reported as the rank of the feature with mean score and standard deviations (mean/standard deviation) in brackets. Mean and standard deviations are based on the 15 repetitions the illustrations were conducted.

A) Outlier-Approach

The intuition behind this approach is that features with abnormal SHAP values are potentially interesting. Therefore, we perform anomaly detection on the distribution of SHAP values and assess the SHAP values for abnormal data points. For simplicity, we assume that the SHAP values approximately form a normal distribution. The outliers then can be detected using mean and standard deviation where the less interesting SHAP values are around the expectation value. However, other anomaly detection methods may be used as alternatives. Assuming a normal distribution, we detect increased SHAP values by determining the SHAP values outside of the normal distribution with at least λ standard deviations $\sigma(\phi_f(X))$ above the SHAP value mean $\bar{\phi}_f(X)$. The importance score g is formally defined as the sum over all outliers $\text{outl}(\lambda, X) = \{ x \in X \mid \phi_f(x) \geq \bar{\phi}_f(X) + \lambda\, \sigma(\phi_f(X))\}$ as:

$$g(f, X, \lambda) = \sum_{x' \in \text{outl}(\lambda, X)} \phi_f(x')$$

Note, $\phi_f(x')$ refers to the SHAP values for feature f computed on data instances x' where the set $\text{outl}(\lambda, X)$ only includes outliers λ standard deviations above the SHAP value mean. The concept is that we consider high SHAP values as interesting because high SHAP values provide a strong indication for errors and therefore hint at error causes.

To illustrate the Outlier-Approach, we now compare the approach with state-of-the-art feature importance measures implemented in the XGBoost library using synthetic data. Metric g is computed with $\lambda = 2$ considering SHAP values 2σ above the features SHAP value mean. As data, we consider the following dataset: Feature A causes a small number of errors within a small value range, i.e., an 8% error rate within a 0.025 quantile range. Feature B causes a decreasing error rate from 4% to 3% over the feature value in a 0.8 quantile range. Thus, feature B has a lower error rate but within a much broader range than feature A. In this situation, we consider feature A with its strong (albeit rare) relation to error events- as more interesting.

The illustration result listed in Table 1 shows the proposed approach Outlier Shap ranks feature A as more important while the classic importance measures do not. That is, all measures except Weight rank feature B higher than A. Note, Weight scores feature A and B very similar. Both features show a difference in mean scores of 19.8 and considering the standard deviations of more than 33.6 both scores of feature A and B are almost equal. Therefore, Weight does not rank feature A clearly higher. Thus, only the proposed Outlier Shap is reliable and detects the more important feature A correctly.

TABLE 1. "ILLUSTRATION RESULT": EVALUATED FEATURE IMPORTANCE SHOWING "OUTLIER SHAP" CORRECTLY RANKS FEATURE A AS MORE IMPORTANT – NOTATED: FEATURE (MEAN/STD).

Rank	Weight	Gain	Cover	Total Gain	Total Cover	Avg. Abs. SHAP	Outlier Shap
1	A (921.2/ 33.66)	B (5.0/ 0.21)	B (1065/ 63.5)	B (4566/ 141)	B (960039/ 50756)	B (0.77/ 0.02)	A (4660/ 137)
2	B (902.3/ 36.85)	A (3.33/ 0.07)	A (781/ 58.6)	A (3072/ 137)	A (720332/ 63755)	A (0.21/ 0.008)	B (429/ 161)

B) Micro-Average Approach

The intuition behind this approach is that features are of interest if they show high SHAP values within a small feature value range. Therefore, we divide the feature value range into equally sized partitions and determine the average SHAP value of each interval. The importance score g is then determined as the maximum average SHAP value of all intervals belonging to the given feature. Formally the importance score is defined as the maximal average SHAP value $\max\{\bar{\phi}_f(X_i)\}$ where $x \in X_i$ of interval i comprises the datapoints $X_i = \{x \in X \mid (i * d) \leq x < (i * d) + d\}$ over the equally sized feature range $d = \frac{1}{n} * range(X_f)$ for the set of feature values X_f and given number of intervals n:

$$g(f, X, n) = \max\{\bar{\phi}_f(X_i) \mid i = 0, \ldots, n-1\}$$

Note, $\bar{\phi}_f(X_i)$ refers here to the mean SHAP value of interval i for given number of intervals n. We consider intervals with higher SHAP values as more important. The concept is that the higher the average SHAP value within an interval, the more important this interval is for the contribution to error events.

An illustration of this approach is an increased error ratio in a tail of a normal distributed feature. Consider the normally distributed $N(0,1)$ features A and B. Feature A causes a 10% error rate in the upper tail of the feature range. Feature B causes a slightly decreasing error rate of 4% to 3% from the 0.3 to the 0.7 feature value quantile. We argue that feature A – even though it explains fewer errors - is more interesting because it leads to more actionable insights. This type of error events is often caused by exceeding a threshold that could be checked in production without much effort.

For this illustration, metric g is computed with a number of intervals $n = 100$. The results listed in Table 2 show that the classical feature importance ranks the less interesting feature B as more important, whereas metric g the Micro-avg Shap correctly ranks feature A as more important. Considering the results for Weight with an absolute difference in scores of A and B of 25 and a standard deviation of 53 for B, both features A and B are attributed with similar importance, with B being ranked slightly higher.

TABLE 2. "ILLUSTRATION RESULT": EVALUATED FEATURE IMPORTANCE SHOWING "MICRO-AVG SHAP" CORRECTLY RANKS FEATURE A AS MORE IMPORTANT – NOTATED: FEATURE (MEAN/STD).

Rank	Weight	Gain	Cover	Total Gain	Total Cover	Avg. Abs. SHAP	Micro-Avg Shap
1	B (921/ 53.6)	B (4.75/ 0.168)	B (1029/ 64.5)	B (4362/ 177)	B (944996/ 48209)	B (0.8/ 0.02)	A (2.62/ 0.579)
2	A (896/ 35.9)	A (3.34/ 0.12)	A (722/ 53.0)	A (2993/ 151)	A (646955/ 46820)	A (0.22/ 0.01)	B (0.997/ 0.294)

C) Slope-Approach

The intuition behind this approach is that rapid changes in SHAP values are of interest. A rapid change of SHAP values within a small interval of feature values indicates a clear threshold at which interpretation as the cause of error events is possible. The rate of SHAP value change can be represented by a slope. Like the former approach equally sized intervals of a feature are constructed but then regression slopes on the means of SHAP values over multiple intervals are computed. To make the approach more precise, further conditions are imposed to accept the slope as admissible solution or the computed slope is not considered for the importance score. Formally, the importance score g is defined:

$$g(f,X,n,w,t) = max\{|slope(w_j)||j = 0,\dots,n-1\}$$

The slope $slope(w_j) = \beta$ is computed over the rolling window $w_j = \{\bar{\phi}_f(\mathrm{X_j}),\dots,\bar{\phi}_f(\mathrm{X_{j+w}})\}$ of size w where β minimizes $\epsilon = \bar{\phi}_f(X_i) - i * \beta$ for $\bar{\phi}_f(X_i) \in w_j$. Here β represents the slope over the averaged shap values of multiple windows w_j. To compute β we used simple OLS regression. Also note that X_i for interval i is similar defined to the previous micro-average approach. The slopes $slope(w_j)$ is considered or discarded, i.e., set to zero, for some threshold t if either condition is fulfilled:

$$\exists\, i = j,\dots,j+w\colon q_{75}(\{\bar{\phi}_f(X_i) \in w_j\}) - q_{25}(\{\bar{\phi}_f(X_i) \in w_j\}) \geq t \quad (1)$$

$$\max(\{\bar{\phi}_f(X_i) \in w_j | i = j,\dots,j+w\}) \geq t \quad (2)$$

Condition (1), called Interquartile (IQR) shap variation, is chosen such that the mean shap values in the window w_j in between the 0.75 quantile q_{75} and the 0.25 quantile q_{25} has to be greater than or equal to given threshold t. For condition (2) the Max Shap variation the maximal mean shap value in the window w_j has to be greater than or equal to a threshold t. If the corresponding condition is fulfilled, the $slope(w_j)$ is accepted. Both conditions suppress steep local slopes covering a too small value range.

To illustrate this metric on a sample case, we consider a change in error rate within a small feature range. We assume two uniform distributed features A and B. Feature A causes an error rate of 15% in a 0.01 feature value quantile range. Feature B causes a decreasing error rate from 10% to 2% over the entire feature value range. Although feature B may be more important globally, we consider feature A as more important to identify actionable insights. To compute the importance score g, we set the numbers of intervals to $n = 300$ and the rolling window of size $w = 10$. The thresholds t are chosen for the IQR variation (1) as $t = 0.1$ and to $t = 0.4$ for the Max Shap variation (2). As such, the interquartile range or the maximum value respectively of the mean SHAP values over the intervals in window w_j has to be greater than or equal to t.

The illustration results listed in Table 3 show the classic importance measures rank feature B as more important. In contrast, both proposed Slope variations correctly rank feature A as more important. Observing Weight with an absolute difference in scores of 2 feature B is slightly ranked better than feature A. However, the values are very similar, given a standard deviation of about 37.

TABLE 3. "ILLUSTRATION RESULT": EVALUATED FEATURE IMPORTANCE SHOWING "SLOPE IQR SHAP" & "SLOPE MAX SHAP" CORRECTLY RANKED FEATURE A AS MORE IMPORTANT – NOTATED: FEATURE (MEAN/STD).

Rank	Weight	Gain	Cover	Total Gain	Total Cover	Avg. Abs. SHAP	Slope IQR Shap	Slope Max Shap
1	B (971/ 37.0)	B (4.41 /0.127)	B (1425 /56.1)	B (4278 /185)	B (1385121/ 84941)	B (0.362 /0.009)	A (0.163 /0.018)	A (0.162 /0.019)
2	A (969/ 37.1)	A (3.32 /0.097)	A (1078 /83.2)	A (3213 /155)	A (1043942/ 73457)	A (0.151 /0.009)	B (0.089 /0.014)	B (0.089 /0.014)

IV. EXPERIMENTS

With the aim to identify features that are interesting in error cause analysis, we conduct an experiment with the Secom dataset [13]. The real-world dataset originates from a semiconductor manufacturing process containing 591 features and 1667 instances of which 106 are error instances.

The learning problem is formulated as a binary classification task and a XGB gradient boosting model with default parameters used for training. For model training and the evaluation of importance metrics, we used the whole dataset. This may resemble an idealized case where the training data perfectly meets the data distribution during prediction but also prevents uncertainty being induced by the model for the evaluation of the importance metrics. The model achieved a perfect training score according to the f1 score (f1=1.0). The SHAP values are computed using the SHAP package (v0.40.0) [14]. The proposed importance metrics were computed using the same parameters described in the illustrations on the synthetic datasets for each proposed approach.

We use the experiments to compare existing and our proposed importance metrics and discuss exemplary features in detail along with their SHAP plots. Figures 1 to 4 show the

TABLE 4. "SECOM EXPERIMENT RESULTS": TOP 5 IMPORTANCE RANKINGS GROUPED COMPARISON WITH HIGHLIGHTED AGREEMENTS TO THE PROPOSED METRICS (GREY) AND UNIQUE FINDINGS (BOLD).

Rank	Classic Metrics					SHAP-based Metrics				Proposed Metrics			
										Slope Approaches			
	Weight	*Gain*	*Cover*	*Total Gain*	*Total Cover*	*Average Abs Shap*	*Max Main*	*Max Shap*	*Range Value*	*Max Shap*	*IQR Shap*	*Micro-Avg Approach*	*Outlier Approach*
1	F59	F210	F168	F59	F59	F59	F59	F59	F59	F59	F59	F64	F59
2	F333	F539	F429	F333	F64	F21	F64	F64	F64	F64	F64	F59	**F423**
3	F103	F29	F426	F64	F426	F333	F40	F426	F333	F429	F33	F103	F64
4	F2	F109	F100	F132	F121	F488	F426	F333	F103	F333	**F130**	F40	F333
5	F33	F304	F331	F33	F574	F103	F153	F40	F33	**F475**	F429	F121	F2

discussed SHAP plots. However, because of the limited space, not all SHAP plots of every feature can be shown. The SHAP plots have the feature values on the x-axes and the corresponding SHAP value on the y-axes. Visually distinguishable are error instances colored red and non-errors colored blue. Colored grey in the background are histograms of the corresponding feature values.

For the following discussion of the results, the metrics are grouped into (1) Classic, (2) SHAP-based and (3) our proposed importance metrics. Table 4 shows the resulting rankings. Highlighted in grey are the agreements of the corresponding group with the proposed metrics. At the first sight, the metrics Gain and Cover have the least overlapping results with the proposed metrics. Since both metrics are commonly used as importance measures this is surprising. On the other hand, the metric Weight has quite a lot in common with the proposed metrics but the previous illustrations on synthetic data already showed that Weight is not a reliable measure. In the following, agreements and disagreements over the grouped rankings of the top three features are discussed in more detail.

A) Agreements of importance

Across all groups of metrics, some features have identical importance. All groups assign similar importance to the features F59, F64, F333 and F103.

Features F59, F64 and 103 are shown in Figure 1 and are examples of interesting features. F59 has increased SHAP values on the right-hand side. A point of interest is the threshold of about 10 of the feature value where the SHAP values are increasing. This hints at a threshold that can be useful for error cause analysis and error explanation. An advanced understanding of such thresholds enables correction in production, like adjustment of parameters or setting machinery alarms. Further assessing the right-hand side of F59 shows high SHAP values, which is an indicator for a cause explanation. Note, this area of increased SHAP values also shows an increased error rate, rendering this an interesting feature. F64 shows these interesting properties too: A distinguishable threshold at which SHAP values are increasing, strong effects, i.e., high SHAP values, and a higher error ratio in the area of increased SHAP values.

Ranked as equally important across all groups – with minor differences – are F103 and F333. Both features are of interest and show equivalent properties as described above. Due to space limitations, just F333 is shown in Figure 1.

Out of the Classic feature importance, F429 (Figure 2) is interesting. It is ranked second by Cover and in the top 3 of the proposed metrics. It shows a moderate effect (more than 0.8) and a clear threshold at which the SHAP values are increasing. This threshold defines the area of an increased error ratio, rendering the feature interesting.

F40 (Figure 2) is ranked as identically important both by the SHAP-based and by the proposed metrics. It has high effects and a good error ratio in an area of increased SHAP values. Note that the feature comprises only a few instances with high effects. It depends on the cost structures and specifics of the production process whether the amount justifies the considerations for a deeper error cause analysis. However, we argue that the observation hints at an interesting phenomenon.

B) Disagreements of importance

Besides commonalities, there are also differences in rankings which are discussed next. Comparing the Classic with the proposed metrics, major differences are revealed by Gain and Cover. Here, we focus on the features F210 and F539 shown in Figure 3 at the bottom of the next page, and F29 as well. Gain ranks all three features high, but we argue that these features are of less interest to determining cause

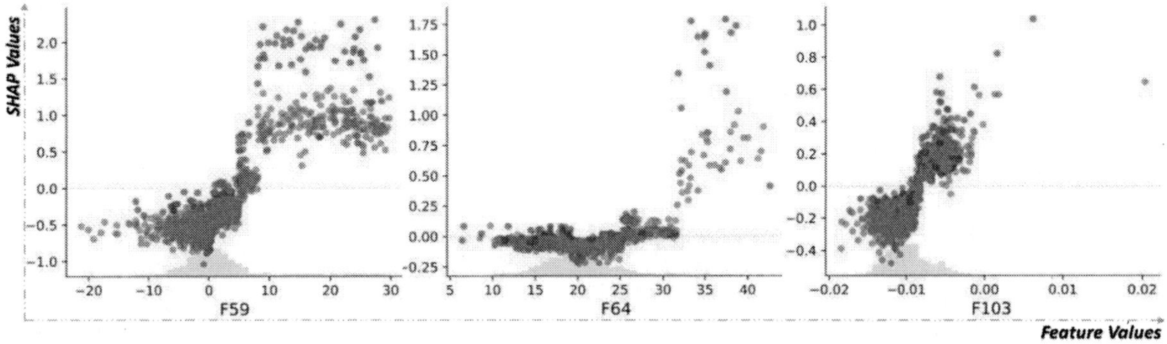

Figure 1. Agreements between importance measures: SHAP plots of features F59, F64 and F103 which have similar rankings across all importance measures and show interesting patterns for cause anlysis – errors-instances (red) and non-errors (blue).

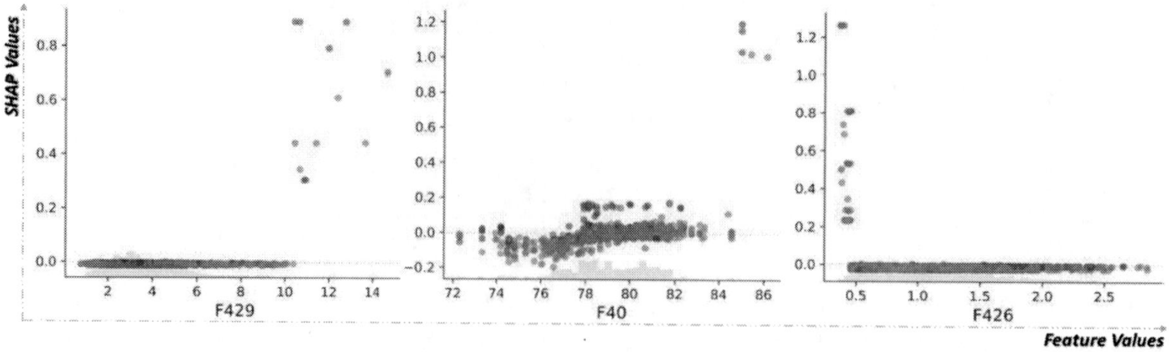

Figure 2. Agreements between importance measures ff: SHAP plots for features F429, F40 with similar rankings over all importance measures. Except feature F426 with low mean average effect falls behind in importance of the proposed metrics – errors-instances (red) and non-errors (blue).

explanations. F210 has an overall weak effect, i.e., the maximal SHAP value is around 0.1. It is also not possible to determine a clear threshold at which SHAP values are increasing, nor to specify a clear threshold of higher error rates. F539 shows a few instances with increased error rate but also with weak effect, i.e., a SHAP value of 0.3 and therefore is not interesting enough for further investigations. Feature F29 is not shown here due to the space limitations but has a similar appearance as both features described above and thus is of less interest.

F168 is shown in Figure 3 and ranked first by Cover, but not ranked in the top 5 by any of the other groups. It shows an area of increased SHAP values with a suitable error ratio but the effect, i.e., of 0.35 is quite low and therefore we argue that this feature also is of low interest.

Feature F426, shown in Figure 2, has interesting properties and ranked as important by the Classic importance but is not ranked in the top five using the proposed metrics. F426 shows a step increase in SHAP values on the left-hand side with a maximal effect of 1.2 which looks sufficient at first glance. Further examinations showed that F426 was ranked seventh by the proposed Slope Max Shap approach. Investigating the region of increased SHAP values revealed also that F426 has a few high effects but the average effect for this region is quite low. This indicates over plotting of the SHAP plot and relativizes the interestingness of F426.

Comparing SHAP-based and the proposed metrics, feature F21 stands out as it ranked as important in the group of SHAP-based measures but neither by the Classic nor by the proposed metrics. F21 (not shown) has a decent effect of 0.6 and a steep increase in SHAP values. Yet, it does not have an area with a high error rate and falls behind in the proposed metrics.

C) Highlights of proposed metrics

F423, F475 and F130, as shown in Figure 4, are only ranked as important by the proposed metrics. F423 has strong positive effects, clear threshold upon which SHAP values increase and a relatively high error ratio in in a specific area. We therefore argue that the feature is interesting. F475 has strong effects, a clear threshold where effects increase, and a good error ratio. Therefore, we argue that it is also interesting for further investigations. F130 shows negative SHAP values in the bottom left corner which indicates a value range where the error rate is much lower. It is also possible to determine a threshold at which SHAP values decrease to a zero effect. This might hint at means to prevent errors and we argue that the feature is therefore interesting.

Overall, the experiments support the usefulness of the proposed metrics. They show that high ranked features have properties that are interesting for a cause analysis of production errors. Furthermore, we have shown that established metrics may rank features high, that do not have such interesting properties. In contrast, the proposed metrics rank features high that are interesting but considered not important by existing metrics. This demonstrates that cause analysis in manufacturing can benefit from the proposed metrics.

V. RELATED WORK

Root cause analysis in the production environment has been well studied [15] and several methods for model

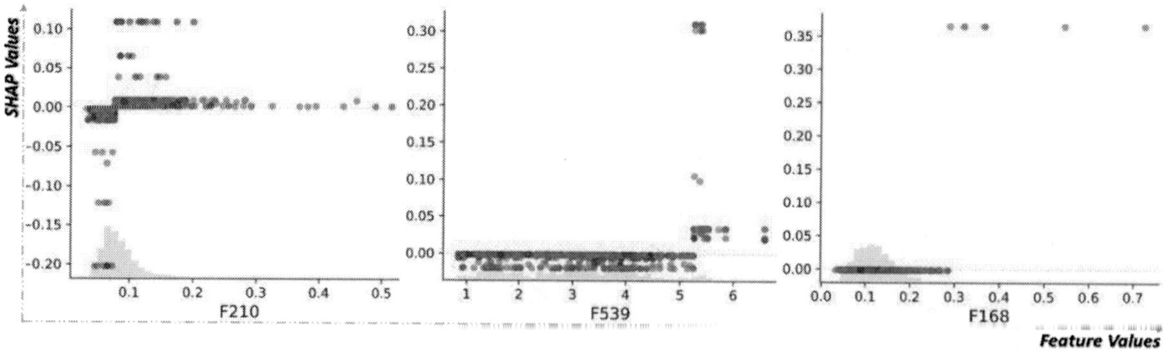

Figure 3. Disagreements between importance measures: SHAP plots for features F210, F539 and F168 ranked by the Classic importance measures as important – errors-instances (red) and non-errors (blue).

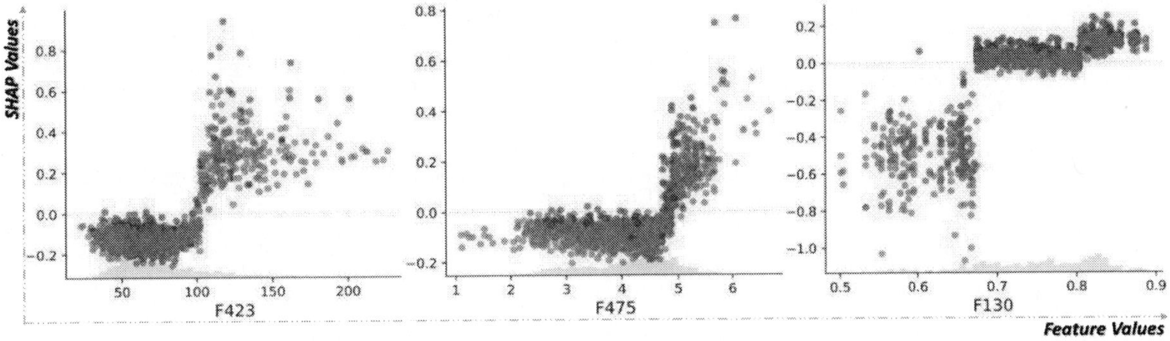

Figure 4. Important features according to proposed metrics: SHAP plots for features F423, F475 and F130 ranked by the proposed importance measures as important – errors-instances (red) and non-errors (blue).

interpretability through xAI have been reported [16]. However, we argue that the proposed metrics are more related to feature importance measures. The metrics may be used in root cause analysis to incorporate expert knowledge. Applied xAI in the manufacturing domain is used to extract explanations from a machine learning model to, e.g., enhance trust in the model, used for model optimization or to assist domain experts taking actions according to the model insights. In [17], saliency maps and class activation maps are extracted from a deep learning model. In [3], the authors use an isolation forest as model to determine normal production line behavior and feature importance to explain the model. Mehdiyev and Fettke apply local and global explanations to examine the impact of different views on the generated insights [18]. However, neither work addresses the problem of which feature provides the most promising insights given the possible tremendous feature space and the corresponding effort required to examine all explanations. To the best of our knowledge, we are the first to provide SHAP-based importance measures tailored to the task for quality management. Lundberg et al., introduced the idea of SHAP-based feature importance [14]. To determine a feature's overall effect, the absolute SHAP value across all considered instances is averaged and thus a global importance measure. In contrast, our proposed measures just consider instances that possibly encompass interesting properties for quality management. Other global importance measures used in the domain have a broad history. A detailed description of the following global importance measures is laid out by Molnar [19]. In [20], Permutation Feature Importance is introduced. A global measure of where the features are perturbated and the resulting performance loss of the model is taken as a measure of the features importance. Mehdiyev and Fettke [18] used Individual Conditional Expectation (ICE) [21] as the global importance. Also possibly used are Partial Dependence Plots (PDP) [22]. However, neither ICE nor PDP accumulates a single importance score. Both are used as visualizations of global model behavior. Overall, one of the most influential global importance measures is the Gini index [23]. According to Lundberg [24], the Gini index is equivalent to the in XGBoost [12] implemented importance measure Gain which *uses the average training loss reduction gained when using a feature for splitting*. Lundberg [24] also describes Weight as *the number of times a feature is used to split the data across all trees* and Cover as *the number of times a feature is used to split the data across all trees weighted by the number of training data points that go through those splits.* Both the total importance scores used for comparison are described in the XGBoost documentation [25] for Total Gain as the *total gain across all splits the feature is used in* and Total Cover as *the total coverage across all splits the feature is used in.* For local feature importance, LIME [11] could also be considered. However, to compute explanations LIME uses sampling which is not restricted to solely interesting areas.

VI. CONCLUSION

In this paper, we have introduced regional feature importance measures that aim at identifying interesting features for quality management in manufacturing. We discussed the underlying notion of interest and provided corresponding formal definitions. Conceptually, our importance measures are between established global and local feature importance measures and highlight regional effects which are helpful in finding production error causes. We illustrate the usefulness of the new measures through experiments using synthetic and real-world data.

Our experiments show that the prosed measures successfully elicit features that – based on our experience [5] – are interesting, but are missed by established methods. Therefore, we conclude that quality managers benefit from adding our proposed importance measures to the pool of xAI methods. We thereby improve xAI for error prediction models in manufacturing. With the help of our importance measures, quality managers get hints about interesting relations that are reflected in the prediction model and drive deeper analysis accordingly.

Subject to future work are questions about the integration of the importance measure in the machine learning pipeline. In this work, we assume that the measures are applied at the end of the pipeline, potentially after automated feature engineering, and model optimization. However, the proposed measures may drive the analysis of features earlier in the pipeline as well. Furthermore, future work may expand on the idea of providing importance measures between global and local measures. With our work, we have presented several heuristics which follow this concept for capturing interesting patterns in features.

REFERENCES

[1] C. Seiffer, A. Gerling, U. Schreier and H. Ziekow, "A Reference Process and Domain Model for Machine Learning Based Production Fault Analysis", *Enterprise Information*

Systems: 22nd International Conference, ICEIS 2020, Springer International Publishing, pp. 140–157, 2021.

[2] A. Gerling et al., "Comparison of algorithms for error prediction in manufacturing with automl and a cost-based metric", *Journal of Intelligent Manufacturing*, 33.2022(2), pp. 555–573, 2022.

[3] M. Carletti, C. Masiero, A. Beghi and G.A. Susto, "Explainable Machine Learning in Industry 4.0: Evaluating Feature Importance in Anomaly Detection to Enable Root Cause Analysis", *IEEE International Conference 2019*, pp. 21–26, 2019.

[4] H. Ziekow, U. Schreier, A. Gerling and A. Saleh, "Interpretable Machine Learning for Quality Engineering in Manufacturing - Importance Measures that Reveal Insights on Errors", *The Upper-Rhine Artificial Intelligence Symposium, UR-AI 2021, Artificial Intelligence - Application in Life Sciences and Beyond*, Germany, Kaiserslautern: Hochschule Kaiserslautern, University of Applied Sciences, pp. 96–105, October 2021.

[5] H. Ziekow et al., "Proactive Error Prevention in Manufacturing Based on an Adaptable Machine Learning Environment", *Artificial Intelligence: From Research to Application: The Upper-Rhine Artificial Intelligence Symposium UR-AI 2019*, Offenburg, Germany, Karlsruhe: Hochschule Karlsruhe - Technik und Wirtschaft, pp. 113–117, March 2019.

[6] R. S. Peres, J. Barata, P. Leitao and G. Garcia, "Multistage Quality Control Using Machine Learning in the Automotive Industry", *IEEE Access*, vol. 7, pp. 79908–79916, 2019.

[7] Y. Wilhelm, U. Schreier, P. Reimann, B. Mitschang and H. Ziekow, "Data Science Approaches to Quality Control in Manufacturing: A Review of Problems, Challenges and Architecture", *Symposium and Summer School on Service-Oriented Computing*, Springer, pp. 45–65, 2020.

[8] A. Gerling et al., "Results from using an Automl Tool for Error Analysis in Manufacturing", *Proceedings of the 24th International Conference on Enterprise Information Systems - Volume* 1, pp. 100–111, 2022.

[9] C. Seiffer, A. Gerling, U. Schreier and H. Ziekow, "A Reference Process and Domain Model for Machine Learning Based Production Fault Analysis", *Enterprise Information Systems: 22nd International Conference, ICEIS 2020*, Springer International Publishing, pp. 140–157, 2021.

[10] S. M. Lundberg and S. I. Lee, "A unified approach to interpreting model predictions", *Proceedings of the 31st International Conference on Neural Information Processing Systems (NIPS'17)*, NY, USA, pp. 4768–4777, 2017.

[11] M. T. Ribeiro, S. Singh and C. Guestrin, "Why Should I Trust You?": Explaining the Predictions of Any Classifier", *Proceedings of the 22nd ACM SIGKDD International Conference on Knowledge Discovery and Data Mining*. New York, NY, USA: Association for Computing Machinery, pp. 1135–1144, 2016.

[12] T. Chen and C. Guestrin, "XGBoost: A Scalable Tree Boosting System", *Proceedings of the 22nd ACM SIGKDD International Conference on Knowledge Discovery and Data Mining*, New York, NY, USA: ACM, pp. 785–794, 2016.

[13] D. Dua and C. Graff, "UCI Machine Learning Repository", Irvine, CA: *University of California, School of Information and Computer Science*, 2019. [Online]. Available from: http://archive.ics.uci.edu/ml.

[14] S. M. Lundberg et al., "From local explanations to global understanding with explainable AI for trees", *Nature machine intelligence, 2(1)*, pp. 56–67, 2020.

[15] E. Oliveira, V. L. Miguéis and, J. L. Borges, "Automatic root cause analysis in manufacturing: an overview & conceptualization", *Journal of Intelligent Manufacturing*, 2022.

[16] G. Sofianidis, J. M. Rožanec, D. Mladenić and D. Kyriazis, "A Review of Explainable Artificial Intelligence in Manufacturing", *Trusted Artificial Intelligence in Manufacturing: A Review of the Emerging Wave of Ethical and Human Centric AI Technologies for Smart Production*, pp. 93–113, 2021.

[17] C. V. Goldman, M. Baltaxe, D. Chakraborty and J. Arinez, "Explaining Learning Models in Manufacturing Processes", *Procedia Computer Science, 180*, pp. 259–268, 2021.

[18] N. Mehdiyev and P. Fettke, "Local Post-Hoc Explanations for predictive Process Monitoring in manufacturing", *29th European Conference on Information Systems - Human Values Crisis in a Digitizing World, ECIS 2021*, Marrakech, Morocco, 2020.

[19] C. Molnar, "Interpretable Machine Learning: A Guide for Making Black Box Models Explainable", *2nd edn.*, 2022. [Online]. Available from: https://christophm.github.io/interpretable-ml-book, retrieved on 08/26/2022.

[20] L. Breiman, "Random Forests", *Machine Learning 45*, pp. 5–32, 2001.

[21] A. Goldstein, A. Kapelner, J. Bleich and E. Pitkin, "Peeking inside the black box: Visualizing statistical learning with plots of individual conditional expectation", *journal of Computational and Graphical Statistics*, 24, pp. 44–65, 2015.

[22] J. H. Friedman, "Greedy function approximation: A gradient boosting machine", *The Annals of Statistics, 29 (5)*, pp. 1189–1232, October 2001.

[23] T. Hastie, R. Tibshirani and J. Friedman, "Random forests", *The elements of statistical learning*, Springer, pp. 587–604, 2009.

[24] S. M. Lundberg, "Interpretable Machine Learning with XGBoost", April, 2018. [Online] Available from: https://towardsdatascience.com/interpretable-machine-learning-with-xgboost-9ec80d148d27, retrieved on 08/26/2022.

[25] XGBoost Documentation, "Python API", *Reference. xgboost developers*. [Online]. Available from: https://xgboost.readthedocs.io/en/latest/python/python_api.html, retrieved on 08/26/2022

Practices for Data Sharing: An Empirical Survey

Andrei-Raoul Morariu, Bogdan Iancu, Jerker Björkqvist
Åbo Akademi University
Faculty of Science and Engineering
Vesilinnantie 3, Turku, Finland
Email: {firstname.lastname@abo.fi}

***Abstract*—The data economy is changing the way companies operate. The largest companies in the world are strong actors in the data economy. Still, the share of data economy of GDP (Gross Domestic Product) is rather small. For industrial operators, data utilization is predicted to increase performance, predictability, and cost-effectiveness. However, to achieve the goals, data often need to be shared between operators, to produce system level gains. This paper analyses the possibilities and barriers for reaching effective data sharing through qualitative interviews with company representatives with technical insights into data sharing. The paper includes aspects such as value proposition, barriers, confidentiality, and technical aspects of data sharing.**

***Index Terms*—data economy, data sharing, industrial operators.**

I. Introduction

The volume of data/information created, captured, copied, and consumed worldwide was in the year 2010 approximately two zettabytes. This volume is forecasted to rise to 181 zettabytes by 2025 [1]. Most of the data is from people's activities where they are happy to share some of their data to improve their experiences. However, companies are more reluctant to share some of their data with other partners [2]. It is usually reduced towards data ownership using policies to prevent harming the participant entities [3].

This motivator made us proceed with a series of interviews with Finnish industry professionals to create an overview of the practicalities of data sharing. The data we refer to is not describing internet traffic data but measurement data from sensors. In most cases, such sensors are usually placed on moving mechanisms or adjacent to them collecting, e.g., vibration measurements.

Companies use data for various purposes, most prominent of which are: supplying it either as a standalone asset or a fundamental component of a product, improving their operational processes, or acquiring new technological or business insights. Data-driven innovation came to the forefront of modern industrial development in the past decade, since various technological advances stimulated data usage through significantly elevated storage capacity, computing power and data transmission speed [4] [5].

Data represents a crucial resource that is yet to be adequately exploited. Modern industrial development already employs prevalent data-intensive technologies such as machine learning, pervasive computing, edge computing, etc. [6]. One critical reason for the adoption of technologies that demand substantial data intake is the development of digital twins when simulating certain processes on physical models is of uttermost complexity. Data generation from diverse machines and devices contributes to datasets which can reach even petabytes per dataset. Companies, especially SMEs (Small and Medium Enterprises), that are reluctant to digitalization or even impede it, compromise their future progress relative to their competitors [4].

While many SMEs have the capacity to design highly innovative solutions to drive their business, in practice often they require data sources they do not have access to. Data sources are developed and analyzed by many companies primarily to advance their own business without an explicit intention to share it. Many data sources remain unexploited to the full of their potential even by the companies that produced them. Moreover, great reluctance towards sharing data with external partners seems to have permeated deep within business development layers as less than 50% of companies in a recent survey show that data sharing is a common practice in their company [7] [6].

In many companies, reluctance towards data sharing is rooted unsurprisingly in the economical aspect. A 2019 OECD (Organisation for Economic Co-operation and Development) report on data sharing identified the main impediments for accessing, sharing and exploiting data through continuous development as data privacy and ownership. Some states do not have currently any clear law that defines data ownership and the benefit of sharing [8]. The complexity is grounded in determining the requirements that need to be met prior to sharing data. Industrial players also find it challenging to estimate the value of data and to assess the risk of sharing it, with many of them being open to share data only if other players reciprocate [6]. Another critical aspect that hinders data sharing among companies is inadequate transparency and a stark imbalance in power between different players in a market sector [5]. One of the most prevalent challenges for data sharing is privacy, which affects several aspects of development within an ecosystem: maintenance of data through its entire life-cycle [9], safeguarding it from corruption, and sustainable development to retain usability [4].

B2B (Busines-to-Business) data sharing is especially scarce, impeding data utilization to its full potential at industrial level [5]. There is a great discrepancy between data sharing and the extensive efforts that are put into collecting it [10].

Notable benefits were attained in some industrial sectors through data sharing. One example is the automotive industry and transport sector, where data sharing promoted smart mapping solutions. For instance, the mapping service HERE [11] provides enhanced spatial data, including geocoding, positioning, map rendering etc., and is endorsed by some of the most prominent automobile manufacturers. While increasing their revenue, HERE also is committed to contribute to safer and more sustainable transportation. Furthermore, automobile manufacturers can capitalize on their data through the HERE marketplace [10]. Another sector where data sharing has brought about tremendous benefits is the healthcare sector, where data sharing is used to promote more rapid diagnostics and more effective treatments by employing machine learning algorithms [12] [13]. Not only does medical data sharing benefit society at large by providing enhanced medical services, but medical providers also capitalize on these solutions, offering more efficient and precise diagnostics [14] [15].

There are two distinct data sharing strategies when it comes to private data, *vertical*, which develops across the supply chain, and *horizontal*, which transpires between competing companies [10] [16]. Vertical data sharing is characterized predominantly by trust between companies along the supply chain and the degree of certainty attributed to certain business needs. Horizontal data sharing, however, is employed to a lower degree due to its sensitivity. Personal data, which concerns largely horizontal data sharing is highly regulated in the European Union by GDPR (General Data Protection Regulation), which requires extensive considerations on various aspects of its content. This, in turn, makes personal data sharing a very intricate matter [10].

To promote data sharing by various companies, it becomes imperious to incentivise the process since it involves an extremely valuable asset. One way to do so could be to purchase it. However, data acquisition raises yet new challenges since selling it at an equitable price can be a difficult endeavour [17] [18]. To address such demands, data marketplaces emerged, such as: Azure Marketplace [19], Japan Data Exchange Inc. [20], Qlik DataMarket [21], etc. However, a considerable variety of data precludes trading it in a fairly regulated manner [22]. To address these challenges, different pricing and trading models showcasing auspicious prospects were introduced in [23] [24].

The paper is organized as follows. Section II depicts the study design and interview questions. Section III illustrates the results of the qualitative analysis of interviews with companies. In Section IV, a few solutions for data exchange are discussed. Conclusions of the study are presented in Section V.

II. Research Questions and Study Design

Sharing data is an integral part of the scientific community as it allows for verification of results and enables researchers to build upon previously discovered information [25]. Interest in this subject came from multiple face to face conversations with industry experts. They assert that cooperation between companies on similar topics can lead to further developments in different areas connected to the industries. Cooperation under non-disclosure agreements would secure the data transactions and enforce the credibility between partners.

The study addresses the following research questions:

RQ1: Is your organisation exercising any data sharing with other company?

- a) If yes, to what extent do you do this and how dependent is your business on data sharing? How long do you store the data you share with others? Do you use a third part service for sharing your data, such as Amazon/cloud services?
- b) If no, what are the reasons for not doing this?

RQ2: What value do you see between sharing your data with other organisations?

RQ3: What are the barriers for performing data sharing? Were there some previous episodes of data sharing with others?

RQ4: Is confidentiality of data an issue?

RQ5: Do you have a data management strategy/policy?

Research questions were used to extract data from a series of interviews with experienced employees from different business areas. We organized Semi-Structured Interviews (SSI) for our research. A semi-structured interview is a meeting where the interviewer asks questions that are meant to evoke open conversations offering participants the chance of bringing up important matters [26]. As part of their experience, SSIs are intended to find out what participants think about their experiences related to the given topic [27]. It provides the advantage of collecting the data needed from topics that can be further developed towards new insights.

A. Threats to validity

The most significant threat to the validity of RQ1 is that data sharing between companies is still limited. Furthermore, companies' guidelines and restrictions drive many respondents to give short and sparse answers to questions. The purpose of RQ1 is to develop a more in-depth understanding of data sharing between companies and other partners. Using this question, we learn how vital data provided by other partners is to a business's success, such as data availability and the platform used for data sharing.

Data value is a subjective opinion that allows for RQ2 to bear a respective degree of uncertainty upon receiving an answer from participants. Although, considering the expertise of the interviewees, the article may provide inspiration for other businesses.

The purpose of the RQ3 is to challenge the specialist to observe the main topic from a different point of view. This question may also bring challenges allowing the respondent to claim that the company is conducting safe data sharing procedures with other external partners. Moreover, RQ3 further investigates whether there have been previous agreements on sharing data with other partners and the resulted outcome. In this case, common factors such as lack of time or limited funding prevent companies from sharing their data with other external partners [25].

RQ4 is counted as a controversial question where many respondents had to take some extra time to respond. Many thought that confidentiality could lead to security concerns since raw data does not display any signs of being private. On the other hand, even number sequences can include, for example, personal identification codes from a specific country.

The validity of our study of RQ5 is compromised by companies keeping the response to the question private. Therefore, companies could decide on some data management strategies internally.

B. Conducting the interview

The selection of respondents was decided internally within the author group on companies that were previous project members in consortiums with the university. Considering their experience and previous connection to us, we interviewed the selected specialists.

When we conducted the interview, the concept of sharing data with other partners was still not a regular practice. Many specialists responded negatively to whether they share company data with external parties. A quarter of the total number of specialists invited for interviews chose not to attend online interviews due to their personal disinterest in discussing any information about company practicalities.

A total of 12 specialists were interviewed during three weeks between 2022-04-02 to 2022-04-28. In selecting the number, we focused on gathering experts from diverse organizations and fields. Interview meetings were agreed upon according to the availability of the specialists. In an email before the interviews, participants were informed that the study would lead to a publication that would enhance university research and provide new business opportunities for companies. Each interview was scheduled for 30 minutes, with an average of 24 minutes per participant. There was an interview guide containing the research questions used listed in Section II. Many questions were meant for an open discussion where the specialists discussed the practicalities of data sharing within the companies where they work. The interviews were transcribed during the conversation in real-time.

III. Results

In this section, we present the main findings of the research. The interview results where categorised in a systematic way based on each question and follow-up discussions.

We aim to create a comprehensive guideline for data sharing that would encourage companies to increase their expertise and revenue from collaborations.

The research starts with domain identification where the respondents were working at the interview date. Figure 1 illustrates these domains. We chose the working domains of the companies with generic names to keep them transparent. We focused on having different areas of expertise of the respondents, but only with applicability to the industry. We chose an even distribution of chart slices for company domains to increase the privacy of the respondents. Several employees working at the same place were interviewed for some of the companies. We decided this way because the experience of the interviewed persons was valuable to our research. Furthermore, to minimize the repeatability of answers, we only chose respondents from different departments of the same company.

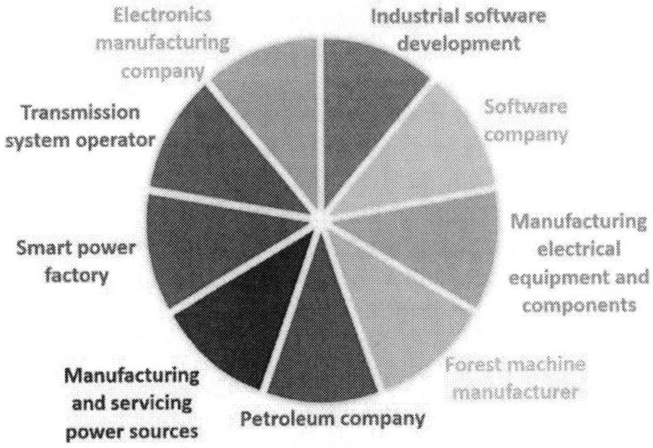

Fig. 1. Application domains of the company representatives who participated in the qualitative interviews.

A. Data sharing between companies (RQ1)

Most of the time, sharing data is hindered by company culture and practices. In addition, individual judgment plays a significant role in influencing later decisions. Today, new mandates relate to data management strategies, which means that new partnerships will be more open.

Considering the first research question, the respondent should share with the researchers whether the company where they work shares any data with outside partners. There are some follow-up questions on the given answers. The purpose of this question is to collect information on reasons for not sharing data or on how dependent the business is on distributing data.

Starting with this, some of the experts responded that sharing data may lead to: further improvements in manufacturing and execution, improve analytics or maintain safe operations. Here, we also asked on how was this performed. The most common answer noted was via project partnership, while others mentioned about verbal agreement, or one time transactions.

It was discussed that confidentiality, general data protection regulation, data ownership, and low business opportunities were some of the risks preventing data sharing. As one individual indicated, their business was not dependent on data sharing. Therefore, it was not taking place. Yet another claimed that data sharing had been attempted with another partner. This practice did not result in a long-term partnership due to the differences between the two partners' technologies.

In addition to the opening question, we asked how long data shared with others is stored. The most common answer is that the data is erased according to customer agreements and when the project ends. A few respondents noted that they typically archive the data for up to 10 years. They added that some reasons involve legal requirements and testing information (e.g., electrical components). Furthermore, some mentioned that they prefer storing data for a longer duration for availability on further improvements to their products and services.

Many respondents noted that they use an in-house private cloud for data sharing. According to Figure 2, Google, Amazon, Microsoft Azure, and OneDrive are services used for data sharing. Others mentioned file transfer protocol (TCP/IP) and email attachments as means for data sharing. This question also brought up an emerging topic from one of the respondents. A respondent stated that they are involved with creating a data lake where companies would be able to access data according to agreements. This illustrates the need for industry companies to develop data sharing frameworks.

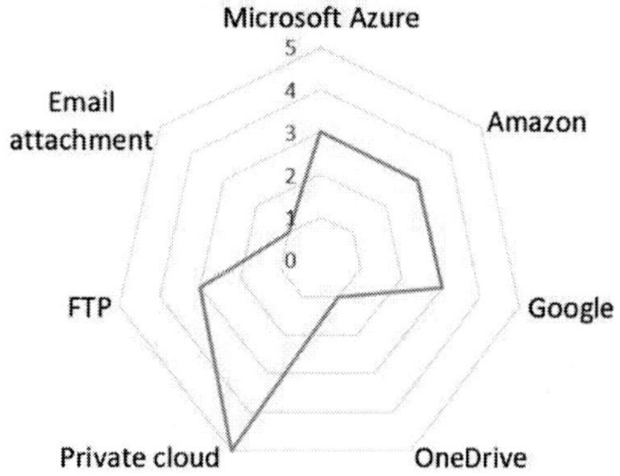

Fig. 2. Means of performing data sharing with external partners.

B. *Value of shared data (RQ2)*

As mentioned in Section II-A, the answer to this question differs even for people from the same company. It aims at experts' opinions on data visualization, which sometimes may only mean a series of numbers aligned in a specific order.

Experts' viewpoint is that the value of shared data comes from reasons such as:

- Money saving from better understanding of the processes
- Forecasting the need for components
- Quick troubleshooting
- Enhancing services to customers
- Development of products
- Increasing value of use cases
- Ensuring customers that sold products will not break

A few interviewees noted that perhaps the value in sharing data with other partners is yet to be discovered or even speculated that there might not be value in doing it at all. They added that the data recipients could have additional benefits from analyzing it and that pre-processing it for sharing purposes typically requires additional resources. Furthermore, sometimes the data the company is working with may belong to clients and is, therefore, more complicated to share externally. In some cases, data refers to the information given via a telephone call from one person to another. Such a situation leads to miscommunication with the other groups interested in the details.

C. *Barriers from performing data sharing (RQ3)*

Obstacles preventing data sharing can sometimes be tied to cultural reasons preventing people from making such decisions. Data sharing is hampered by intellectual property rights due to ownership of data. Some companies are service providers using data from partners according to contracts. In this case, sharing customer data would mean creating new agreements, contacting the customer, and other connected processes.

In Figure 3, we extracted some of the reasons preventing companies from exercising data sharing. In many cases, experts contend that the heavy process, confidentiality, and Non-Disclosure Agreement (NDA) are some of the main reasons for not executing data sharing. Usually, it takes a long time to agree on the revised terms of the contract with customers, and the process becomes extremely tedious. It is crucial to consider privacy and access when it comes to data sharing to prevent breaches, identity theft, or other security threats.

Therefore, some respondents mentioned that before sharing the data with others, they perform data masking in various ways such as cleaning, averaging, anonymizing, and removing the means. There is no harm intended to occur to the company sharing the data through those filtering methods.

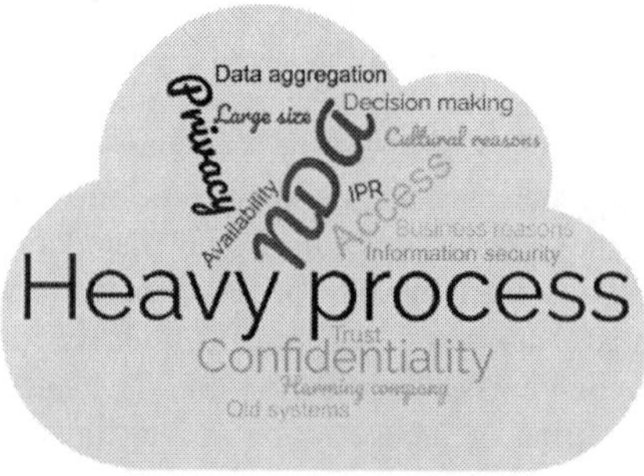

Fig. 3. Barriers preventing data sharing between companies.

D. *Is data confidentiality an issue? (RQ4)*

Having information about a company's process work may be of significant importance to the company. However, that same piece of information may not be of any importance to another company. This leads to a comprehensive definition of confidentiality. This interview question raised many affirmative answers on validating that data confidentiality is an issue. Experts mentioned that data sharing is always executed under NDA contracts and trust. The NDA contracts usually contain agreements that include:

- Common collaboration on improvements

- Complete list of information about shared data
- Data leaking prevention measures
- Access limitations

E. Data management strategies/policies (RQ5)

Three-quarters of the respondents mentioned that the company where they work has data management strategies. Distributed control systems and in-house data management are the most common strategies related to cyber security. Data systems in many companies are only used within a closed network without an external data sharing interface.

Equipment manufacturers typically create an Application Programming Interface (API) to facilitate customers' installation of their protocols. One respondent mentioned that the data management policy implies retrieving data up to ten years old.

IV. Strategies for performing data exchange

Machine learning models that use the output to change the operation of a real-world device may be patentable since they are integrated into changing the actual state of the device. Artificial intelligence systems are now able to solve problems more effectively due to new developments. But a novel solution may still be patentable if it improves upon a conventional manual process as well. Last but not least, it is crucial for companies to prepare detailed disclosures describing the low-level details of the system [28].

Two core challenges affect the deployment of AI solutions in companies. Firstly, industrial partners store data in silos and do not implement regulated exchange frameworks, and secondly they prefer a more traditional approach to data privacy and security, which limits considerably data sharing or exchange, sometimes to an astounding degree. Given the highly competitive nature of various industrial sectors, enhanced privacy requirements and demanding data management specifications, companies find it often challenging to implement data integration even within their own organisation. One approach to address the aforementioned hindrances is *federated learning*, which promotes the idea of developing Machine Learning (ML) models by exploiting data originating from multiple sources, while obstructing data breaches [29].

An important challenge that federated learning faces is the *traceability* of ML models throughout their life-cycle. Given a prediction value from an ML process, if one cannot trace which input values (originating in which datasets) determined it, we encounter a situation when the ML model is essentially a black-box, hence its traceability cannot be ensured [30]. To address this topic, several frameworks employing blockchain technology emerged, which tackle the development of more transparent deep learning models with enhanced traceability [31] [32].

Gaia-X [33] is a standard for data exchange across companies. Its role is to be a mediator in agreements between companies and to ensure cooperation. One of these data ecosystems is Catena-X [34], which is responsible for creating a standalone data exchange standard across the entire automotive supply chain. The core values of their standards are to ensure data protection, security, and fairness for participating companies.

Toolchains have been standardized by numerous non-profit organisations, such as ASAM (Association for Standardization of Automation and Measuring Systems), to ensure better quality for their underlying processes, testing and development in the automotive sector [35]. The members of ASAM standards are companies involved in the car manufacturing process as manufacturers, suppliers, etc. ASAM is the owner of the standards that enable data exchange or the necessary tools required. In order to share data within the ASAM group, partners need to comply with the definition of the test data provided by the application model and to have the data in XML (Extensible Markup Language) file format. Since every company has its application model, the ASAM standard extends toward company-specific metadata [36].

V. Conclusion

Data economy is an emerging topic where many companies are currently working to improve their operability and increase revenue through the development of various systems.

Many companies and allied businesses begin to exchange data in order to increase the number of services they offer and solve unknown customer problems.

This article aims to provide an overview of various companies' capabilities to collaborate with external partners across multiple sectors. We interviewed 12 employees of various companies in industrial sectors that gave us insights on practices they employ regarding data sharing with external parties.

It is common nowadays to see an increase in external collaboration, but unfortunately, companies are backed-up on collaborating only under projects. Collaboration between two companies is usually time-consuming when NDA contracts are involved. For the purpose of avoiding damaging company information, companies prefer to send single batches of data that are averaged and partially removed.

In order to increase the number of services offered, young emerging businesses must make their customers aware of the potential data sharing.

Acknowledgments

This work was partially supported by projects funded by Business Finland.

References

[1] Statista. https://www.statista.com/, Accessed on June 2022.

[2] N. Pearce and A. H. Smith. Data sharing: not as simple as it seems. *Environmental Health*, pp. 1–7, vol. 10(1), 2011.

[3] F. Aggestam. Setting the stage for a shared environmental information system. *Environmental Science & Policy*, pp. 124–132, vol. 92, 2019.

[4] S. Yin et al. Data-based techniques focused on modern industry: An overview. *IEEE Transactions on Industrial Electronics*, pp. 657–667, vol. 62(1), 2014.

[5] H. Richter and P. R. Slowinski. The data sharing economy: on the emergence of new intermediaries. *IIC-International Review of Intellectual Property and Competition Law*, pp. 4–29, vol. 50(1), 2019.

[6] A. Krotova, A. Mertens, and M. Scheufen. Open data and data sharing: An economic analysis, IW-policy paper. Technical Report 21, Institut der deutschen Wirtschaft (IW) Köln, 2020.

[7] H. Huttunen et al. What are the benefits of data sharing? uniting supply chain and platform economy perspectives. *Uniting Supply Chain and Platform Economy Perspectives (September 19, 2019)*, 2019.
[8] X. Li and Y. Cong. A systematic literature review of ethical challenges related to medical and public health data sharing in china. *Journal of Empirical Research on Human Research Ethics*, pp. 537–554, vol. 16(5), 2021.
[9] H. F. Atlam and G. B. Wills. Iot security, privacy, safety and ethics. In *Digital twin technologies and smart cities*, pp. 123–149. Springer, 2020.
[10] N. Stüdlein. Developing a framework for strategic data sharing barriers among competitors. *Data as a Common Good*, pp. 16, 2022.
[11] HERE. https://www.here.com, Accessed on August 2022.
[12] G. Cammarota et al. Gut microbiome, big data and machine learning to promote precision medicine for cancer. *Nature reviews gastroenterology & hepatology*, pp. 635–648, vol. 17(10), 2020.
[13] K. Y. Ngiam and W. Khor. Big data and machine learning algorithms for health-care delivery. *The Lancet Oncology*, pp. 262–273, vol. 20(5), 2019.
[14] S. Rutella et al. Society for immunotherapy of cancer clinical and biomarkers data sharing resource document: volume i—conceptual challenges. *Journal for immunotherapy of cancer*, vol. 8(2), 2020.
[15] D. Kerr et al. The oncology data network (odn): A collaborative european data-sharing platform to inform cancer care. *The Oncologist*, pp. 1–4, vol. 25(1), 2020.
[16] F. Cruijssen, W. Dullaert, and H. Fleuren. Horizontal cooperation in transport and logistics: a literature review. *Transportation journal*, pp. 22–39, vol. 46(3), 2007.
[17] D. Iwasa, T. Hayashi, and Y. Ohsawa. Development and evaluation of a new platform for accelerating cross-domain data exchange and cooperation. *New Generation Computing*, pp. 65–96, vol. 38(1), 2020.
[18] M. Zhang et al. Pricing fresh data. *IEEE Journal on Selected Areas in Communications*, pp. 1211–1225, vol. 39(5), 2021.
[19] Azure Marketplace. https://azuremarketplace.microsoft.com/en-u, Accessed on July 2022.
[20] J-DEX. https://j-dex.co.jp/en/index.html, Accessed on July 2022.
[21] Qlik. https://www.qlik.com/us/, Accessed on July 2022.
[22] F. Liang et al. A survey on big data market: Pricing, trading and protection. *IEEE Access*, pp. 15132–15154, vol. 6, 2018.
[23] J. Yang, C. Zhao, and C. Xing. Big data market optimization pricing model based on data quality. *Complexity*, 2019.
[24] Z. Zheng et al. Arete: On designing joint online pricing and reward sharing mechanisms for mobile data markets. *IEEE Transactions on Mobile Computing*, pp. 769–787, vol. 19(4), 2019.
[25] C. Tenopir et al. Data sharing by scientists: practices and perceptions. *PloS one*, pp. e21101, vol. 6(6), 2011.
[26] C. Schmidt. The analysis of semi-structured interviews. *A companion to qualitative research*, pp. 7619–7374, vol. 253(258), 2004.
[27] M. J. McIntosh and J. M. Morse. Situating and constructing diversity in semi-structured interviews. *Global qualitative nursing research*, pp. 2333393615597674, vol. 2, 2015.
[28] E. L. Sophir and R. E Glass. Key strategies for patenting big data solutions. https://www.foley.com/en/insights/publications/2022/key-strategies-for-patenting-big-data-solutions, Accessed on July 7 2022.
[29] Q. Yang et al. Federated machine learning: Concept and applications. *ACM Trans. Intell. Syst. Technol.*, pp. 1–19, vol. 10(2), Jan 2019.
[30] V. Mothukuri et al. A survey on security and privacy of federated learning. *Future Generation Computer Systems*, pp. 619–640, vol. 115, 2021.
[31] H. Kim et al. Blockchained on-device federated learning. *IEEE Communications Letters*, pp. 1279–1283, vol. 24(6), 2019.
[32] K. Salah et al. Blockchain for ai: Review and open research challenges. *IEEE Access*, pp. 10127–10149, vol. 7, 2019.
[33] Gaia-X. https://gaia-x.eu/, Accessed on July 2022.
[34] Catena-X. https://catena-x.net/en/, Accessed on July 2022.
[35] ASAM. https://www.asam.net/, Accessed on July 2022.
[36] ASAM. Asam solutions guide. http://citeseerx.ist.psu.edu/viewdoc/download?doi=10.1.1.738.2707rep=rep1type=pdf, Accessed on July 10 2022.

Using Deep Learning for Automated Tail Posture Detection of Pigs

Jan-Hendrik Witte
Very Large Business Applications
University of Oldenburg
Oldenburg, Germany
jan-hendrik.witte@uni-oldenburg.de

Johann Gerberding
Very Large Business Applications
University of Oldenburg
Oldenburg, Germany
johann.gerberding@uni-oldenburg.de

Jorge Marx Gómez
Very Large Business Applications
University of Oldenburg
Oldenburg, Germany
jorge.marx.gomez@uni-oldenburg.de

***Abstract*—Tail biting is one of the biggest problems in pig livestock farming. One indicator that can be observed before an outbreak is the change in tail posture. Studies have shown that days before a tail biting outbreak, a steady increase in hanging tail postures can be observed. A continuous monitoring of this indicator could, therefore, be used to inform farmers of potential problems arising within respective pens. This paper presents a first step in the development of automated monitoring systems for early detection of tail biting indicators by evaluating different approaches for tail posture detection using image data and Deep Learning. Using a dataset consisting of 1000 annotated images, different YOLOv5 object detection models were trained to detect upright and hanging tail postures. The results show that there are significant differences in performance for the detection of upright and hanging class. To further investigate the problem, an EfficientNetv2 image classification model was trained to examine if similar performance differences for the two classes could be observed. Considered in isolation, these differences could be mitigated. However, potentials could not be utilized, as the results of the comparison of the one-step detection of tail posture using YOLOv5 and the introduced two-step detection using YOLOv5 for tail detection and EfficientNetv2 for tail posture classification shows. Based on the discussion of the possible explanations for the inferior performance as well as the summary of the key findings of this paper, we present approaches that can be used as a basis for future research.**

***Keywords*—precision livestock farming; tail biting; tail posture; deep learning; computer vision.**

I. Introduction

Structures of modern pig livestock farming, and pork production have been undergoing major changes in recent years. Data from the Federal Statistical Office in Germany shows the contrary trend of steadily decreasing numbers of farms [1] with simultaneously increasing numbers of animals per farm [2], which makes individual animal management and welfare monitoring increasingly difficult. Meanwhile, the slaughter price has remained volatile for several years [3], making it also more challenging for farmers to maintain pig livestock farming economically viable. At the same time, politics and society alike are calling for more sustainable and more animal-friendly husbandry [4], putting additional pressure on the farmer. These challenges cannot be met with conventional methods, which is why new and innovative solutions are needed. As a result, research in the domain of Precision Livestock Farming (PLF) has increased in recent years. PLF describes systems that utilize modern camera and sensor technologies to enable automatic real-time monitoring in livestock production to supervise animal health, welfare, and behavior [4] [5]. This involves the automated acquisition, processing, analysis, and evaluation of sensor-based data like temperature, ammonia, or CO_2 concentration [6] as well as video data [7] [8]. The combination of these different types of information and data sources hold the potential to enable data-driven assistance systems that support farmers in their daily work, creating more time again for more animal- and welfare-oriented husbandry.

One of the biggest problems in conventional pig livestock farming is tail biting [9]. Tail biting describes a behavioral disorder in pigs and is defined as the intentional damaging of the tail of one pig by another pig, which can result in injuries of varying severity [10]. Not only can this have significant consequences for the health and welfare of the individual pig, but the farmer can also suffer economic damage as a result. Tail biting can negatively impact the growth of affected pigs, which, in addition to incurring additional veterinary costs and labor, also has adverse economic consequences for the farmer [11]. Tail biting is a multifactorial problem that potentially results from a number of different internal as well as external factors and can be separated into two phases: the pre-injury phase and the post-injury phase [12]. To detect tail biting before the actual outbreak, the indicators of the pre-injury phase are of particular importance. In their literature review, Schukat and Heise aggregated animal-specific indicators observed in different studies prior to the onset of tail biting [9]. They concluded that especially the change in tail postures was a consistent indicator that could be observed before an outbreak of tail biting. In each of the investigated studies, it was examined that the number of stuck tails increased steadily in the course leading up to the outbreak and that the ratio of curled and lowered or stuck tails shifted strongly [9].

Current developments in Deep Learning (DL) and Computer Vision (CV) could provide the tools to potentially detect and analyze these indicators automatically using video data. Video data is already being used as a basis for a variety of comparable use cases in pig PLF, many of which can be found in literature. Considering practical applications such as the counting of pigs [13], the tracking of pigs over specific time intervals [14], the detection of aggressive behavior among group housed pigs [7], or the automatic weight estimation [15], there are a number of use cases which are addressed by utilizing image data based on camera recordings. For this reason, this paper will present a method for automated recognition of tail posture based on video data.

The paper is structured as follows: In Section II, the current state of the art in the field of tail posture detection and classification is presented. The primary focus lies on papers that apply DL models and architectures, their respective performance as well as the general state of research regarding the observation of pre-injury indicators aside from the DL and CV domain. In Section III, materials and methods are presented. This section covers the data acquisition, model selection, definition of classes as well as label strategy, dataset description and creation as well as the description of the general test environment and setup. In Section IV, the results are presented based on quantitative evaluation metrics, applying standard evaluation metrics for bounding box prediction. The results of the trained tail posture detection models are also examined and evaluated in this section. Section V offers a discussion of the obtained results and Section VI summarizes the key findings of this paper and presents an outlook on how further research can be conducted on the topic of tail posture classification in the future.

II. Related Work

Tail biting is a subject that has been extensively researched in the literature. Already in 1969, van Putten investigated tail biting among fattening pigs and concluded, that tail biting is induced by various factors and hence describes a multi-factorial problem [16]. Since then, other studies have investigated the issue in greater depth. In 2001, Schrøder-Petersen and Simonsen summarized the research published on the issue of tail biting up to that time. It gives an additional overview of both internal and external risk factors that could induce tail biting [12]. In a similar study, Moinard, Mendl, Nicol and Green also investigated different risk factors that can increase the likelihood of tail biting as well as factors that can potentially reduce it [17]. However, tail posture as a potential indicator for early detection of tail biting is not mentioned in any of the previous referenced studies. Schukat and Heise provide the most recent overview of indicators that can be observed prior to the onset of tail biting [9]. In addition to a general increase in activity inside the pen, an increase in various behaviors such as chewing or other hostile interactions and other specific behaviors such as the tail-in-mouth behavior, the change in tail posture prior to the onset of tail biting was particularly observed in the examined studies.

Although many different use cases have already been investigated in the context of pig PLF using methods from the field of DL and CV, the issue of tail biting or the tail detection in general appears to be a vastly underrepresented subject compared to other topics in that domain. In our literature search, we were only able to identify six papers that investigated the prediction of tail biting or other related topics such as tail detection or tail posture classification based on methods from the field of machine learning (ML), DL and CV. The query that was used to search the scorpus literature database can be found in Table I. During review of the obtained

TABLE I
Search Query

TITLE-ABS-KEY((”pig” OR ”piglet”) AND (”tail biting” OR ”tail detection” OR ”tail posture”) AND (”deep learning” OR ”computer vision” OR ”machine learning” OR ”machine vision”))

papers based on the literature search, one paper was discarded as it only presented a concept for developing an early warning system for tail biting and did not yet present results regarding the performance of different models in detecting tails and their posture [18]. The remaining five papers could be categorized into two groups depending on the type of data that has been used in the respective use case: *sensor-based* and *image-based* approaches. In the following, the results of the papers of the respective category are presented.

A. Sensor-based use cases

Domun and Pedersen used sensor data like water consumption of individual pigs, pen level temperatures and different indoor climate data like ventilation, cooling, heating, and humidity to train an algorithm based on a bidirectional Long Short-Term Memory (LSTM) and feedforward neural network architecture to predict tail biting with an Area under the Curve (AUC) of 0.782 [19]. Larsen and Pedersen adopted a similar approach and achieved comparable results by using water consumption of individual pigs and temperature data at pen level to train an Artificial Neural Network (ANN) to predict the outbreak of tail biting with an AUC of 0.75, while producing false alarms in 30% of the days [20]. The authors concluded that future research should focus on more event-specific predictors like the tail posture and the development of systems to monitor these indicators, which we adopt in the scope of this paper.

B. Camera-based use cases

Two different approaches for data collection and data usage can be found in this category. In [5], 3D cameras in combination with Linear Mixed models were used to classify tail posture of individual pigs. The cameras were located above the feeder and pointed vertically down, covering one third of the pen. Validated against human observers, the proposed algorithm did best in the detection of tucked tails with an accuracy of 88.4%. However, the detection accuracy for curly tails, which was the most commonly observed class in the dataset, resulted in a score of 41.7%, which leaves room for improvement. It should also be noted that 3D camera systems are much more expensive than conventional 2D cameras, which also makes it difficult to transfer these systems into agricultural practice. Ocepek et al. [21] present the only research that is comparable to the approach followed in this paper. Using 2D cameras mounted under the roof for data collection, they applied a YOLOv4 object detection model to detect *straight* and *curled* tail postures with an Average Precision (AP) of 90%. However, the model was only trained on 30 images and other important metrics for performance evaluation of object detection models such as Precision (P), Recall (R) and mean Average Precision (mAP) for different Intersection over Union (IoU) thresholds are missing, which makes the results not representative in our opinion.

Based on the identified and analyzed literature, clear research gaps can be identified in the area of tail detection, tail posture detection, and general use cases in the field of tail biting, especially when using image data. Therefore, this paper will address the following research gaps:

a) Usage of a larger, more representative data set consisting of 1000 manually annotated images.
b) Provision of relevant metrics that allow for a better evaluation of model performance.
c) Evaluation of differently complex model architectures in terms of size and number of parameters and their influence on performance.

III. Materials and Methods

A. Data acquisition

Data collection was conducted within the DigiSchwein project at the agricultural research farm for pig husbandry of the Chamber of Agriculture Lower Saxony in Wehnen. Within the project, video recordings from both piglet rearing and fattening were collected and stored for analysis. An AXIS M3 16-live network camera was used for video recording in the piglet rearing pens, while the VIVOTEK IB9367-H model was used for the fattening pens. In both cases, the cameras were mounted beneath the ceiling to capture the entire pen from a top-down view. Since piglets in piglet rearing are much more active, move much faster compared to pigs in fattening pens and are also a lot smaller, recording within piglet rearing was conducted with 30 Frames Per Second (FPS) and a resolution of 2688×15120, while in fattening pens recording was done with 10 FPS and a resolution of 1920×1080. The higher resolution enabled us to capture the more rapid and spontaneous movements of the piglets, and to provide the necessary level of detail to ensure that the tails were always clearly visible in the images. Since the pigs in the fattening are much larger and slower, we lowered resolution as well as the number of FPS to reduce the amount of memory needed to store the videos. Figure 1 shows some example images that were extracted from the video recordings.

B. Model selection

The model selection for the task of tail posture detection was conducted based on defined selection criteria. These criteria were derived based on models and architectures that were already used in pig PLF literature as well as on the requirements for PLF systems that have been mentioned in the PLF literature. The following criteria were defined:

1) **Prediction accuracy**: The prediction of the respective models should be as accurate as possible [22].
2) **Prediction speed**: Model inference should be in real-time [23].

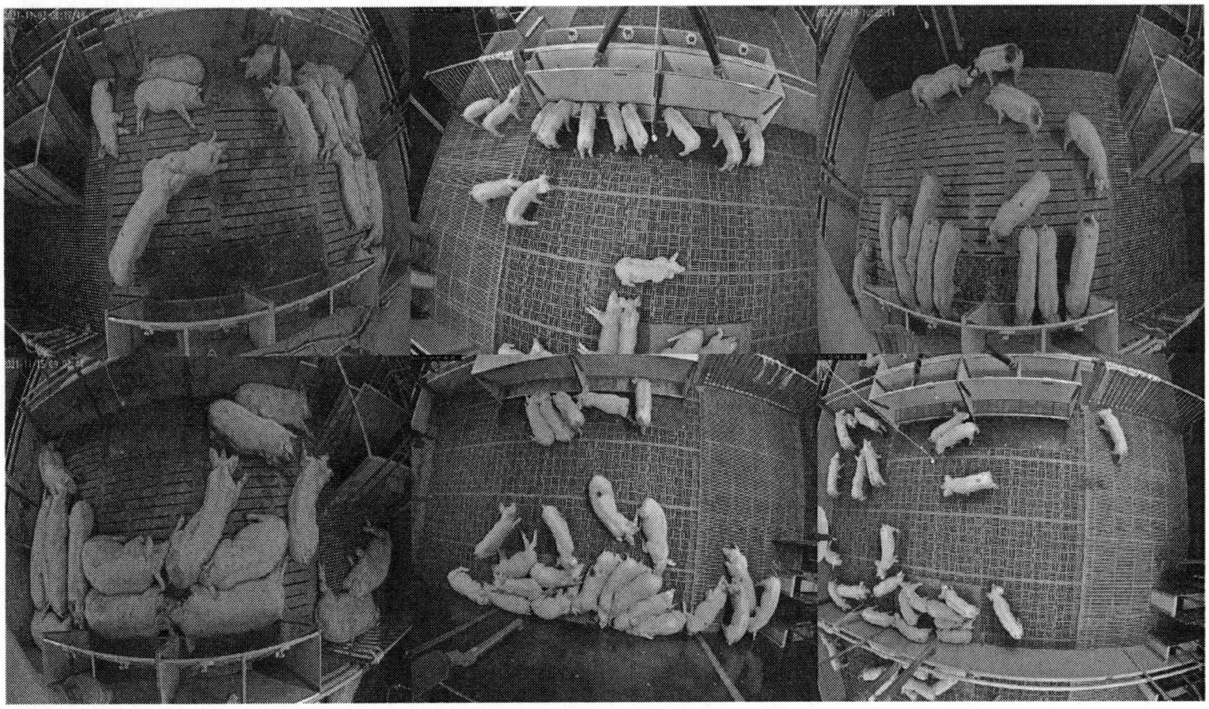

Fig. 1. Example images.

3) **Cost efficiency**: The respective models should be as resource efficient as possible to allow a potential deployment to low-cost hardware [24].

Since the YOLO architecture has already been used in the PLF literature, matches the established criteria by balancing performance, speed, and resource requirements, and has an extensively documented repositories as well as an active community, YOLO was chosen as a baseline architecture for further analysis. YOLOv5 is the latest instalment of the YOLO architecture, but there is currently no official paper for this release. The latest paper release is related to YOLOv4 [25]. YOLOv4 applies specific methods and concepts summarized under the terms bag of freebies and bag of specials to improve accuracy and execution speed compared to YOLOv3 and other architectures such as EfficientDet. The performance was further improved by introducing a network scaling approach by modifying model depth, width, resolution, and structure [26]. The comparison of the two official implementations of YOLOv4 and YOLOv5 resulted in the selection of the YOLOv5 implementation, as it was more suitable for the context of this paper.

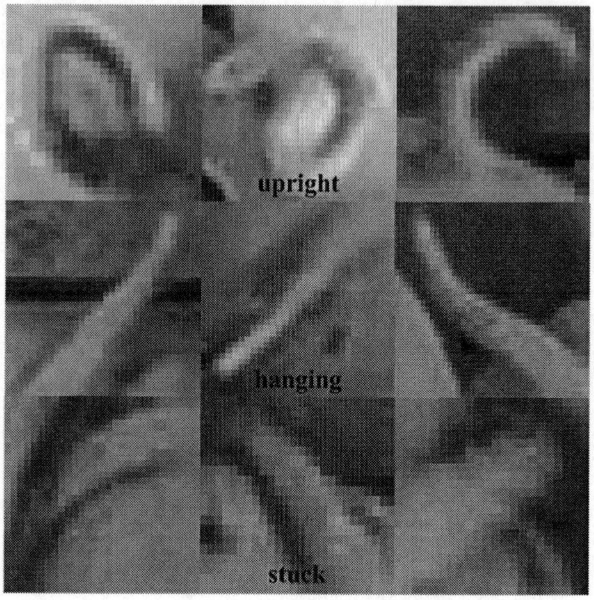

Fig. 2. Tail posture examples.

C. Label strategy

Before we started to create the dataset, we defined a label strategy in which we specified class selection, image selection and other aspects regarding dataset annotation. To select the label classes, we first identified and compared the different tail postures previously mentioned in the literature and subsequently validated them by an expert group consisting of farmers, veterinarians, and researchers within the DigiSchwein project. Schukat and Heise [9] mention the *curled*, *hanging*, and *stuck* tail posture [9]. D'Eath et al. [5] defined similar tail postures, with the difference that instead of *hanging* they specified the class *loose*, which was further separated into the classes *low loose* and *high loose*. Ocepek et al. [21] distinguish tail posture into *straight* and *curled*, with the *straight* class including tucked tails as well. Furthermore, it is described that both classes were only annotated if the respective pig in the image was standing. If it was lying, the respective pig was not annotated. After a discussion in the expert group of the DigiPig project, it was initially decided to separate the posture classes into three classes similar to [9] and [5]: *upright*, *hanging* and *stuck*. Figure 2 shows examples for each defined class. However, unlike [21], we decided to annotate every visible tail object and its respective posture on the images, regardless of whether it is lying or standing. Reason for this is the assumption that the distinction of the pigs' posture and hence the decision whether to annotate an object or not is not being represented in the training dataset. Thus, there is a possibility that the algorithm may also not learn these relationships. Furthermore, if the tail objects are labelled inconsistently without a reason for the distinction being represented in the dataset, it could negatively impact the performance of the model. The raw images used for dataset creation were extracted from the video recordings that were captured inside the DigiSchwein project. For video and frame selection, we specified the following guidelines:

1) Inclusion of images from piglet rearing and fattening as well as different camera angles, backgrounds, and perspectives to ensure as much data heterogeneity as possible.
2) Inclusion of images with different activity levels within the respective pens to ensure a balanced ratio of standing and lying pigs and a balanced distribution of pig positions and locations inside the pen to further increase data heterogeneity.
3) Balancing the number of each defined tail posture so that none of the defined classes are over- or underrepresented.

Especially the last point caused problems during the data collection and annotation process. The class *stuck* was extremely underrepresented in the extracted images and it was difficult to find additional video recordings in which the respective class could be identified. Additionally, initial results based on a prototypically trained model showed that the class *stuck* was difficult to detect because of this class imbalance. Based on a dataset containing 400 images, a YOLOv5m model trained with an image size of 1280×1280 achieved a mAP0.5:0.95 of 0.277, which also improved just slightly as the number of images increased. To deal with this imbalance, we decided to merge the *stuck* class into the *hanging* class, creating a better balance between the defined classes.

Another challenge that emerged during the annotation process was the annotation of the tails of lying pigs. In some cases, it could not be clearly determined to which class the respective tail could be assigned to. Figure 3 shows some examples for these cases. Even after discussing the issue within the expert group of the DigiSchwein project, no

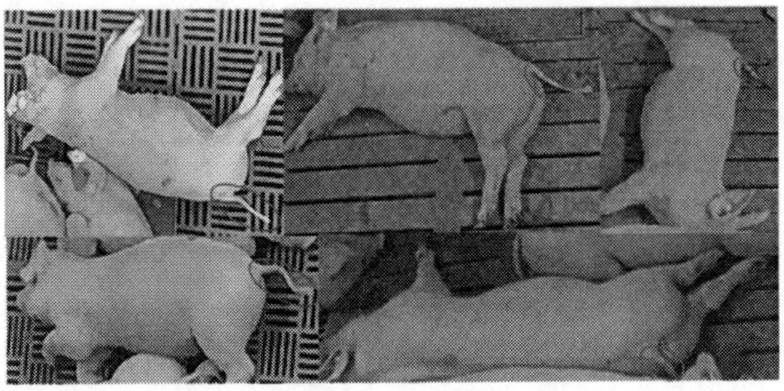

Fig. 3. Difficult to distinguish classes.

clear consensus could be reached. In essence, two separate approaches have emerged when explaining the determination of the class: One group argued that lying pigs, as the ones shown in Figure 3, must have a hanging tail posture because, when in a relaxed or almost relaxed state, the tail would have a hanging position due to gravity alone. The other group argues based on the orientation of the tail of the lying pigs and tends to classify these tail postures as upright. It was difficult to decide how to translate the results of this discussion into the label strategy, as both ways of reasoning are comprehensible. Ultimately, it was decided to assign these instances to the *hanging* class.

D. Dataset description

A dataset consisting of 1000 images with a total of 12802 high quality bounding box annotations was created. By following the data extraction and label strategy, a proper class balance of 6391 *upright* and 6412 *hanging* annotations was ensured. The open-source tool *Labelme* was used to annotate the images for model training and evaluation [27]. Images were extracted from video recordings that were collected in the DigiSchwein project and subsequently annotated according to defined label strategy described in Section III-C. To reduce the overall annotation time, the dataset creation process was divided into different phases:

1) A sample of 200 out of the total 1000 images were manually annotated. This sample was first randomly extracted from the overall data pool and then inspected to ensure data variety was sufficient in the sample
2) A pretrained YOLOv5 model based on the YOLOv5m checkpoint was trained using the annotated sample. The model was subsequently applied on the unlabeled data to generate predictions.
3) The predictions of the model were transformed into the Labelme JSON format and loaded into the annotation tool, where the predictions were subsequently checked by a human annotator. If the given annotations for the respective image were inaccurate or incorrect, they were adjusted manually within the Labelme tool. After the 200 images were reviewed, the model was re-trained with the additional data and the process re-started from step 1) until all 1000 images were annotated. This ultimately reduced the amount of manual label work.

E. Test environment

Model training was performed on a desktop workstation with two Nvidia RTX 3090 with 24 GB VRAM each, a Threadripper 3960X and 64 GB RAM. For the object detection task of detecting tail postures of pigs, the YOLOv5 implementation of Jocher et al. [28] was applied. Standard parameters were used for training of each selected model variant. Data augmentation is applied in form of image mosaic and mix-up, random image flip, image rotation, image scaling as well as hue saturation value augmentation. Each model was trained for a maximum of 300 epochs with a batch size of 64 for the 640×640 models and 16 for the 1280×1280 image size models. The YOLOv5 model checkpoints *s*, *m* and *l* as well as the updated versions *s6*, *m6* and *l6* of the respective variants were selected for training and evaluation. Training was stopped early if performance did not improve over several epochs or if validation losses was increasing over several epochs to avoid overfitting. For each trained model, the epoch with the best result on the validation set was saved and used for evaluation. We used an 80-20 split for train and test data.

IV. Results

A. Evaluation metrics

The commonly used metric for evaluation and benchmarking object detection models is the mAP, which is the mean of the AP averaged over all defined classes based on a set of different IoU thresholds [29]. IoU is defined as the similarity between the ground truth annotation and the predicted annotation present in the image and is determined by dividing the intersection with the area of union [30]. Common thresholds to calculate the mAP are values in the range 0.5 to 0.95 with a threshold step size of 0.05, represented in this paper as mAP0.5:0.95 [31]. The higher the IoU threshold, the less margin is allowed in the deviation of the ground truth bounding box and predicted bounding box to be labelled as correct, so the AP is usually lower at higher thresholds. P and R for each tested model variant are also provided, describing what portion of the positive predictions were correct and what portion of the positive predictions was detected correctly, respectively. We also included inference time as well as the number of parameters for each tested model variant. The number of parameters describes the model size and can affect the required hardware to train and operationalize the respective model, having direct effect on the inference time.

B. Quantitative results

The results are shown in Table II, while Table III shows the inference time of each evaluated model variant as well as their number of parameters. The old and updated model variants showed a similar inference time within the experiments when using the 1280 image size, which is why they are merged with the updated variants. During testing, different inference times were observed when performing the same evaluation run multiple times. The table, therefore, shows the respective

TABLE II
RESULTS TAIL POSTURE DETECTION.

		Tail Posture Detection													
		640				*1280*									
Class	*M*	*P*	*R*	*mAP0.5*	*mAP:0.95*	*M*	*P*	*R*	*mAP0.5*	*mAP:0.95*	*M*	*P*	*R*	*mAP0.5*	*mAP:0.95*
all		0.802	0.675	0.716	0.301		0.875	0.813	0.857	0.459		0.865	0.813	0.852	0.460
upright	**s**	0.849	0.778	0.822	0.356	**s6**	0.923	0.862	0.911	0.505	**s**	0.906	0.853	0.802	0.511
hanging		0.755	0.572	0.610	0.246		0.827	0.763	0.803	0.412		0.824	0.772	0.802	0.410
all		0.835	0.755	0.801	0.394		0.861	0.840	0.872	0.486		0.883	0.838	0.867	0.491
upright	**m**	0.907	0.827	0.884	0.445	**m6**	0.901	0.883	0.919	0.526	**m**	0.922	0.887	0.915	0.540
hanging		0.763	0.684	0.718	0.342		0.822	0.797	0.825	0.446		0.845	0.789	0.819	0.443
all		0.850	0.720	0.790	0.366		0.871	0.828	0.857	0.487		0.885	0.844	0.879	0.511
upright	**l**	0.897	0.816	0.879	0.424	**l6**	0.906	0.876	0.903	0.531	**l**	0.919	0.885	0.922	0.552
hanging		0.803	0.624	0.700	0.309		0.836	0.780	0.811	0.444		0.85	0.803	0.836	0.469

TABLE III
NUMBER OF PARAMETERS AND INFERENCE TIME.

Model	*Parameter (m)*	*Inference (ms)*	
s	7.2		1.2
m	21.2	640	2.9
l	46.5		4.4
s6	12.6		5.2
m6	35.7	1280	9.3
l6	76.8		17.9

mean of the observed inference times. Each trained model was evaluated three times after we noticed the problem in order to investigate the deviations in the inference times in more detail. However, an exact cause could not be determined. Overall, it can be observed that, with one exception, the performance of tail posture detection can be increased when a greater image size and a larger model variation is used. The training of the YOLOv5l model with an image size of 640 had to be stopped early because performance did not improve after several epochs as well as overfitting that could be observed after around 100 epochs, which subsequently resulted in an overall reduction of the measured performance compared to the YOLOv5m variant. This could be due to the fact that the YOLOv5l model is too complex and too big for the considered use case, which is why this model and image size combination seems unsuitable. In general, it can be observed that the performance results for the *s*, *m* and *l* model variants trained on a 640 image size are insufficient. With an mAP0.5:0.95 of 0.394 a P and R of 0.835 and 0.755 over all classes, the YOLOv5m achieves the best results in this image size category. Although this combination has the fastest inference time with 2.9 ms per frame as well as the lowest number of parameters and, therefore, has the lowest hardware requirements, the results are not sufficient enough to further investigate this combination of model and image size. However, an improvement in all measured metrics can be observed when using the 1280 image size for the *s*, *m* and *l* model variants. Compared to the YOLOv5s 640 combination, a mAP0.5:0.95 of 0.46 can be achieved when increasing the image size to a 1280×1280 resolution, resulting in an overall increase in performance of almost 52% in terms of mAP0.5:0.95. This also significantly increases the number if parameters of the model as well as the inference time, which increases to 9.3 ms in comparison to the 2.9 ms. Despite this, real time inference can still be ensured when using appropriate hardware, which is why the YOLOV5m with an image size of 1280×1280 offers the best balance between accuracy, speed, and hardware requirements out of the tested model variants. When comparing the performances of the *s*, *m* and *l* versions with the updated *s6*, *m6* and *l6* variants, it is noticeable that the updated models are, with the exception of minimal improvements in P and partial R in some cases, consistently lower than the measured performances of the older variants. For this reason, the updated variants are not further considered in the quantitative analyzes of the results. Overfitting, which was previously observed for the YOLOv5l 640 variant, does not occur when using the larger image resolution. In fact, using the larger model variant improved performance in all measured metrics, but the difference is much smaller than when changing from the YOLOv5s to the YOLOv5m variant. This might mean that in terms of parameter number and model complexity, a bottleneck has been reached and further performance improvements cannot be achieved by just using more complex models, but rather by providing better training data, more training data, or different approaches for tail posture detection in general. This becomes even more evident when comparing the performance of the *upright* and *hanging* class. For each model variation evaluated, P, R, mAP, and mAP0.5:0.95 are significantly lower for the *hanging* class compared to the *upright* class, although both classes are relatively balanced in the train and test set. This may be due to the higher complexity of the *hanging* class caused by the merging of the *hanging* and *stuck* class, previously discussed in Section III-C as part of the label strategy.

To further investigate this problem, the method presented in [32] was adapted by separating the tail posture detection into two separate stages: A detection step, where only the *tail* class is detected and an subsequent image classification step, where the detected bounding boxes of the *tail* detection model are classified into the defined posture classes *upright* and *hanging*. The idea behind this is that by further merging the classes *upright* and *hanging* into the class *tail*, the highest possible level of representation could be obtained, so that the classes would no longer be considered disjoint from each other and thus performance in tail detection could potentially increase. The actual classification of the posture will then be moved to an image classification model, which will eventually also be used to investigate whether the same differences in performance can be observed for the *upright* and *hanging* classes as with the tested YOLOv5 model variants. In the final step, the two presented methods of one-step tails posture detection and two-step tail posture detection consisting of an object detection and image classification model will be compared and benchmarked based on their performance. The results are presented in the following sections.

C. Results image classification

We first wanted to determine whether image classification models have similar problems in classifying the *hanging* class. Based on the selection criteria defined in Section III-B as well as in [32], we selected the EfficientNetV2-B0 model for training. Based on the annotated object detection dataset described in Section III-D, we created an image classification dataset by extracting the bounding boxes from the object detection dataset using the annotated coordinates and subsequently saved them as separate files. For model training, the official Keras implementation of EfficientNetV0 has been used. Transfer learning was applied by first freezing all but the top layers when initializing the model and utilizing pre-trained ImageNet weights. Second, the layers were unfrozen to fit the model on the new data. In both steps, the model was trained for 30 epochs with a batch size of 128 and an input size of 224×224. Data augmentation was applied in form of random horizontal flipping, random zoom, random rotation as well as random crops and random contrast changes. Training was stopped early when accuracy and validation accuracy intersected, and accuracy continued to increase while validation accuracy stagnated or decreased to avoid overfitting. Sigmoid activation function was used in the last layer while Adam was used as optimizer. Binary cross entropy was specified as the loss function. The results are shown in Table V. Performance in terms if *P*, *R* and *F1* are almost identical for both classes. With a *P* of 0.970, the *hanging* class even achieves a slightly higher performance than the *upright* class, while *R* is still slightly lower for the *hanging* class. Unlike the YOLOv5 model, the problem of distinguishing and classifying the *hanging* class do not seem to be present here, but to ultimately verify whether the approach of separating tail posture detection into an object detection and image classification step can improve performance, the entire process must be considered. Therefore, the following presents the results of the object detection model, which only detects the merged *tail* class and that serves as a preceding step before the image classification step.

D. Results tail detection

To create the data set for detecting the higher-level class *tail*, the *upright* and *hanging* labels of the object detection data set were merged and overwritten in the label files. To ensure a direct comparison, the same combinations of YOLOv5 model variants and image sizes were applied as in Section II for model training and evaluation. The results, presented in Table IV, show that merging the two classes can improve the performance of every measured metric. Comparing the two YOLOv5m 1280 variants, a mAP0.5:0.95 of 0.530 can be achieved compared to the mAP0.05:0.95 of 0.491, resulting in a significant increase in performance. P and R can also be improved, while R still remains lower than P. Up to this point, it can be concluded that separating the tail posture detection into an object detection and an image classification step can, in isolation, lead to performance improvements in the respective tasks. However, the results are only beneficial if the combination of the *tail* object detection model and the image classification model translate into a performance improvement that surpasses the results of the model presented in SectionII. This will be examined in the following section.

E. Comparison

In order to verify whether the presented approach can lead to performance improvements, we compared the performance

TABLE V
RESULTS TAIL CLASSIFICATION.

		Tail Classification		
		224		
Class	*Model*	*Precision*	*Recall*	*F1*
all	B0	0.965	0.970	0.970
upright		0.960	0.980	0.970
hanging		0.970	0.960	0.970

TABLE IV
RESULTS TAIL DETECTION

		Tail Detection													
		640				*1280*									
Class	*M*	*P*	R	mAP0.5	mAP0:0.95	M	P	R	mAP0.5	mAP:0.95	M	P	R	mAP0.5	mAP:0.95
tail	**s**	0.879	0.778	0.831	0.381	**s6**	0.905	0.848	0.898	0.474	**s**	0.919	0.861	0.905	0.493
tail	**m**	0.879	0.813	0.851	0.418	**m6**	0.899	0.880	0.916	0.522	**m**	0.926	0.877	0.918	0.530
tail	**l**	0.888	0.805	0.857	0.422	**l6**	0.917	0.881	0.921	0.531	**l**	0.921	0.884	0.924	0.547

of the one-step YOLOv5m and YOLOv5l tail posture detection trained on a 1280×1280 image size with the two-step approach consisting of the YOLOv5m and YOLOv5l model for *tail* detection and the EfficientNetV2-B0 model for subsequent image classification of the detected bounding boxes into *upright* and *hanging*. Since the YOLOv5m variant offers the best balance of performance, speed, and hardware requirements and the YOLOv5l variant gives the best overall performance when disregarding speed as well as hardware requirements, these model variations were selected for comparison. We use a customized version of the *val.py* script of the YOLOv5 repository, which we adapted to integrate the *tail* detection model as well as the EfficientNetV2-B0 model for image classification in the evaluation pipeline.

The comparison of both approaches, presented in Table VI, shows that the combination of the object detection and image classification methods cannot improve the performance for tail posture detection. The opposite is true, as the direct comparison of the results of the YOLOv5m model variants reveals a decrease in performance for all measured metrics. The difference in performance between the *upright* and *hanging* class is also still present, it even increased in direct comparison. The same observations apply when comparing the results for the YOLOv5l model variations. However, it can also be observed that, as the accuracy of the predicted bounding boxes of the *tail* object detection model used in the pipeline increases, the overall classification of tail posture can also be increased. Although the difference between the map0.5:0.95 of 0.530 and 0.547 for *tail* detection with YOLOv5m and YOLOv5l respectively is not significant, it can lead to a similar performance increase for the two-step tail posture detection based on the combination of object detection and image classification. This results in almost identical performance of the YOLOv5l model variant in combination with the EfficientNetv2-B0 compared to the YOLOv5m variant for one-step tail posture classification.

V. Discussion

Given that, in isolation, both the merging of the *upright* and *hanging* class into the *tail* class led to a more accurate detection and that the subsequent image classification for tail posture classification into *upright* and *hanging* was able to avert the problems regarding the detecting of the *hanging* class presented in Section IV-B, it was surprising that the combination of the two approaches achieved inferior results in comparison. However, a closer look at the data as well as the results reveals a possible explanation, which will be discussed in the following. The results of Section IV-E already demonstrated that the accuracy of the object detection and image classification pipeline is dependent on the accuracy of the object detection model. The more accurate the object detection is, the more accurate the final classification by the image classification model will be. Possible explanation for the inferior performance is that the image classification model was trained using perfectly cropped image data for the *upright* and *hanging* classes, which cannot be provided in that form in inference mode due to the currently existing inaccuracy of the *tail* detection. The image crops provided by the *tail* detection, on the basis of which the posture classification model is supposed to categorize the tail posture, are in terms of the mAPO.5:0.95 of 0.530 and 0.547 for the YOLOv5m model and the YOLOv5l model insufficiently accurate, which is why the image classification model is provided with input images that may not fully capture the targeted *tail* object. Thus, the provided input data by the object detection model may deviate from the actual training data, in which the targeted *tail* object could be represented under ideal conditions. This discrepancy in the data may lead to inferior results when comparing the two approaches. However, this will need to be further validated in future research.

VI. Conclusion

In summary, the following findings can be derived from the results obtained in this paper. Table IV as well as the examination of the results in Section IV-B each show, that performance for one-step tail posture classification based on the YOLOv5 object detection architecture can be increased when larger models and larger image sizes are used for training. However, this performance increase does not scale infinitely, but seems to decrease as the number of model parameters increases. Thus, performance cannot simply be increased by using larger models and larger image sizes. It was also observed that there are large performance differences between the *upright* and *hanging* class. The results in Section IV-C show that, in isolation, the observed differences in performance can be mitigated by using image classification

TABLE VI
Comparison of approaches.

	Tail Posture Detection									
		Object Detection				***Object Detection + Image Classification***				
Class	*M*	*P*	*R*	*mAP0.5*	*mAP:0.95*	*M*	*P*	*R*	*mAP0.5*	*mAP:0.95*
all	**m**	0.883	0.838	0.867	0.491	**m + B0**	0.851	0.803	0.808	0.473
upright		0.922	0.887	0.915	0.540		0.853	0.886	0.862	0.522
hanging		0.845	0.789	0.819	0.443		0.849	0.720	0.754	0.424
all	**l**	0.885	0.844	0.879	0.511	**l + B0**	0.847	0.807	0.823	0.492
upright		0.919	0.885	0.922	0.552		0.846	0.892	0.869	0.537
hanging		0.850	0.803	0.836	0.469		0.848	0.722	0.778	0.447

for tail posture classification. In general, tail detection, as the results in Section IV-D show, can also be improved by merging the *upright* and *hanging* class into the higher-level class *tail*. However, when considered as a whole, the indicated potentials of the object detection model for tail detection and the image classification model for tail posture classification cannot be utilized, as the comparison of the results of the one-step and two-step tail posture classification approach in Table VI revealed. The *hanging* class is not only a problem in terms of detection, but also in terms of annotation, which is also reflected in the obtained model results in Table II. Especially lying pigs seem to aggravate this problem, since it is not always evident to which class the object under consideration can be assigned to. In general, it is questionable whether the tail posture of lying pigs should be included at all as a relevant indicator for tail posture monitoring or, if included, how to properly handle them.

One approach to deal with the identified problems could be to simply include more training data, more diverse training data, better training data or, if the previous solution approaches indicate that the problem is not data related, to find or select a different approach for tail posture detection. The former could particularly help to improve the performance of the presented two-step tail posture classification approach, since the performance of the two-step approach is positively correlated with the performance of the tail detection model, so that an improvement in accuracy for the tail detection model can lead to a better classification of the cropped bounding boxes. However, it is also possible that the problem in detecting the *hanging* class cannot be solved by simply adding more training data. This is where the latter of the mentioned approaches comes into play. One solution approach could be to exclude lying pigs from the tail posture detection process or treat them separately. However, the exclusion of lying pigs is not a trivial task, as it cannot be achieved by simply not annotating lying pigs and their respective tail postures, since for object detection tasks, every object of a defined target class should be annotated in the training set. Thus, the exclusion must be realized in form of a preceding or subsequent step within the tail posture detection process. In future work, we will investigate the approaches of excluding lying pigs from the tail posture detection process or separate handling them based on a preceding pig posture classification step, where we classify detected pigs into *lying* and *notLying* and examine whether performance improvements can be achieved in that way.

VII. Acknowledgments

The project is supported (was supported) by funds of the Federal Ministry of Food and Agriculture (BMEL) based on a decision of the Parliament of the Federal Republic of Germany. The Federal Office for Agriculture and Food (BLE) provides (provided) coordinating support for digitalisation in agriculture as funding organisation, grant number 28DE109A18.

References

[1] Statistisches Bundesamt, "Number of pig farms in Germany from 1950 to 2021," 2021. https://de.statista.com/statistik/daten/studie/1175101/umfrage/betriebe-in-der-schweinehaltung-deutschland/.

[2] Statistisches Bundesamt, "Number of pigs per farm in Germany from 1950 to 2021," 2021. https://de.statista.com/statistik/daten/studie/1174729/umfrage/anzahl-der-schweine-je-betrieb-in-deutschland/.

[3] Bundesministerium für Ernährung und Landwirtschaft, "Slaughter prices of pigs, cattle and lambs," 2022. https://www.bmel-statistik.de/preise/preise-fleisch/.

[4] D. Berckmans, "Precision livestock farming technologies for welfare management in intensive livestock systems," *Revue scientifique et technique (International Office of Epizootics)*, vol. 33, no. 1, pp. 189–196, 2014.

[5] R. B. D'Eath *et al.*, "Automatic early warning of tail biting in pigs: 3D cameras can detect lowered tail posture before an outbreak," *PloS one*, vol. 13, no. 4, p. e0194524, 2018.

[6] J. Cowton, I. Kyriazakis, T. Plötz, and J. Bacardit, "A Combined Deep Learning GRU-Autoencoder for the Early Detection of Respiratory Disease in Pigs Using Multiple Environmental Sensors," *Sensors (Basel, Switzerland)*, vol. 18, no. 8, p. 2521, 2018.

[7] C. Chen *et al.*, "Recognition of aggressive episodes of pigs based on convolutional neural network and long short-term memory," *Computers and Electronics in Agriculture*, vol. 169, p. 105166, 2020.

[8] C. Chijioke Ojukwu, Y. Feng, G. Jia, H. Zhao, and H. Ta, "Development of a computer vision system to detect inactivity in group-housed pigs," *International Journal of Agricultural and Biological Engineering*, vol. 13, no. 1, pp. 42–46, 2020.

[9] S. Schukat and H. Heise, "Indicators for early detection of tail biting in pigs - a meta-analysis.," 2019.

[10] N. R. Taylor, D. C. J. Main, M. Mendl, and S. A. Edwards, "Tail-biting: a new perspective," *Veterinary journal (London, England : 1997)*, vol. 186, no. 2, pp. 137–147, 2010.

[11] R. B. D'Eath *et al.*, "Changes in tail posture detected by a 3D machine vision system are associated with injury from damaging behaviours and ill health on commercial pig farms," *PLOS ONE*, vol. 16, no. 10 October, 2021.

[12] D. L. Schrøder-Petersen and H. B. Simonsen, "Tail biting in pigs," *The Veterinary Journal*, vol. 162, no. 3, pp. 196–210, 2001.

[13] G. Chen, S. Shen, L. Wen, S. Luo, and L. Bo, "Efficient Pig Counting in Crowds with Keypoints Tracking and Spatial-aware Temporal Response Filtering."

[14] J. Cowton, I. Kyriazakis, and J. Bacardit, "Automated Individual Pig Localisation, Tracking and Behaviour Metric Extraction Using Deep Learning," *IEEE Access*, vol. 7, pp. 108049–108060, 2019.

[15] Y. Cang, H. He, and Y. Qiao, "An Intelligent Pig Weights Estimate Method Based on Deep Learning in Sow Stall Environments," *IEEE Access*, vol. 7, no. 99, pp. 164867–164875, 2019.

[16] G. van Putten, "An Investigation into Tail-Biting among Fattening Pigs," *British Veterinary Journal*, vol. 125, no. 10, pp. 511–517, 1969.

[17] C. Moinard, M. Mendl, C. Nicol, and L. Green, "A case control study of on-farm risk factors for tail biting in pigs," *Applied Animal Behaviour Science*, vol. 81, no. 4, pp. 333–355, 2003.

[18] P. Wißkirchen *et al.*, "Early detection of tail biting among pigs on the basis of deep learning: Development concept of a practical early warning system," pp. 343–348, Gesellschaft fur Informatik (GI), 2021.

[19] Y. Domun, L. J. Pedersen, D. White, O. Adeyemi, and T. Norton, "Learning patterns from time-series data to discriminate predictions of tail-biting, fouling and diarrhoea in pigs," *Computers and Electronics in Agriculture*, vol. 163, p. 104878, 2019.

[20] M. L. V. Larsen, L. J. Pedersen, and D. B. Jensen, "Prediction of Tail Biting Events in Finisher Pigs from Automatically Recorded Sensor Data," *Animals : an open access journal from MDPI*, vol. 9, no. 7, 2019.

[21] M. Ocepek, A. Žnidar, M. Lavrič, D. Škorjanc, and I. L. Andersen, "Digipig: First developments of an automated monitoring system for body, head and tail detection in intensive pig farming," *Agriculture (Switzerland)*, vol. 12, no. 1, 2022.

[22] T. Norton, C. Chen, M. L. V. Larsen, and D. Berckmans, "Review: Precision livestock farming: building 'digital representations' to bring

the animals closer to the farmer," *animal*, vol. 13, no. 12, pp. 3009–3017, 2019.

[23] S. Lee, H. Ahn, J. Seo, Y. Chung, D. Park, and S. Pan, "Practical Monitoring of Undergrown Pigs for IoT-Based Large-Scale Smart Farm," *IEEE Access*, vol. 7, pp. 173796–173810, 2019.

[24] Banhazi, H. Lehr, J. L. Black, H. Crabtree, and D. Berckmans, "Precision Livestock Farming: An international review of scientific and commercial aspects," *International Journal of Agricultural and Biological Engineering*, vol. 5, no. 3, pp. 1–9, 2012.

[25] A. Bochkovskiy, C.-Y. Wang, and H.-Y. M. Liao, "YOLOv4: Optimal Speed and Accuracy of Object Detection," 2020.

[26] C.-Y. Wang, A. Bochkovskiy, and H.-Y. M. Liao, "Scaled-YOLOv4: Scaling Cross Stage Partial Network," 2020.

[27] K. Wada, "labelme: Image Polygonal Annotation with Python," 2016.

[28] Jocher, Glenn et al., "ultralytics/yolov5: v5.0 - YOLOv5-P6 1280 models, AWS, Supervise.ly and YouTube integrations," 2021.

[29] K. He, G. Gkioxari, P. Dollár, and R. Girshick, "Mask R-CNN," *2017 IEEE International Conference on Computer Vision (ICCV)*, pp. 2980–2988, 2017.

[30] M. A. Rahman and Y. Wang, "Optimizing Intersection-Over-Union in Deep Neural Networks for Image Segmentation," in *ISVC*, 2016.

[31] R. Padilla, W. L. Passos, T. L. B. Dias, S. L. Netto, and E. A. B. da Silva, "A Comparative Analysis of Object Detection Metrics with a Companion Open-Source Toolkit," *Electronics*, vol. 10, no. 3, p. 279, 2021.

[32] J.-H. Witte and J. Marx Gómez, "Introducing a new Workflow for Pig Posture Classification based on a combination of YOLO and EfficientNet," in *Proceedings of the 55th Hawaii International Conference on System Sciences* (T. Bui, ed.), Proceedings of the Annual Hawaii International Conference on System Sciences, pp. 1135–1144, Hawaii International Conference on System Sciences, 2022.

The Use of Multi-Step Markov Chains in the Characterization of English Literary Works

Clement H. C. Leung
School of Science and Engineering &
Guangdong Provincial Key Laboratory of Future
Networks of Intelligence
The Chinese University of Hong Kong, Shenzhen
Shenzhen, China
Email: clementleung@cuhk.edu.cn

Chenjie Zeng
School of Humanities and Social Science
The Chinese University of Hong Kong, Shenzhen
Shenzhen, China
Email: chenjiezeng@link.cuhk.edu.cn

***Abstract*—Typical English literary works tend to include a wide variety of different dimensions and features, and these would constitute the apparatuses which enable individual authors to express their personal sentiments and perspectives in different eras and cultural settings. We make use of iambic pentametre to quantify and characterize such dimensions by the use of Markov chains. Here, we adopt a machine learning approach by processing and extracting the characteristics of known passages and ultimately represent these as a signature transition matrix. We develop a multi-step Markov chain to characterize the time evolution of stress levels. In this approach, arbitrary amount of memory on previous stress levels may be incorporated into the model. It is expected that this method may be further developed and leveraged to enhance understanding and appreciation of English literary works, which will eliminate the application of subjective human judgments.**

Keywords - English literature; Markov model; Multi-step Markov chain; Shakespearean plays; sparse matrix.

I. INTRODUCTION

The richness of literary passages possesses multi-faceted characteristics, and such characteristics would allow different authors to express their unique emotions and outlook in different periods of time and cultural environments. In computational literary analysis, differing aims include determining authorship, sentiments, emotional contents, outlook, motif, rhythm, metre and purpose. Due to the complex dimensions, features and genres in English literature, there remain two especially significant obstacles in computer-aided literary attribution, respectively, practical and philosophical, which are related [7].

As literary works can be viewed from a machine learning perspective [8]-[12], we first introduce a one-step Markov chain where the future stress level is dependent only on the present one. While this is useful, its limitation being that it is largely memoryless and ignore earlier stress levels. To overcome this restriction, we develop a multi-step Markov chain to characterize the evolution of stress levels. Through the combined use of one-step and multi-step Markov chain, show that certain characteristics of these works remain fairly uniform.. The examples include polarity of emotions, average sentence length, the arrangement of words, the occurrences of a particular word and punctuations.

We use machine learning approaches to learn the characteristics of known passages using big data and ultimately encode these as a signature. In these approaches, arbitrary amount of memory on previous stress levels may be incorporated, with the caveat that the number of possible states would grow exponentially. By exploiting such sparsity, we are able to generate a numerical signature to characterize a passage. We also improve the traditional way of manually using human judgments to analyze literature into a faster and more space-efficient one.

The rest of this paper is organized as follows. The next section, with the help of specific examples, gives the motivation of studying English literary works by using Markov chains as a first approximation. As a second approximation, since the simple Markov chain is limited in memory of the past, the multi-step Markov chain is developed in Section III, which is followed by experimentations in Section IV. The paper concludes in Section V.

II. A MARKOV CHAIN CHARACTERIZATION

Poems in one sense may be viewed as apparatus for the expression of human sentiments and emotions which are often manifested and closely intertwined in the poetic structure, metre, and rhyme scheme. To fix ideas, we consider Wordsworth's poem "Daffodils" by first examining its emotional elements, and then consider the poetic structure.

Daffodils are usually the symbol of "physically weak or impotent" [14] in English literature, and the lexical "daffodils" is a dactyl trisyllable with a stress on the first syllable. In the poems and a journal entry "Daffodils" [17]-[19], Ted Hughes, William Wordsworth, and Dorothy Wordsworth present the traits of daffodils by employing various rhetorical patterns and linguistic features. The characters can think and feel. European romanticism claims it is a new model of presence and emphasizes centrality [15]. The characters' feelings and emotions could be related to Zen's paradoxical philosophy of "fullness and emptiness" because 'up comes to a flower and a world is born' [16]. This "fullness and emptiness" philosophy is like the waxing and the waning of the Moon. It shows how the characters see the "happiness and sadness" and "fullness and emptiness" in their space time. Through the eyes of the characters, it could also bridge the gap between the sentiment lexicon analysis and the cross-cultural interpretation of literary works.

TABLE 1. POLARITY AND EMOTIONS

Polarity	Verse	Emotion
Positive	Tossing their heads in sprightly dance	Sprightly
	A poet could not but be gay	Gay
	In such a jocund company	Jocund
Negative	Which is the bliss of solitude	Bliss; Solitude
	I wandered lonely as a cloud	Lonely
	In vacant or in pensive mood	Vacant; Pensive

a. "Daffodils" by William Wordsworth [17]

From a language aspect, among the 24 lines (153 words) in William Wordsworth's poem "Daffodils", there are nine emotional lexicons, which are further tagged as "positive" or "negative". The five positive words include "sprightly, gay, jocund, bliss, and pleasure", which are the similar expression of "happiness" but with different degrees of "happiness". The varying degree of "happiness" could be the interpretation of Zen's "fullness" in eastern culture. In contrast, the four negatives are "lonely, vacant, pensive, and solitude", which represent the paradoxical pair of "sadness" or Zen's "emptiness". The same method is applied to the analysis of Ted Hughes' poem "Daffodils" and Dorothy Wordsworth's journal entry of "Daffodils". Hughes' poem [18] has three explicit emotions: eagerness, happiness, death, and being overwhelmed. In Dorothy Wordsworth's journal entry [19], the positive emotion lexicons of the characters are "fancied, laughed, gay, good, enjoyed", whereas the negatives are "cheerless" and "sour". In these English literary pieces, the emotions are the paradoxical pair of "happiness and sadness" and its varying degree of "fullness and emptiness".

In English literary writings, iambic pentameter plays a key role. In particular, one of the most important aspects of Shakespeare's language is his use of stress, the way certain syllables are emphasized in words more than others. In a line of a poem, a foot is a certain number of stressed and unstressed syllables, forming distinct units, as a musical measure consists of a certain number of beats. Delimitation of the sounds of the spoken chain can be based on auditory impressions, but the description of these sounds is an entirely different process. Description can be carried out on the basis of the articulatory act, for it is impossible to analyze the units of sound in their own chain [2].

Stressed syllables vary in strength, while unstressed syllables vary in weakness; and a third group can strike us as uncertain as falling into a range that seems stronger than unstressed but weaker than stressed [2]. Therefore, it is common to notate the stressed sound with a "/" marking ictic syllables and a "×" marking nonictic syllables. In this notation, a standard line of iambic pentameter would look like, "× / × / × / × / × /" where each line of verse is made up of five two-syllable iambs for a total of ten syllables. This is used for many of Shakespeare's most famous lines. As the metre is mainly about sound, not spelling, scansion adds numbers to indicate a variety of stress levels to realize beats and offbeats (1=lightest stress, 4=heaviest stress).

In relation to the poetic structure, metre and rhyme scheme, William Wordsworth's poem "Daffodils" [17] also exhibits correspondence with "fullness and emptiness". Here, the stressed sounds are in bold and labelled as "/", whereas the unstressed sounds are marked as "u".

u /u / u / u /

*They **flash upon** that **in**ward **eye***

u /u / u/u/

*Which **is** the **bliss** of **so**li**tude**;*

u / u / u / u /

*And **then** my **heart** with **plea**sure **fills**,*

u /u / u/u/

*And **dances with** the **daff**o**dils**.*

b. "Daffodils" by William Wordsworth [17]

III. Multi-Step Markov Chain Characterization with Memory

In the above, if we break down the unstressed groupings, then a one-step Markov chain will not be adequate as the situation retains a certain amount of memory. More precisely, it remembers how many unstressed metres occurred in the past before it can determine whether the next one should be stressed or unstressed: if the past three metres were all unstressed, then the next one should be stressed; if the past three metres were not all unstressed, then the next one should be unstressed. Thus, knowing only the current state will not be able to predict what happens next.

Hence, to remove the limitations on the above simple model, we can proceed in two directions: we can increase the number of possible states; and to reduce the memoryless property in the Markov chain. Let us initially concentrate on the first direction as Markov model recognition systems can effectively be realized for classification systems at large scales [1]

Consider Part I of Shakespeare's play "King Henry the Sixth", where the rebel Jack Cade beheads a lord for printing books and setting up a grammar school to teach young men to read instead of leaving them to tally their business accounts, we have

1 4 1 4 1 4 1 3 1 4

× / × / × / × / × /

*His **brandisht Sword** did **blinde** men **with** his **beames**.*

c. The Sonnets [13]

The transition matrix of the above line, where the four states indicate the stress levels of 1, 2, 3, 4 respectively, is

$$\begin{pmatrix} 0 & 0 & 0.2 & 0.8 \\ 0 & 0 & 0 & 0 \\ 1 & 0 & 0 & 0 \\ 1 & 0 & 0 & 0 \end{pmatrix}$$

It is possible to perform a simplification of this enhancement from the following observation. While the English syllables we speak can be spoken with many degrees or shades of emphasis of loudness, sharpness, duration, and other ways of signaling importance, it seems likely that in most English speech we perceive mainly two major levels of stress, and that we hear a continuous series of relatively stressed and relatively unstressed syllables [2]. Hence, the following

1 4 1 4 1 4 1 4 1 4

× / × / × / × / × /

*His **sparkling eyes, repleat** with **wrathfull fire**.*

d. The Sonnets [13]

can be constructed simply as

$$\begin{pmatrix} 0 & 0 & 0 & 1 \\ 0 & 0 & 0 & 0 \\ 0 & 0 & 0 & 0 \\ 1 & 0 & 0 & 0 \end{pmatrix}$$

using binary entries for the transition matrix.

Assuming these come from the same piece of work, and if the first pattern occurs with probability r, and the second pattern occurs with probability *s*, and that there are no other patterns, then we have the following combined transition matrix T

$$T = r\begin{pmatrix} 0 & 0 & 0.2 & 0.8 \\ 0 & 0 & 0 & 0 \\ 1 & 0 & 0 & 0 \\ 1 & 0 & 0 & 0 \end{pmatrix} + s\begin{pmatrix} 0 & 0 & 0 & 1 \\ 0 & 0 & 0 & 0 \\ 1 & 0 & 0 & 0 \\ 1 & 0 & 0 & 0 \end{pmatrix}$$

which results in the transition matrix

$$T = \begin{pmatrix} 0 & 0 & 0.2r & 0.8r + s \\ 0 & 0 & 0 & 0 \\ 1 & 0 & 0 & 0 \\ 1 & 0 & 0 & 0 \end{pmatrix}$$

Such a transition matrix may be used to characterize authorship.

As suggested by Cheney Patrick [5], a laureate entitled *counter-authorship* is a form of authorship that exists not in isolation but also in reaction, and when we profitably speak of Shakespeare, another laureate has been phrased as *counter-lauréate authorship* [5]. One example of the *counter-lauréate authorship* in "King Henry the Fourth" as following is pivotal in the action of the play because it is first verification that the character Hal is in the process of reforming from tavern wastrel to national hero.

0 4 1 4 1 4 1 4 1 4
× / × / × / × / × /
Wanton *as* ***youthful goats****,* ***wild as*** *young* ***bulls****.*

1 4 1 4 1 4 1 4 1 4
× / × / × / × / × /
I saw *young* ***Harry with*** *his* ***beaver on****,*

1 4 1 4 1 4 1 4 1 2
× / × / × / × / × /
His ***cushes*** *on his* ***thighs****,* ***gallantly arm'd****,*

1 4 1 4 1 4 1 4 1 3
× / × / × / × / × /
Rise ***from*** *the* ***ground*** *like* ***feathered Mercury****,*

1 4 1 3 1 4 1 4 1 4
× / × / × / × / × /
And ***Vaulted with*** *such* ***ease onto*** *his* ***seat***

1 4 1 4 1 4 1 4 1 4
× / × / × / × / × /
As ***if*** *an* ***angel dropp'd down*** *from the* ***clouds***

1 4 1 4 1 4 1 4 1 3
× / × / × / × / × /
To ***turn*** *and* ***wind*** *a* ***fiery Pegasus****,*

1 4 1 4 1 4 1 4 1 3
× / × / × / × / × /
And ***witch*** *the* ***world*** *with* ***noble horsemanship****.*

e. Henry IV, Act I, 103-110 [3]

The above passage, disregarding the first line, may be characterized by the following transition matrix

$$\begin{pmatrix} 0 & 0.03 & 0.11 & 0.86 \\ 1 & 0 & 0 & 0 \\ 1 & 0 & 0 & 0 \\ 1 & 0 & 0 & 0 \end{pmatrix}$$

Another form of *counter-lauréate authorship* emerges in a more obvious place, Theseus's speech in the mid-1590s romantic comedy "A Midsummer Night's Dream". It is noticeable that Shakespeare's self-reflexive revision, such as the inserting discourse about the 'poet' as company for "lunatic" and the "lover", turns a speech about the madness of love into one about the poet's role in forming an eternizing state of consciousness [5].

1 4 1 4 1 4 1 4 1 4
× / × / × / × / × /
More **strange** than **true**. I **never** may be**lieve**

1 4 1 4 1 4 1 4 1 4
× / × / × / × / × /
These **antic** fa**bles**, **nor** these **fairy** to**ys**.

1 4 1 4 1 4 1 4 1 4
× / × / × / × / × /
Lo**vers** and **mad**men have **such** see**thing** **brains**,

1 4 1 4
× / × /
Such shaping **fantasies**, that **apprehend**

1 4 1 4 1 4
× / × / × /
More **than** cool **reason** ever **comprehends**

1 4 1 4 1 4
× / × / × /
The **lunatic**, the **lover**, and the **poet**

1 4 1 4
× / × /
Are of **imagination** all **compact**.

1 4 1 4 1 4 1 4 1 4
× / × / × / × / × /
One **sees** more **devils** than vast **hell** can **hold**;

1 4 1 4 1 4 1 4 1 4
× / × / × / × / × /
That **is** the **mad**man. The **lover**, **all** as **frantic**,

1 4 1 4 1 4 1 4
× / × / × / × /
Sees **Helen**'s **beau**ty in a **brow** of **Egypt**.

1 4 1 4 1 4 1 4 1 4
× / × / × / × / × /
The **poet**'s **eye**, in a **fi**ne frenzy **rolling**,

1 4 1 4 1 4 1 4 1 4
× / × / × / × / × /
Doth **glance** from **heaven** to **earth**, from **earth** to **heaven**;

1 4 1 4 1 4 1 4
× / × / × / × /
And **as** imagi**na**tion **bo**dies **forth**

1 4 1 4 1 4 1 4 1 4
× / × / × / × / × /
The **forms** of **things** un**known**, the **poet**'s **pen**

1 4 1 4 1 4 1 4 1 4
× / × / × / × / × /
Turns **them** to **shapes**, and **gives** to **aery** **nothing**

1 4 1 4 1 4
× / × / × /
A **local** habi**ta**tion and a **name**.

1 4 1 4 1 4
× / × / × /
Such **tricks** hath **strong** imagi**nation**,

1 4 1 4 1 4 1 4
× / × / × / × /
That **if** it would **but** appre**hend** some **joy**,

1 4 1 4 1 4
× / × / × /
It **comprehends** some **bringer** of that **joy**;

1 4 1 4 1 4
× / × / × /
Or **in** the **night**, **ima**gining some **fear**,

1 4 1 4 1 4 1 4 1 4
× / × / × / × / × /
How **easy** is a **bush** sup**pos'd** a **bear**?

f. A Midsummer Night's Dream, Act V, Scene I, 2-22 [3]

The above passage may be characterized by the following matrix

$$\begin{pmatrix} 0 & 0 & 0 & 1 \\ 0 & 0 & 0 & 0 \\ 0 & 0 & 0 & 0 \\ 1 & 0 & 0 & 0 \end{pmatrix}$$

In general, the transition matrix U for a given piece of literary work may be represented as, assuming there are m patterns, each occurring with probability p_i,

$$U = \sum_{j=1}^{m} p_j T_j$$

where each T_j corresponds to the characteristic matrix of pattern j.

Thus, with vast text collections, Markov matrices can be systematically built and it provides a unique characterization of each period and author and nature of work.

In the above, a one-step Markov chain is used, but in more general situations, as pointed out above, a multi-step Markov chain (with a longer past memory chain) is required. Let us consider the following fragment from "King Henry the Fourth",

1 4 1 4 1 4 1 4 1 2
× / × / × / × / × /
*His **cushes** on his **thighs**, **gallantly** **arm'd**,*

1 4 1 4 1 4 1 4 1 3
× / × / × / × / × /
*Rise **from** the **ground** like **feathered** **Mercury**,*

1 4 1 3 1 4 1 4 1 4
× / × / × / × / × /
*And **Vaulted** **with** such **ease** onto his **seat***

We see here that state 1 does not always make a transition to state 4; it sometimes goes to state 2 and sometimes go to state 1. In fact, it retains memory of the past states in addition to the current state.

Let us amalgamate two consecutive states into one single state, thereby injecting more memory into the chain. In doing so, we incorporate memory of the immediate past state as well as the current state to determine the future transition. Thus, from the primitive states of $S = \{1, 2, 3, 4\}$, we now have the new set of states Ω,

$$\begin{aligned} \Omega = S \times S = \{ & (1, 1), (1, 2), (1, 3), (1, 4), \\ & (2, 1), (2, 2), (2, 3), (2, 4), \\ & (3, 1), (3, 2), (3, 3), (3, 4), \\ & (4, 1), (4, 2), (4, 3), (4, 4) \}, \end{aligned}$$

with $|\Omega| = 16$. Thus, by including memory of the past state, we can construct a 16 × 16 transition matrix.
For the above situation, let us reduce the number of states and omit those that do not occur as follows,

$$\begin{aligned} \Omega = S \times S = \{ & \cancel{(1, 1)}, (1, 2), (1, 3), (1, 4), \\ & (2, 1), \cancel{(2, 2), (2, 3), (2, 4)}, \\ & (3, 1), \cancel{(3, 2), (3, 3), (3, 4)}, \\ & (4, 1), \cancel{(4, 2), (4, 3), (4, 4)} \}. \end{aligned}$$

Doing so will reduce the number of states from 16 to 6, with the reduced set of states Ω' as,

$$\Omega' = \{ (1, 2), (1, 3), (1, 4), (2, 1), (3, 1), (4, 1) \}.$$

By considering the frequency of occurrence, we obtain the following signature transition matrix, where the states are ordered according to the above sequence of Ω',

$$H' = \begin{pmatrix} 0 & 0 & 0 & 1 & 0 & 0 \\ 0 & 0 & 0 & 0 & 1 & 0 \\ 0 & 0 & 0 & 0 & 0 & 1 \\ 0 & 0 & 1 & 0 & 0 & 0 \\ 0 & 0 & 1 & 0 & 0 & 0 \\ 0.09 & 0.18 & 0.73 & 0 & 0 & 0 \end{pmatrix}$$

In general, if $|S| = n$, this will result in a $n^2 \times n^2$ matrix before any reduction. The form and values of the entries in the matrix may be regarded as a characteristic signature of the passage in question, and we also note that such a matrix tends to be a sparse matrix.

Admittedly, the determination of transition probabilities, especially for extended memory situations, can be quite laborious. Other less computationally intensive methods exist, however, such as measuring the number of different types of lines, such as interrogative lines or exclamatory lines. A recommended procedure is to apply these less computationally intensive methods first, and then for fine tuning, apply the signature method above for greater accuracy.

IV. EXPERIMENTATION

Here, we examine and analyze Shakespeare's work "Henry VI" and focus on his use of interrogative and exclamatory lines because it is rare to always identify the extent of a particular writer's work beyond a significant margin of error [6]. From our analysis of the passage, the results are plotted in Figures 1 and 2.

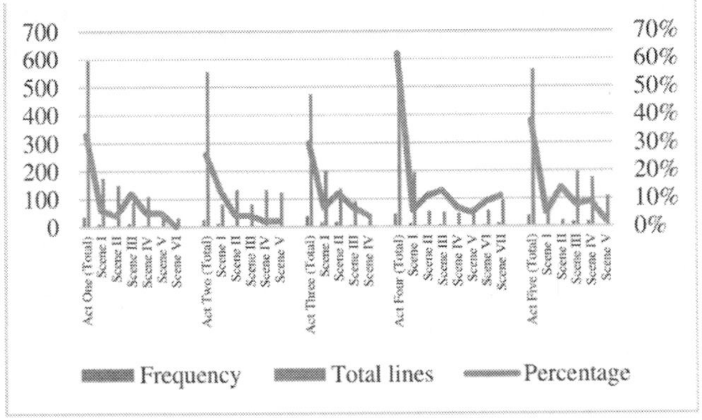

Figure 1. Exclamatory lines in Henry VI, Part I

It would be uneasy with the claim that Shakespeare wrote nothing in Part One [4], because from Figure 1, it is noticeable that Acts One, Two, Three and Five share relatively a stable 30% of using exclamatory lines, and the frequencies are roughly lower than 39, whereas in Act Four the figure largely varies from the previous ones, reaching the highest 62% and standing a figure of 47 in frequency.

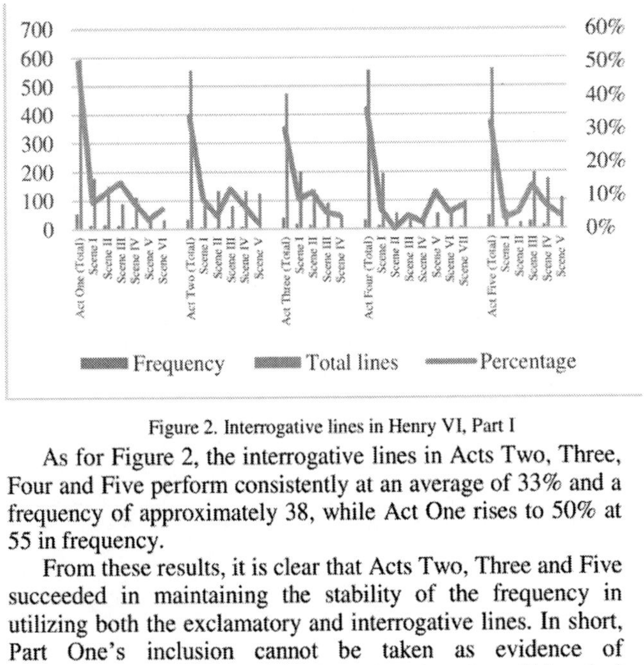

Figure 2. Interrogative lines in Henry VI, Part I

As for Figure 2, the interrogative lines in Acts Two, Three, Four and Five perform consistently at an average of 33% and a frequency of approximately 38, while Act One rises to 50% at 55 in frequency.

From these results, it is clear that Acts Two, Three and Five succeeded in maintaining the stability of the frequency in utilizing both the exclamatory and interrogative lines. In short, Part One's inclusion cannot be taken as evidence of Shakespeare's sole authorship [4], and conjunction of historical and analytical evidence suggests that it might be collaborative. Furthermore, Act One and Four contain indication regarding the collaboration of other authors as the analyzed data "betrayed" the works that bear Shakespeare's name. If Part One postdates its two companions, then the primitive style of most of it can hardly be attributed to Shakespeare, and the "trilogy" is an artistic afterthought, not the product of the aspiring vision of a young prodigal genius [4].

V. CONCLUSION

English literary works tend to include many dimensions and features, and these would constitute the apparatuses that enable different authors to express and articulate their personal sentiments and perspectives in different eras and emotional settings. In the analysis of literary works, there are differing aims, which include determining such aspects as the authorship, the emotional contents, sentiments, outlook, motif and purpose. We have made use of iambic pentametre to quantify and characterize such dimensions by the use of Markov chains.

In place of using human judgments, which is largely a manual process and a time-consuming process, we have proposed the use of a machine learning approach by learning the characteristics of known passages using big data and ultimately encode these as a signature. We first introduce a one-step Markov chain where the future stress level is dependent only on the present one. While this is useful, its limitation being that it is largely memoryless and ignores earlier stress levels. To overcome this restriction, we develop a multi-step Markov chain to characterize the evolution of stress levels. In this approach, arbitrary amount of memory on previous stress levels may be incorporated, However, a caveat concerning this method is that by extending the memory too far into the past may lead to overfitting in some situations which makes it sometimes difficult to effectively generalize. It is recommended that the memory extension should not be more than four steps.

The present method is able to significantly eliminate error-prone and relatively subjective human elements, and it is expected that this approach may be further developed and leveraged to enhance understanding and appreciation of English literary works.

REFERENCES

[1] T. Plotz and G. A Fink, Markov Models for Handwriting Recognition. London: Springer London, 2011.

[2] G. T. Wright, Shakespeare's metrical art. Berkeley: University of California Press, 1988.

[3] W. Shakespeare and P. Alexander, William Shakespeare; the complete works. London: Collins, 1964.

[4] G. Taylor, "Shakespeare and Others: The Authorship of Henry the Sixth, Part One". Medieval & Renaissance Drama in England, 1995, Vol. 7 (1995), pp. 145-205. Rosemont Publishing & Printing Corp DBA Associated University Presses.

[5] C. Patrick, Shakespeare's literary authorship. Cambridge: Cambridge University Press, 2008.

[6] P. Edmondson and S. Wells, Shakespeare Beyond Doubt. Cambridge: Cambridge University Press, 2013.

[7] G. Taylor and G. Egan, The New Oxford Shakespeare: Authorship Companion. Oxford: Oxford University Press, 2017.

[8] D. Berend and A. Kontorovich, A Finite Sample Analysis of the Naive Bayes Classifier. Journal of Machine Learning Research, Vol. 16(1), pp.1519-1545, 2015.

[9] C. M. Bishop, Pattern Recognition and Machine Learning (Information Science and Statistics). Springer-Verlag, 2006.

[10] N. L. J. Kuang and C. H. C. Leung, "Analysis of Evolutionary Behavior in Self-Learning Media Search Engines," in Proceedings of the IEEE International Conference on Big Data, Los Angeles, USA, 643-650, 2019.

[11] N. L. J. Kuang and C. H. C. Leung, "Dynamics and Termination Errors in Reinforcement Learning - A Unifying Perspective," In Proceedings of the

IEEE International Conference on Artificial Intelligence and Knowledge Engineering, pp. 129-133, 2018.

[12] N. L. J. Kuang and C. H. C. Leung, "Leveraging Reinforcement Learning Techniques for Effective Policy Adoption and Validation". in Misra S. et al. (eds) in Computational Science and Its Applications – ICCSA 2019, 311-322, Lecture Notes in Computer Science, Vol. 11620. Springer, 2019.

[13] W. Shakespeare, The Sonnets. London: Macmillan Collector's Library, 2016.

[14] P. Rose, Dances With Daffodils. The Atlantic, 2002.

[15] A. Bennett and N. Royle, An introduction to literature, criticism and theory, 3rd ed., Harlow: Longman, 2004.

[16] U. Shizuteru, J. W. Heisig, and F. Greiner. Emptiness and Fullness: Śūnyatā in Mahāyāna Buddhism. The Eastern Buddhist,15(1), pp. 9–37, 1982.

[17] W. Wordsworth, Daffodils, 1807.

[18] T. Hughes, Daffodils, Birthday Letters, 1998.

[19] D. Wordsworth, Journals of Dorothy Wordsworth, Vol. I (of 2), London: Macmillian and Co., Ltd., 1897.

Towards Style Classification for Fashion Recommender Systems

René Kessler
Department of Computing Science
University of Oldenburg
Ammerländer Heerstr. 114-118, 26129 Oldenburg
rene.kessler@uol.de

Jorge Marx Gómez
Department of Computing Science
University of Oldenburg
Ammerländer Heerstr. 114-118, 26129 Oldenburg
jorge.marx.gomez@uol.de

***Abstract*—In recommender systems, products can be recommended based on customer modeling. Especially in fashion e-commerce, recommendations can be a solution for many business and sustainability challenges. This paper presents how deep learning can be used for style classification in fashion e-commerce. The style of a person is classified based on a photo. Furthermore, this paper analyzes which data preprocessing and augmentation techniques can positively impact a style classification model. In order to be able to explain recommendations based on this, it was analyzed to what extent the resulting model provides accurate results and the predictions can be explained.**

***Keywords*—E-Commerce, Recommender Systems, Style Classification, Deep Learning, Explainable AI.**

I. INTRODUCTION

While direct consultation can occur in stationary retail, for example, by sales staff, this point is almost entirely omitted in online retail. Whenever a customer is not looking for a specific product they already know and has not yet made a clear product decision, this advice may still be necessary. For this reason, e-commerce retailers work with recommender systems, i.e., they try to present a specific product based on existing customer information in such a way that the user does not have to search through the entire product catalog but can reach the desired product quickly and effortlessly [1]. At the same time, targeted recommendations can also create incentives to buy. The recommendation quality always depends on the quality and quantity of the existing customer information. The more data available and the higher the information value of this data, the more accurate the customer profiling can be [2] [3]. The importance of recommendations becomes particularly clear regarding products that cannot be described exclusively textually by their properties. There is a high demand for individual advice, particularly in the case of stylistic features or visual characteristics, which can only be represented to a limited extent by textual descriptions or categorizations. For example, such products can be found in the fashion sector, which represents the highest share of all e-commerce sectors in terms of sales with 20.0 billion euros (Germany) in 2021 [4]. Compared to 2020, the online share in the fashion industry has risen by 3.21 %, from 39.8 % to 46.5 % - in absolute terms, this represents an increase of 3.21 billion euros, underscoring the importance and future potential of recommendations in online retail [3] [4].

The basis for recommender systems is the profiling of customers. The overall goal of customer profiling is to collect relevant data from the customer, extract information from this data, build a customer model, and use this model to predict the customer's future behavior to support purchase decisions [5]–[7]. Stereotyping or clustering of customers represents an important strategy here in order to be able to realize personalization for a group of customers [8]–[10].

Customer-relevant data sources (e.g., master data, transaction data, or data from marketing campaigns) can be used to gain information about the customer [11] [12]. In research and practice, mainly master data, personal data such as age, gender, or data related to origin or place of residence are used [13]. While these data provide essential information, transactional data, such as purchase history or other touchpoints, can be used to model and subsequently predict buying behavior in an online store or even user preference [13] [14]. In contrast, a more recent approach is the analysis of click paths in online platforms. This can be used to model the interaction behavior of customers without purchases having already taken place [15] [16]. Thus, the priority is to evaluate structured data in current approaches to model customer characteristics, behavior, and preference.

The paper is structured as follows: The introduction is followed by the introduction to the problem addressed. The third section describes related work, while the fourth section describes the research objectives and methodology. In the main body, the fifth section, the data basis is first described. Based on this, the experiments, their evaluation and the interpretability of the results are explained. Finally, the results are discussed and a short outlook for further research is given.

II. PROBLEM STATEMENT

To recommend a product to customers at all, the relationships between customers and products must be known. A distinction can be made between micro and macro behavior factors. The analysis of transaction data, e.g., purchases of products or product reviews, describes the macro behavior, i.e., the user's behavior that led to a purchase. The micro behavior is fundamentally more refined in its structure. Here, the user's interactions with products that are not directly linked to a purchase are also analyzed, i.e., in addition to transaction data, behavioral patterns are also analyzed. The insights gained are incorporated into the recommendation process [1] [14]–[16]. In addition to transaction and interaction data, many approaches also process data about creating the product and demographic data (or master data, such as age or gender) [13]. The data sources used in recommender systems can be roughly divided into three types: user-related data, product-related data, and transaction- or behavior-related data. These data are primarily available in a structured form. Data of an unstructured nature has hardly played a role in existing approaches. When unstructured data is used, it is mainly product-related information, i.e., visual features of the products or textual descriptions, and product- and user-related information, i.e., textual product reviews [17]–[19]. The approaches considered mainly look at simple, individual products rather than product bundles (such as outfits) [20]–[22]. Therefore, these approaches can only be classified in the analysis of relationships between users and products.

Unstructured personal data (e.g., customer images) have been considered relatively rarely, although they can be crucial for modeling user preferences [18]. The subject of current research is processing customer images to extract new information that can be used to improve recommendations, as publications show [3] [23]. Although visual recommender systems exist, the focus is mainly on product images. Analyzing and using this data to generate recommendations has added value but cannot solve the cold start problem [24]. Various studies have shown that explainability can positively contribute to the quality of recommendations. Existing approaches indicate that explaining recommendations (e.g., via historical transactions, similarity metrics between products, or customer ratings and reviews) can increase customer satisfaction [24]–[27]. However, it is also a prerequisite in these approaches that historical transaction data of the customer is already available. In particular, accurately recognizing a clothing style can provide an essential building block for successful recommendations in fashion e-commerce. Nevertheless, clothing style can rarely be determined simply by utilizing textual information or purchase history; the customer's visual characteristics must be processed for this purpose.

III. Related Work

In order to make the best possible recommendations to a customer, the customer must be known as well as possible. In fashion e-commerce, it is essential to know the style in which the customer dresses to assist them in finding a product or to recommend products that they will probably like because they match their style. Especially in aesthetic use cases such as the determination of a clothing style, which cannot be described one hundred percent textually, deep learning or, in particular, computer vision offers a possibility to process these aesthetic features via images. There are already previous approaches in style classification, but they differ from the focus of this paper.

In a literature study, the literature databases *Scopus*, *ScienceDirect*, *Web of Science*, *arXiv*, *ACM*, *IEEE* were searched for relevant articles from 2013. The retrieved hits were then filtered by title and abstract screening.

Gu et al. (2017) combine traditional recommender system approaches with autoencoder-based processing of visual fashion features, so-called fashion coordinates. Sets of product images (three products each: outerwear, pants, and shoes) serve as input [28]. A similar approach is taken by McAuley et al. (2015). Here, the authors also consider product images and developed a prototype matching products to a product (input) [29]. Liu et al. (2017) in their approach try to classify fashion images into clusters representing a style via different clustering methods. In addition to individual product images, image details of people are also included [17].

An approach based on product data but which differs significantly is described by Guan and Qin (2019). In their work, product images are analyzed, and descriptive attributes are extracted from the images. These descriptive attributes (e.g., colors or contrast) are then associated with human concepts, feelings, or other customer characteristics to make product recommendations [30]. Properties and attributes of a style can also be modeled as a knowledge graph to represent styles from multiple properties and their interrelationships [31].

Ma et al. (2017) show an interesting approach in their paper that uses images to show a spectrum of different clothing styles to make them more understandable. In this approach, style features are first extracted from images, then processed by an autoencoder to cluster the autoencoder results. The resulting clusters were then classified in a Fashion Semantic Space [32]. Schindler et al. (2018) are similarly concerned with extracting features from images. Here, they use images of people and products crawled from online stores. These images are then classified using a pre-trained Convolutional Neural Network [33].

Existing work makes a valuable contribution to research in visual recommender systems but looks at the underlying problem of fashion style classification from a different angle. In the context of this work, an attempt will be made to assign a style to product images directly and dispense with the prior extraction of features. The resulting fashion style classification can then be used for further steps in the recommendation process.

IV. Research Objectives and Methodology

This paper presents a novel fashion style classification approach that analyzes users' image data (assuming consent of the user) in fashion e-commerce and extracts the fashion style. The detected fashion style can then be incorporated into the recommendation process, for example, garments that match the person's clothing style could be recommended. The focus is on the one hand on solving the cold start problem and expanding the database of recommendation systems, and on the other hand on improving the recommendations by making the generated recommendations explainable.

For this purpose, images first had to be collected and labeled. Based on the use case, three different datasets are created here. Based on this, various deep learning experiments

Fig. 1. Visualization of the different style classes in the dataset

were conducted. Deep Learning models were implemented and trained using different image preprocessing and augmentation techniques and critically compared. In addition to a qualitative evaluation of the models, a quantitative, technical evaluation of the deep learning experiments was also performed. To complement this, the best model was then selected, used, and the extent to which the model's results could be explained was examined.

V. STYLE CLASSIFICATION

This section describes the design and implementation of style classification. First, the creation of the dataset is discussed. This is followed by the description of the Deep Learning experiments and the evaluation of the resulting models. Finally, the procedure for evaluating the explainability of the models is described, and the results are presented.

A. Dataset

In the first step of creating the datasets for style classification, possible, suitable public data sources were researched, i.e., datasets containing images of people and, in the best case, labels about the person's clothing or style. This revealed that a large number of datasets are freely available (e.g., Figaro-1k, Appareal, CelebA, iMaterialist Fashion 2018, and 2019). However, a closer look at the datasets showed that while they can be used for some related tasks, they cannot be used as a basis for the intended classification of customer style, as none of the datasets focus on people in real scenes. There are no labels for the person's style. Therefore, the creation of a separate dataset was necessary.

Before data collection, a catalog of 7 style classes was created by researching fashion magazines/portals and interviewing three fashion experts. The three fashion experts are employees of a cooperating online fashion retailer. The seven different styles and their characteristics are described below:

- **Athleisure:** The style *Athleisure* describes mainly sporty styles, i.e. people who wear sportswear in everyday life. Examples may include plain, tighter-fitting, muscle-toned shirts or leggings.
- **Boho:** In the *Boho* style, wider-fitting, less muscle-emphasizing clothes are mainly worn. In addition, earth tones or eye-catching patterns, such as mandala patterns, are often features of the garments worn.
- **Casual:** The *Casual* style represents the typical everyday style, that is, the style that most people wear in everyday life. Examples include simple jeans, white shirts, or sweaters in shades of gray.
- **Elegant:** The *Elegant* style is mainly worn business clothes. Often suits, blouses or elegant hats can be found. Patterns are rather rare here (if, then, more inconspicuous check patterns) and colorwise, rather calm, neutral colors are to be found, such as black, gray or beige.
- **Rebel:** The *Rebel* look makes heavy use of punk and rock elements. Ripped jeans, studs, leather jackets or band shirts are often found.
- **Retro:** The *Retro* style describes clothing styles that seem to have fallen out of time, i.e., mainly classic clothing items, such as corduroy pants, hats or long coats.
- **Romantic:** The *Romantic* style describes playful looks and is mainly found on women. Core elements are, for example, dresses in pastel colors or floral patterns.

The defined styles were used in the next step to crawling public search engines and portals. In this course, the search engine *Bing* and the fashion social media portal *Chictopia* were used, and a total of 11200 images of people, as close to reality as possible, were collected. The images were manually sifted to clean them up (erroneous crawls or duplicates) and then annotated by a team of eleven, with the majority defined as label strategy. Each image was assigned exactly one style. In some cases, more than one person could be recognized in the image. If all persons to be seen could be assigned to one style, the image was kept in the dataset; otherwise, it was removed.

The resulting images were then used to form a data set (in

TABLE I
ACCURACY OF MODELS USING DIFFERENT DATASETS AND AUGMENTATION TECHNIQUES

Augmentation	Accuracy		
	Original	**Without Background**	**Cropped**
No Augmentation	0.698	0.698	0.755
Horizontal Flip	0.679	0.679	0.751
Blur	0.698	0.680	0.738
CLAHE	0.689	0.699	0.729
Coarse Dropout	0.698	0.699	0.738
Elastic Transform	0.699	0.704	0.739
Grid Distortion	0.707	0.694	0.729
Motion Blur	0.704	0.683	0.737
Optical Distortion	0.704	0.697	0.734
Random Resized Crop	0.692	0.683	0.739
Shift Scale Rotate	0.709	0.701	0.727
All Augmentations	**0.726**	0.706	0.749
AutoAugmentation	0.717	**0.733**	**0.825**

the further course: original) for the experiments. A 70/30 split was used, i.e., 70 % of the images were used for training, while 30 % of the images formed the validation dataset. This resulted in 1120 images per class for training and another 480 images per class to validate the models. Some examples of the resulting dataset and the annotated styles can be seen in Figure 1.

In a further step of data preprocessing, additional datasets were built. First, images with multiple people were split, i.e., object detection was used to detect people on images and extract the resulting bounding box. This resulted in smaller images but more images forming the dataset. The second dataset (Cropped) consisted of 13500 images (70/30 - Training/Validation-Split). On the other hand, we went one step further and completely removed the background of the person. For this purpose, we implemented a background removal service that detects the background of an image and removes all pixels except those belonging to the person to be seen. The resulting dataset (without background) also included a total of 13500 images. An example of the data preprocessing steps is shown in Figure 2.

B. Modeling Experiments

Numerous experiments were conducted to develop the style classification model. The EfficientNet architecture developed by *Google* was used as the model architecture. This architecture was chosen because it can be used and adapted flexibly and because it offers state-of-the-art results in the field of image classification [34]. The b0 variant of EfficientNet was tested for resource reasons. However, it can be assumed that the different architectures can show even better results due to the higher number of parameters and the possibility of processing larger images. For implementation, the *PyTorch*-implementation in the framework *timm* of EfficientNet was used. The following hyperparameters were used: Epochs 10, Batchsize 64, Learning rate 1e-2, Optimizer Adam, Finetuning (last 100 layers), Activation (Output-Layer) Softmax, Loss-Function Categorical Cross Entropy.

Based on the architecture, further experiments were conducted using various image augmentation and preprocessing

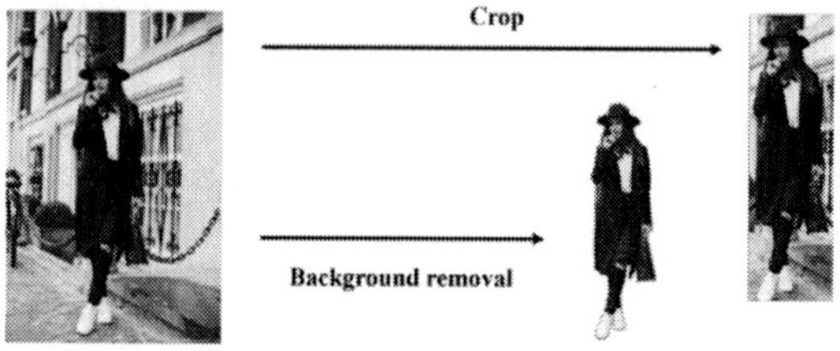

Fig. 2. Removing the background and cutting out persons to create the different datasets

techniques. In total, ten established, different techniques for image enhancement (Horizontal Flip, Blur, CLAHE, Coarse Dropout, Elastic Transform, Grid Distortion, Motion Blur, Optical Distortion, Random Resized Crop and Shift Scale Rotate) were evaluated. For this purpose, the image augmentation framework *albumentations* was used, and a custom data loader was implemented to augment the input images with a defined probability of p=0.5 with the respective technique [35]. Models without augmentation were also implemented as baselines to ensure comparability. In addition, the ten different techniques were applied in combination (All Augmentations). As an alternative augmentation strategy, the AutoAugmentation approach from Google Brain was implemented and examined in more detail [36]. AutoAugmentation describes a procedure to learn an optimal data augmentation strategy based on the existing data material. The algorithm searches for the optimal strategy and adapts it individually in sub-strategies.

C. Evaluation of the Models

Looking at the results in Table I, it quickly becomes apparent that some augmentation techniques can positively affect the quality of the results (measured by the accuracy). The effects of the respective techniques also differ depending on the dataset used. For the *original* dataset, i.e., the dataset without further image preprocessing, all augmentation techniques perform relatively equally well. The manual combination of all augmentation techniques is the best, with an accuracy of 72.6 %. A similar picture emerges at first glance when looking at the individual augmentation techniques for the dataset without *Without background* and *Cropped*. Thus, all individual techniques and their combinations within the dataset perform relatively similarly. However, it can be shown that the *Cropped* dataset performs much better than the other two datasets (about 5 % across all augmentation techniques). It is particularly striking, however, that for both datasets, the AutoAugmentation technique performs best. Overall, the best model in the experiments was the model trained on the *Cropped* dataset using AutoAugmentation. In addition, it is noticeable that only the AutoAugmentation approach shows an improvement in this dataset. This can be explained by the fact that the other augmentations may change the images too much. It is conceivable that the algorithmic search for the best strategy selects more realistic augmentation intervals.

Overall, the experiments show promising results with the best accuracy of 82.5 %. Manual evaluation of additional images that were not included in the training set shows that the models can solve the style classification problem (see Figure 3). In particular, the manual evaluation shows that outfits that can be localized (e.g., a complete sports outfit) are reliably classified. In contrast, mixed styles can be problematic for the model, e.g., when people deliberately combine elements of different styles. It can be stated from the experiments that a style classification benefits from a large amount of data, and the more data available, the better results can be obtained. Additionally, it shows that AutoAugmentation can be a promising strategy for data augmentation. The approach minimizes the manual effort, and at the same time, very good results are shown.

D. Explainability of the Models and Predictions

Now that an initial model for style classification has been developed, it will be examined to what extent the model's predictions can also be explained. In doing so, it will be investigated which areas of an image lead to the classification into a specific style. Furthermore, it is to be investigated whether the resulting model recognizes the correct image contents or, for example, learns styles from an image's context (e.g., the image background).

For this purpose, the widely used framework *lime* is used [37]. *lime* provides methods to provide so-called locally interpretable model-agnostic explanations. To this end, another experiment used the model previously identified as the best model and built an *lime* explanatory model based on it.

The results of this explanatory model can be seen in Figure 4. Clearly, the model learns the expected signal of an image, i.e., image areas where the person whose style can be classified can be seen. At the same time, it is noticeable that background areas are also perceived as a signal or partial areas of the person (see upper example on figure 4) are learned as a negative influence on the classification. This becomes especially clear if one looks closely at the Explanation Map.

In principle, explanatory models can be expected to produce better results if the model also produces more robust and better results since explainability depends on model performance. The results of the explanatory models can be used in the further course of development to enrich the generated recommendations with a visual explanation and thus create additional user acceptance.

VI. Conclusion and further Steps

In this state of research, it has already been shown that unstructured data can provide added information value for recommender systems and underlying customer profiling. A first approach to style classification is shown here. The results of the models so far are promising and already show practicality. Moreover, it becomes apparent that the manual search for an optimal augmentation strategy is not trivial. Especially in the case of complex elements in an image, as is the case with the detection and classification of fashion styles, changes to the image can lead to positive effects, but also to negative effects if the changes are incorrectly selected, as the results were able to show. The AutoAugmentation approach shows promise, where a very realistic augmentation strategy adapted to the data set can be found, which could lead to better results in our experiments.

In defining styles, it became clear that styles cannot always be clearly distinguished from one another. Often, fashion-conscious people deliberately combine different styles to make a fashion statement. On the other hand, certain clothing items are often worn in different styles. It can be assumed that styles are almost always associated with fashion elements but that the boundaries between styles can sometimes become blurred. This led to the fact that the developed models for style classification may have difficulties, although providing good results, especially in these mixed clothing styles. On the one hand, a more extensive and improved data set will be built for this purpose, as described earlier. On the other hand, further experiments will be conducted to investigate whether multi-label classification can solve this problem.

The technical evaluation of the different models by the developers and the manual visual inspection has shown that the results of the models can be considered promising and will therefore be followed up and extended. In the future, this very technical and subjective evaluation will be complemented by an empirical study to test the methods' suitability objectively. To this end, various test scenarios will be developed and conducted. This study will also measure whether the explainability of the approach can positively contribute to the perceived goodness of the models and whether they are advantageous compared to classical, non-explained recommendations.

References

[1] P. Kumar and R. Thakur, "Recommendation system techniques and related issues: a survey," *Int. j. inf. tecnol. (December 2018)*, 2018.

[2] Y.-J. Park and K.-N. Chang, "Individual and group behavior-based customer profile model for personalized product recommendation," *Expert Systems with Applications*, vol. 36, no. 2, Part 1, pp. 1932–1939, 2009.

[3] H. Zheng, K. Wu, J.-H. Park, W. Zhu, and J. Luo, "Personalized fashion recommendation from personal social media data: An item-to-set metric learning approach," *2021 IEEE International Conference on Big Data (Big Data)*, pp. 5014–5023, 2021.

[4] HDE Handelsverband Deutschland, "Online monitor 2022," Web, 2022. https://einzelhandel.de/index.php?option=com_attachments&task=download&id=10659, retrieved on 28.08.2022.

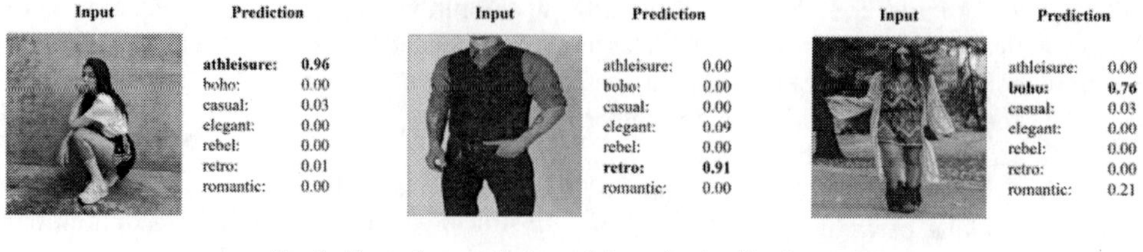

Fig. 3. Exemplary predictions of the style classification model

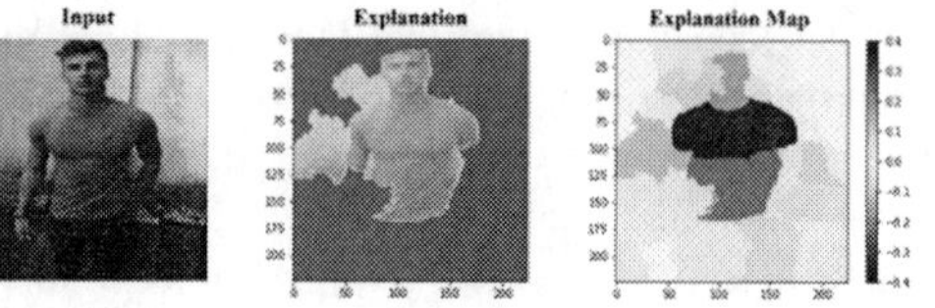

Fig. 4. Visualization to explain the predictions of the model

[5] S. Berkovsky, "Ubiquitous user modeling in recommender systems," in *User Modeling 2005* (L. Ardissono, P. Brna, and A. Mitrovic, eds.), (Berlin, Heidelberg), pp. 496–498, Springer Berlin Heidelberg, 2005.

[6] K. Lakiotaki, N. F. Matsatsinis, and A. Tsoukias, "Multicriteria user modeling in recommender systems," *IEEE Intelligent Systems*, vol. 26, no. 2, pp. 64–76, 2011.

[7] H.-N. Kim, A. Alkhaldi, A. E. Saddik, and G.-S. Jo, "Collaborative user modeling with user-generated tags for social recommender systems," *Expert Systems with Applications*, vol. 38, no. 7, pp. 8488–8496, 2011.

[8] E. Rich, "User modeling via stereotypes," *Cognitive Science*, vol. 3, no. 4, pp. 329–354, 1979.

[9] H. Rijn, A. Johnson, and N. Taatgen, *Cognitive user modeling.*, pp. 523–538. Handbook of human factors in web design, CRC Press, 2 ed., 2011.

[10] A. Johnson and N. Taatgen, *User modeling.*, pp. 424–438. Handbook of human factors in web design, Lawrence Erlbaum Associates Publishers, 2005.

[11] A. Kobsa *User Modeling and User-Adapted Interaction*, vol. 11, no. 1/2, pp. 49–63, 2001.

[12] A. Goy, L. Ardissono, and G. Petrone, *Personalization in E-Commerce Applications*, vol. 4321, pp. 485–520. Berlin, Heidelberg: Springer Berlin Heidelberg, the adaptive web. lecture notes in computer science ed., 2007.

[13] K. Wei, J. Huang, and S. Fu, "A survey of e-commerce recommender systems," in *2007 International Conference on Service Systems and Service Management*, pp. 1–5, IEEE, 2007.

[14] S. Sivapalan, A. Sadeghian, H. Rahnama, and A. M. Madni, "Recommender systems in e-commerce," in *2014 World Automation Congress (WAC)*, pp. 179–184, IEEE, 2014.

[15] Y. Gu, Z. Ding, S. Wang, and D. Yin, "Hierarchical user profiling for e-commerce recommender systems," in *Proceedings of the 13th International Conference on Web Search and Data Mining*, pp. 223–231, ACM, 2020.

[16] M. Zhou, Z. Ding, J. Tang, and D. Yin, "Micro behaviors," in *Proceedings of the Eleventh ACM International Conference on Web Search and Data Mining*, pp. 727–735, ACM, 2018.

[17] Q. Liu, S. Wu, and L. Wang, "DeepStyle," in *Proceedings of the 40th International ACM SIGIR Conference on Research and Development in Information Retrieval*, pp. 353–361, ACM, 2017.

[18] P. Pérez-Núñez, "Taking advantage of images and texts in recommender systems: semantics and explainability," in *Fourteenth ACM Conference on Recommender Systems*, pp. 792–796, ACM, 2020.

[19] S. Wang and J. Qiu, "A deep neural network model for fashion collocation recommendation using side information in e-commerce," *Applied Soft Computing*, vol. 110, p. 107753, 2021.

[20] B. O. Viso, "Evolutionary approach in recommendation systems for complex structured objects," in *Fourteenth ACM Conference on Recommender Systems*, pp. 776–781, ACM, 2020.

[21] M. F. Dacrema, P. Cremonesi, and D. Jannach, "Are we really making much progress? a worrying analysis of recent neural recommendation approaches," in *Proceedings of the 13th ACM Conference on Recommender Systems*, pp. 101–109, ACM, 2019.

[22] K. Laenen and M.-F. Moens, "Attention-based fusion for outfit recommendation," in *Fashion Recommender Systems* (N. Dokoohaki, ed.), (Cham), pp. 69–86, Springer International Publishing, 2020.

[23] W.-C. Kang, E. Kim, J. Leskovec, C. Rosenberg, and J. McAuley, "Complete the look: Scene-based complementary product recommendation," in *Proceedings of the IEEE/CVF Conference on Computer Vision and Pattern Recognition (CVPR)*, pp. 10524–10533, 2019.

[24] X. Chen, Y. Zhang, H. Xu, Y. Cao, Z. Qin, and H. Zha, "Visually explainable recommendation,"

[25] X. Chen, Y. Zhang, and Z. Qin, "Dynamic explainable recommendation based on neural attentive models," *Proceedings of the AAAI Conference on Artificial Intelligence*, vol. 33, pp. 53–60, 2019.

[26] V. Dominguez, P. Messina, I. Donoso-Guzmán, and D. Parra, "The effect of explanations and algorithmic accuracy on visual recommender systems of artistic images," in *Proceedings of the 24th International Conference on Intelligent User Interfaces*, pp. 408–416, ACM, 2019.

[27] D. Pan, X. Li, X. Li, and D. Zhu, "Explainable recommendation via interpretable feature mapping and evaluation of explainability," in *Proceedings of the Twenty-Ninth International Joint Conference on Artificial Intelligence*, IJCAI'20, p. 2690–2696, 2021.

[28] S. Gu, X. Liu, L. Cai, and J. Shen, "Fashion coordinates recommendation based on user behavior and visual clothing style," in *Proceedings of the 3rd International Conference on Communication and Information Processing*, ICCIP '17, (New York, NY, USA), p. 185–189, Association for Computing Machinery, 2017.

[29] J. McAuley, C. Targett, Q. Shi, and A. van den Hengel, "Image-based recommendations on styles and substitutes," in *Proceedings of the 38th International ACM SIGIR Conference on Research and Development in Information Retrieval*, SIGIR '15, (New York, NY, USA), p. 43–52, Association for Computing Machinery, 2015.

[30] C. Guan, S. Qin, and Y. Long, "Apparel-based deep learning system design for apparel style recommendation," *International Journal of Clothing Science and Technology*, vol. 31, no. 3, pp. 376–389, 2019.

[31] C. Zhang, X. Yue, W. Liu, and C. Gao, "Fashion style recognition with graph-based deep convolutional neural networks," in *Artificial Intelligence on Fashion and Textiles* (W. K. Wong, ed.), (Cham), pp. 269–275, Springer International Publishing, 2019.

[32] Y. Ma, J. Jia, S. Zhou, J. Fu, Y. Liu, and Z. Tong, "Towards better understanding the clothing fashion styles: A multimodal deep learning approach," in *AAAI*, Proceedings of the Thirty-First AAAI Conference on Artificial Intelligence (AAAI-17), pp. 38–44, 2017.

[33] A. Schindler, T. Lidy, S. Karner, and M. Hecker, "Fashion and apparel classification using convolutional neural networks," *CoRR - Forum Media Technology*, vol. abs/1811.04374, 2018.

[34] M. Tan and Q. V. Le, "Efficientnet: Rethinking model scaling for convolutional neural networks," 2020.

[35] A. Buslaev, V. I. Iglovikov, E. Khvedchenya, A. Parinov, M. Druzhinin, and A. A. Kalinin, "Albumentations: Fast and flexible image augmentations," *Information*, vol. 11, no. 2, 2020.

[36] E. D. Cubuk, B. Zoph, D. Mane, V. Vasudevan, and Q. V. Le, "Autoaugment: Learning augmentation policies from data," 2018.

[37] M. T. Ribeiro, S. Singh, and C. Guestrin, ""why should I trust you?": Explaining the predictions of any classifier," in *Proceedings of the 22nd ACM SIGKDD International Conference on Knowledge Discovery and Data Mining, San Francisco, CA, USA, August 13-17, 2016*, pp. 1135–1144, 2016.

Detecting Signs of Mental Disorders on Social Networks: a Systematic Literature Review

Ayrton Herculano, Glauco Gomes, Damires Souza, Alex Rêgo
Professional Master's in Information Technology (PPGTI)
Federal Institute of Education, Science and Technology of Paraiba (IFPB)
João Pessoa, Brazil
Email: {ayrton.herculano, glauco.gomes}@academico.ifpb.edu.br, Email: {damires, alex}@ifpb.edu.br

***Abstract*—Social networks have been used more and more by people to share feelings and emotions. This scenario helps to create an environment which may provide additional information regarding signs of mental disorders users carry. In this light, this study investigates the state of the art on how the literature has considered techniques or strategies related to identifying signs of mental disorders on social networks. Some analyses have been made to answer questions regarding methods, data, labelling and other aspects related to such identification. Challenges and gaps are also discussed in this work.**

Keywords–mental health; social media; pre-processing; labeling; systematic review.

I. INTRODUCTION

The use of social networks has increasingly gained more and more popularity. By joining communities on social networks, users have provided more information about themselves including, sometimes, feelings and opinions. Feelings or opinions are published on these platforms by means of texts, photos, emoticons or videos [1]. The emotion and language used on social media by means of such posts may, at times, indicate feelings of worthlessness, guilt, loneliness, helplessness, and self-hatred that may characterize, for example, a propensity for depression or for other kinds of mental disorders [2].

A mental disorder is characterized by a clinically significant confusion in an individual's cognition, emotional regulation, or behaviour [3]. Research on mental health in the areas of psychiatry, psychology, sociolinguistics and neuroscience, combined with computational support from specific tools of, for instance, sentiment analysis, can increase the understandings about the relationship between human behavior and the feelings expressed on social profiles. This is due to the fact that users with mental disorders tend to present different online behaviors from users who do not suffer from any disorder when using social networks [2] [4].

With this scenario in mind, this work presents a Systematic Literature Review (SLR) with the objective of investigating how works are identifying signs of mental disorders on social networks. In this sense, this work provides some findings on methods, data and features, data labeling strategies and other related aspects to the theme at hand. It also provides answers to some defined research questions and a list of 19 studies, which have been selected on the topic. As a result, it is able to discuss some identified impacts, challenges and critical success factors described by the selected works when working on identifying signs of mental disorders. An important finding concerns the still recurrent lack of more appropriate and effective strategies when labeling training data in this scenario.

The remaining parts of the paper are organized as follows: Section 2 introduces some theoretical background. Section 3 discusses some related work. Section 4 describes the methodology used in this study. Section 5 presents the results obtained and a discussion relating these findings to the research questions. Finally, Section 6 provides some concluding remarks and indicates future work.

II. THEORETICAL FOUNDATION

A mental disorder is conventionally defined as a syndrome with characteristics that cause significant clinical changes in a person's cognition, emotion or behavior, causing psychological and biological diseases [5]. The most common mental disorders are [6] [7]: depression, insomnia, anxiety disorders, eating disorders (e.g., anorexia), bipolar disorder, schizophrenia, self-harm, post-traumatic stress disorder and drug or alcohol use disorders. The term "disorder" is used to characterize symptoms and/or behaviors that can be clinically identified and, in most cases, are linked to an individual's suffering and cognitive disturbance [7]. The discovery of these signs in advance can help in clinical assistance and treatments, making it possible to prevent recurrences or even hospital admissions [8].

To help matters, sentiment analysis strategies have been used to identify signs of some mental disorders such as depression. Sentiment analysis seeks to establish and/or use techniques capable of extracting subjective information from data such as text, images, emoticons, emojis, or audios. Examples of these data include opinions or feelings that are usually provided in natural language, which implies the need of creating structured data from those. The idea is using such data to assist some kind of decision [9]–[11].

Through these strategies, it can be determined whether a piece of writing or image is positive, negative, or neutral. The definition of a sentiment is a combination of beliefs and emotions, which, in general, may be considered good or bad according to a given real scenario (e.g., depression). In the light of depression, for instance, "loss of interest or pleasure" may be a sign of negative sentiment. On the other hand, a neutral sentiment occurs when there is a lack of emotion or opinion in such a way that it can not be detected. A sentiment analysis strategy for text, for instance, usually combines Natural Language Processing (NLP) and Machine Learning Techniques to assign weighted sentiment scores to the entities, topics, themes, and categories within a sentence or phrase [12].

NLP is a subfield of computing dedicated to the natural understanding of human language by computational machines [13]. It includes techniques capable of analyzing and characterizing texts in order to perform language processing similar to the way human beings perform [14]. NLP strategies include a set of pre-processing tasks to obtain a structured representation of a less sparse set of words in the text for computational processing. Another approach used in NLP is the use of lexicons. Lexicons provide a vocabulary with preceding information about the type and intensity of each phrase or word and correlate it to a degree of polarity [15]. Words or phrases that have meaning in a lexicon are called lexemes. Such strategy is accomplished by the examination of a document or text looking for words that express a positive (e.g., good, perfect, nice, beautiful, etc.) or negative (e.g., bad, sad, etc.) feeling. In addition, automatically discovering topics from noisy and short texts posted on social networks is paramount. Due to this fact, topic modeling methods, based usually on classical probabilistic or recent neural approaches, have been considered [16]. As an illustration, the Latent Dirichlet Allocation (LDA) method is one of the most adopted in the literature. It is a generative and probability approach based on word co-occurrences [17].

The Machine Learning (ML) field relies on computational algorithms which is used to optimize a performance criterion using example data or past experience [18]. To this end, a model is produced up to some parameters, and learning is obtained by means of the model using the training data or past experience. The model may be predictive to make predictions in the future, or descriptive to gain knowledge from data, or both [18]. Supervised learning relies on using examples to provide predictions. Unsupervised learning does not use a target variable thus, instead of telling the machine to predict Y for specific data X, it asks what is possible to understand from data X [19]. Supervised learning is usually accomplished by classification or regression tasks [19]. For unsupervised ML, one of the most used tasks is clustering. According to [20], its objective is grouping objects that are similar to each other in clusters, based on the characteristics that these objects have. Considered as a subfield of ML, deep learning is a category of techniques that allows processing various levels of data abstractions using computational models, which can be applied in various tasks, such as associating posts and products with user preferences and also selecting content on social networks [21].

III. Related works

In this section, some secondary works related to the SLR previously mentioned are discussed.

In [22], the authors carried out a SLR in order to discuss the state of the art on how studies used techniques for analyzing feelings and emotions to identify depressive mood disorders. The researchers analyzed which social networks, techniques, emotions and feelings were used most in discovering predecessors of depression. The SLR showed that text is the most used kind of data to identify depressive disorders. In addition, the research revealed that the selected works, for the most part, proposed strategies joining ML classifiers to lexical ones. Some gaps were also identified in the studies found, such as the little exploration of data as images, videos and emojis.

The systematic mapping produced by [23] aimed to provide insights on sentiment analysis and ML techniques used to identify profiles with a depressive tendency on social networks. This work identified which types of labeling techniques were proposed to the datasets of the studies found. The authors analyzed papers published from 2013 to 2019 and found that most of the works used supervised ML algorithms for the task of classifying depressive profiles on social networks. Lexical dictionaries, such as the Linguistic Inquiry and Word Count (LIWC), Affective Norms for English Words (ANEW) and NRC Emotion Lexicon (Emolex) were also used by the works found for the same purpose. The research showed that only one study used a dataset in Portuguese, while English was the most used language.

The research developed by [6] carried out a literature review seeking to analyze works that used social media texts for mental health surveillance, with greater attention to studies that approached depression and suicide. The researchers investigated which data collection techniques were used as well as features used in training ML models to predict population-level mental illness. They also considered which classifiers were adopted for training models. The results showed that the selected works collected data from questionnaires, such as the PHQ-9 (Patient Health Questionnaire), and scales, such as the Depression Scale Center for Epidemiological Studies (CES-D) used in psychiatry. Other forms of data collection highlighted by the review authors were the self-reports of people with depression or suicidal ideation on social networks, in addition to mental health support forums. The articles found indicated that most of the works used supervised ML algorithms combined with lexicons, exploring linguistic, semantic, behavioral and user profile features such as post volume and time.

In [7], the authors conducted a survey looking for works that proposed computational methods in the assessment of mental state from posts on social media. Most of the studies found by the researchers analyzed depressive, eating and post-traumatic stress disorders. The authors highlighted that the discussed articles performed resource extraction using topic models, such as the Latent Dirichlet Allocation (LDA) and lexical approaches such as LIWC or ANEW. They also employed techniques such as bag-of-words, word embeddings, writing behavior (frequent use of 1st person pronouns), social engagement (frequency and time of posts) and syntactic structures such as the use of negative words. The research also revealed that supervised ML algorithms, such as Support Vector

Machines (SVM), Naïve Bayes, Logistic/Linear Regression, Random Forest, Ada Boost and K-Nearest Neighbours (KNN), were the most applied ones by the works to online mental state assessment. Some articles proposed the use of deep learning models as the ones which are currently expanding. Regarding the usage of deep learning, some works used simple neural networks such as the Multilayer Perceptron (MLP) to identify mental disorders, while others adopted more complex networks, such as the Long Short-Term Memory (LSTM) and Convolutional Neural Network (CNN). In addition to ML models, some articles used rule-based approaches such as Character Language Models (CLMs), Sequential Incremental Classification (SIC), Decision List, and Temporal Mood Variation.

The current work extends some of the aspects discussed in previous related works. This work investigates various kinds of mental disorders on social networks. It also studies issues and aspects related to data, pre-processing methods, NLP techniques, labeling strategies and languages usually used to build corpora. Another concern regards the identification of linguistic terms or pronouns which may help identifying a mental disorder (e.g., depressive terms, first person pronouns). Likewise, behavioral (e.g., engagement, interval between posts) and social media features (e.g., number of reposts, comment tree) which may also be used are discussed in this work.

IV. Research Method

This work complies with the guidelines and practices established by [24] for conducting SLR. Thus, the research process accomplishes the following steps: (i) research planning, (ii) data search, and (iii) data selection, data extraction and data synthesis.

A. Research planning

The main research question that motivates this work is RQ: What is the state of the art on identifying signs of mental disorders on social networks profiles? Given the broad scope of such question, the following specific research questions may provide evidence to help answering RQ:

RQ1. What sentiment analysis strategies have been proposed/applied to detect signs of mental disorders on social media posts?

RQ2. Which behavioral characteristics or features have been used most in discovering predecessors of mental disorders?

RQ3. Which languages are most commonly used to build corpora?

RQ4. What data pre-processing strategies have been proposed/employed?

RQ5. What kind of techniques have been proposed/used for post training data labeling? What types of labels have commonly been used?

RQ6. What evaluation metrics have been used to assess the quality of results?

RQ7. What challenges and gaps have been found?

B. Data search

From the research questions presented along with some synonym adaptations, the authors extracted the constructs to be used to enable the data search, as follows:

("sentiment analysis" OR "text mining" OR "emotion") AND ("social networks" OR " social media" OR "social posts") AND ("depression" OR "depressive disorder" OR "mental disorder").

The strategy of this research used the following scientific web databases (libraries or proceedings): ACM Digital Library, IEEE Xplore Digital Library, Science Direct, Brazilian Journal of Information Systems (iSys), Journal of Information and Data Management (JIDM), Brazilian Conference on Intelligent Systems (Bracis), Symposium on Knowledge Discovery, Mining and Learning (KDmile), Brazilian Symposium on Multimedia and Web Systems (WebMedia), Brazilian Workshop on Social NetWork Analysis and Mining (Brasnam) and Brazilian Database Symposium (SBBD).

Two inclusion criteria were applied to filter the articles: (I1) works that answer at least one of the research questions and (I2) primary studies. The exclusion criteria used were: (E1) studies without scientific relevance; (E2) secondary or tertiary works; and (E3) articles published prior to 2016.

C. Data selection, data extraction and data synthesis

The studies collected by the search string went through a filtering process set in three phases. In Phase 1, the protocol analyzed the studies' title, abstract, and keywords. The articles selected in this first phase went to Phase 2, in which researchers read the studies' introduction and conclusion. In the same manner as Phase 1, this phase eliminated studies that did not answer at least one of the research questions (RQ1 to RQ7), i.e., studies that did not address the subject of this systematic review. In Phase 3, the authors read the papers completely and selected the ones which complied with the inclusion and exclusion criteria.

To assess the level of agreement among the authors and in order to rank the works which would be the most relevant to this research, an adaptation of the Likert scale was employed. Thus, three levels of evaluation were defined along with a respective value, as follows: (i) works that contributed little - value 5; (ii) works that contributed reasonably - value 10; (iii) works that contributed a lot - value 15. In addition, some quality dimensions were added to score articles based on the following criteria: 1 point, if only one of the research questions was answered, 2 points, if the work answered two or more research questions, 3 points, if it answered two or more questions and used machine learning techniques, lexical dictionaries (important to answer the RQs), and 4 points, if in addition to the criteria already mentioned, the work used the Portuguese language to build corpora.

After data extraction, some synthesis tasks were performed. The synthesis was then carried out for each RQ following specific methods adapted to each question's proposal.

V. Results and Discussion

In total, 19 papers were found likely to contribute to this review. Table I shows the number of works collected or selected along the review process, grouped according to the scientic data source and phases employed. Figure 1 shows the publication timeline of the final selected papers. There has been an increase in works published in recent years on this subject. This may be due to the fact that the theme "metal disorders" has been increasingly highlighted on social networks in recent times, specially in the context of pandemics.

Some general findings of this SLR are pointed out in the following. Then, each one of the research questions is discussed. Table II shows the list with the references and titles of the selected works. References are used as identifiers of the selected papers in this section.

TABLE I
Number of selected studies: digital library vs phase.

Digital library	Phase 1	Phase 2	Phase 3	Final result
ACM Digital Library	477	100	24	8
IEEE Xplore	34	19	9	6
Science Direct	11	9	2	1
iSys	4	0	0	0
JIDM	7	1	0	0
Bracis	3	2	1	0
Brasnam	7	7	3	2
KDMile	2	2	1	1
SBBD	1	2	1	1
Webmedia	3	2	0	0
Total	**549**	**147**	**44**	**19**

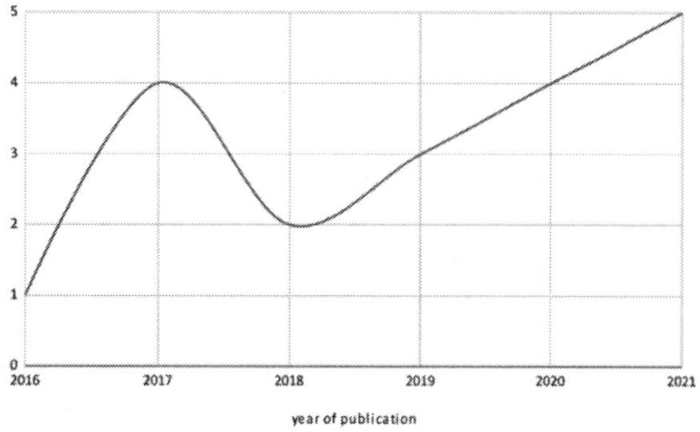

Fig. 1. Timeline of publications.

Regarding mental disorders, the selected articles revealed that depression (60%) is the most studied one. Articles that addressed anxiety (4%), bipolar disorder (4%), borderline personality disorder (4%) and stress (4%) were also found. Some studies have tried to identify positive or negative feelings, excessive sadness and behavioral change through posts on social networks. The research developed by [26] deserves to be highlighted for using data from Reddit (specific subcommunities) to analyze indicators of depression, self-harm and anorexia. In the work of [28], the authors proposed to use

TABLE II
Selected studies.

	Title
[25]	A knowledge-based recommendation system that includes sentiment analysis and deep learning
[26]	An emotion and cognitive based analysis of mental health disorders from social media data
[27]	Sentiment analysis in brazilian portuguese tweets
[28]	Characterization of anxiety, depression, and their comorbidity from texts of social networks
[29]	Depression detection using machine learning techniques on Twitter data
[30]	DepressionNet: Learning multi-modalities with user post summarization for depression detection on social media
[31]	Detecting stress based on social interactions in social networks
[32]	Early detection of depression: social network analysis and random forest techniques
[33]	Emotional and linguistic cues of depression from social media
[34]	Identifying depression among Twitter users using sentiment analysis
[4]	Mining Twitter data for signs of depression in Brazil
[35]	Modeling and detecting change in user behavior through his social media posting using cluster analysis
[36]	User emotional tone prediction models in mental health communities on Reddit
[37]	Multimodal sentiment analysis to explore the structure of emotions
[38]	Semi-Supervised approach to monitoring clinical depressive symptoms in social media
[39]	Subconscious Crowdsourcing: a feasible data collection mechanism for mental disorder detection on docial media
[40]	Tracing the emotional roadmap of depressive users on social media through sequential pattern mining
[41]	Using Twitter social media for depression detection in the Canadian population
[42]	What about mood swings: identifying depression on Twitter with temporal measures of emotions

deep learning to identify depression and anxiety. Figure 2 shows the disorders found in the 19 works that stood out the most.

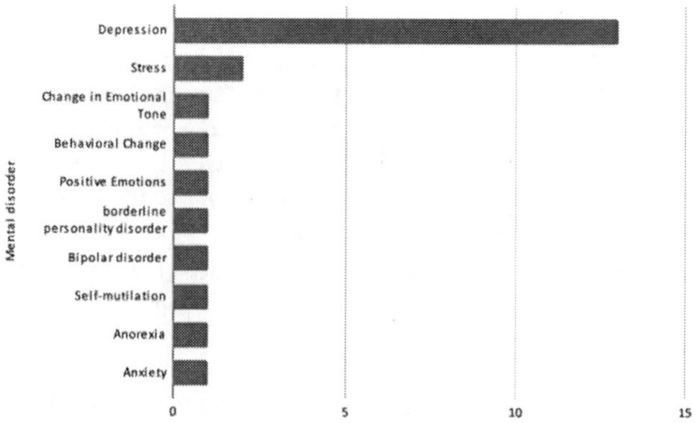

Fig. 2. Most studied mental disorders.

Most of the selected works used Twitter posts as data source (58%). The second most mentioned social network was Reddit (27%), followed by Facebook (5%). The study by [37] used the blogging platform Tumblr (5%). The authors of [31] obtained their data from Sina Weibo (5%), which is a kind of Chinese Twitter. In the following, we present the RQs and the results found by the teams in the data extraction and synthesis activities.

RQ1: For the task of predicting symptoms of mental disorders from social media posts, most researchers used combined ML approaches and lexical dictionaries, such as LIWC, VADER, ANEW and NRC Emolex. The vast majority of works used supervised ML algorithms, such as SVM, Naive Bayes, KNN and ensembles, such as Random Forest, Gradient Boosting and AdaBoost. Three works used unsupervised ML with the K-means algorithm. The work developed by [38] proposed a topic modeling using LDA to detect clinical depression from Twitter posts. Articles that applied deep learning through neural networks were also selected: CNN, LSTM and MLP. Figure 3 depicts some topic modeling and ML methods found, grouped by supervised, unsupervised and deep learning that were most used in the 19 highlighted works. It is also noticed that the use of deep learning models for this type of task has been increased. The reason underlying that may be linked to how these methods perform the analysis and learning.

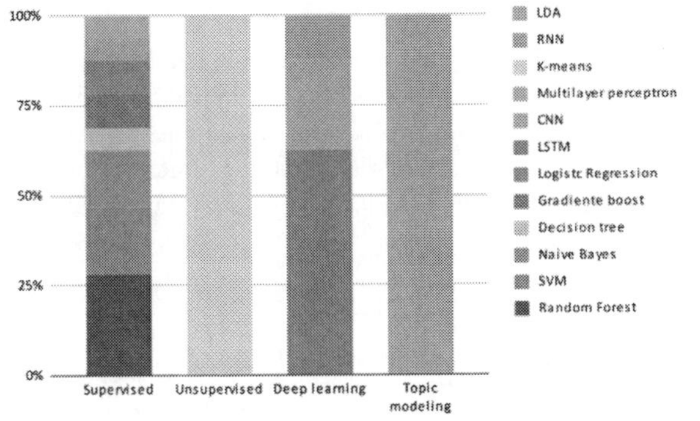

Fig. 3. Topic modeling and machine learning methods.

RQ2: Research has identified features to perform data analysis and explore them through some sentiment analysis strategy. The behavior patterns of users on social networks were essential in identifying some mental disorders. Table III presents the main features found that are grouped into 3 categories: Behavioral, that means how people act on networks; Linguistics, regarding the way they write their posts; and Features in the social network about information related to personal profiles. However, such properties were little explored over a certain period in the timeline of user posts on their profile. Interaction-related features, such as responses and comments between users with mental disorders and their friends, were also under-examined. The analysis of these characteristics taking into account the timeline of posts can bring new characteristics and discoveries of behavioral patterns to the study of mental disorders from social networks.

RQ3: The language most found in the data analyzed by the works was English (79%). For the Portuguese language, there were 3 articles (16%), highlighting the research by [4] that analyzed Twitter posts to predict signs of depression, and [25] that used facebook posts to predict signs of depression

TABLE III
FEATURES CATEGORIES.

Category	Feature
Behavioral	Time of posts, engagement, interval between posts, frequency on the networks, insomnia index, number of publications;
Linguistics	Antidepressant drug names, depressive terms, first person pronouns, syntactic features (verb, adverb);
Social network	Number of followers, number of reposts, comment tree, interaction with friends.

and stress. Only one study evaluated data by considering the Chinese language. There is a lack of research focused on studying mental disorders from social networks, exploring, in particular, datasets in Portuguese. This might be due to the difficulty in working with this language that has nuances, such as slang and regional dialects. According to the region of the country, the same word has different meanings, and can express different feelings according to the place where the user of the social network lives. For a more accurate computational diagnosis, this cultural diversity becomes a challenge, as the linguistic variety needs to be taken into account in steps such as pre-processing and labeling, when using ML algorithms. Otherwise, there is the possibility of erroneous analysis, and, consequently, false computational diagnoses. In addition, there is a shortage of lexical dictionaries in the Portuguese language, specifically to deal with mental disorders. Thus, here is an open field to improve existing solutions. The development of lexicons in the Portuguese language, for specific domains e.g. depression, anxiety, anorexia, presents itself as a promising line of research.

RQ4: Before being analyzed by models such as ML algorithms, the data collected from social media posts usually go through the pre-processing step. The selected works showed that techniques, such as stopword removal, tokenization, lemming, stemming and Term Frequency - Inverse Document Frequency (TF-IDF) are the ones that appear the most. The articles also showed that it was necessary to anonymize the posts by removing user names, mentions, URLs or any information that could identify the owner of the profile on the social network. Emojis and emoticons in most of the works were removed or transformed into text. The work of [34] stands out, using the demoji, a library developed in Python, and transformed the emoticons and emojis that appear in text. The exclusion or conversion of hashtags, emojis and emoticons in texts, or even exclusion of words with repeated letters, indicating intensity, could be better handled to provide a dataset with more subsidies and characteristics that would help in the evaluation of ML models.

RQ5: Labeling strategies used in the selected studies were largely done through self-reports of social network users, parsing and identifying sentences, such as: "I was diagnosed with depression" on their profiles. Some research carried out the labeling manually and had the help of experts to identify whether or not a particular post showed signs of a mental disorder. Only one article found focused on a proposal for automatic labeling using Textblob to punctuate the sentence and label it. We highlight the work of [29] who used Textblob, a library used by Python to calculate the sentiment score of a text according to subject and polarity, thus classifying sentences as -1 (negative), 0 (neutral) and 1 (positive). When the calculated value was less than 0, the sentences were labeled as depressive and when greater than 0, non-depressive. Regarding labeling training data, works have demonstrated that this is indeed the largest bottleneck in deploying machine learning models applied to sentiment analyses. Manual labeling can present subjectivity and different interpretations by human annotators. Experts are supposed to significantly enhance this process, although it demands a lot of time and effort to accomplish this task. The volume of data may be a restriction. In turn, the use of libraries such as Textblob can speed up the labeling step, however, it needs to be developed in such a way that may provide specificities to the data domain at hand. Thereby, there is a lack for more research and proposals to label training data to the mental disorders scenario. An automated or even semi automated strategy for labeling training data on mental disorders may bring two main benefits: (a) reducing the effort employed in the usual labeling step; and (b) contributing to find out new examples that could not be easily found by performing manual labeling. As a result, it may also increase the performance of the classifier used to predict signs of mental disorders.

RQ6: In order to measure the performance of ML models, evaluation metrics were used. Most articles used precision, recall, accuracy and F-measure. A possible explanation for this is that for the task of predicting signs of mental disorders, the classification problem is usually binary. Besides the mentioned metrics, in [26], the Area under the Receiver Operating Characteristic curve (AUC) was used to evaluate the performance of the models proposed in the research. The authors considered this metric to be less sensitive to the imbalance of the data set used in the work. Another highlight was the research in [33] which, in addition to accuracy, calculated the micro-F1 and macro-F1 scores to evaluate the Gradient Boosted Decision Trees classifier in the task of identifying emotional and linguistic signs of depression on Twitter.

RQ7: The main challenges are related to the development of approaches that can allow a more automated training data labeling, perhaps using lexical dictionaries specific to the mental disorder. Automatic training data labeling avoids the situation of depending on user reports on their networks or the need of performing manual annotations in large datasets. Likewise, there is lack of studies specifically focused on signs, emotions and linguistic, behavioral and associated with the timeline of user posts. Thus, it is worth studying some specific chronology on users to enhance such analysis on the propensity to mental disorders. The construction of a lexical dictionary in Portuguese specialized on a mental disorder such as depression as well as the investigation of behavioral resources and social interaction over a period of time using a database in Portuguese are gaps that still need to be filled.

VI. Conclusion

The analysis of data from social networks focused on research to detect signs of mental disorders emerges as a promising topic in the field of sentiment analysis. This work carried out an SLR with the objective of investigating how the literature presents the sentiment analysis techniques proposed to identify mental disorders from posts on social networks. The characteristics and languages used were analyzed, revealing that few studies with data in Portuguese were found. The pre-processing methods were also analyzed, showing that features such as emoticons and emojis can be further explored. Training data labeling was accomplished manually or through user reports. Furthermore, it was revealed that the works are proposing the combination of ML methods and lexical dictionaries to detect signs of propensity to mental disorders. The most discussed disorder found in the studies was depression. The works identified behavioral and linguistic characteristics that helped in the early detection of depression. Thus, future investigations of this disorder are relevant. We also sought to find out which metrics evaluated the performance of the strategies proposed in the works. Finally, challenges and gaps to be filled according to the work obtained were identified. In future work, we can explore the development of automated or semi-automated training data labeling strategies, which are indeed important to detect mental disorders such as depression on social media.

References

[1] J. W. G. Duque, A. L. Raymundo, and P. F. Neto, "An application of big data for twitter depressive sentence classification," *H-TEC humanities and technology magazine*, vol. 2, no. 1, pp. 82–95, 2018.

[2] M. De Choudhury, M. Gamon, S. Counts, and E. Horvitz, "Predicting depression via social media," in *Seventh international AAAI conference on weblogs and social media*, 2013, pp. 128–137.

[3] WHO, "World health organization," 2022, https://www.who.int/news-room/fact-sheets/detail/mental-disorders Last accessed 04 Sep 2022.

[4] O. V. Sperling and M. Ladeira, "Mining twitter data for signs of depression in brazil," in *Anais do VII Symposium on Knowledge Discovery, Mining and Learning*. SBC, 2019, pp. 25–32.

[5] American Psychiatric Association, *Diagnostic and statistical manual of mental disorders: DSM-5*. American psychiatric association Washington, DC, 2013, vol. 5.

[6] R. Skaik and D. Inkpen, "Using social media for mental health surveillance: a review," *ACM Computing Surveys (CSUR)*, vol. 53, no. 6, pp. 1–31, 2020.

[7] E. A. Ríssola, D. E. Losada, and F. Crestani, "A survey of computational methods for online mental state assessment on social media," *ACM Transactions on Computing for Healthcare*, vol. 2, no. 2, pp. 1–31, 2021.

[8] S. Abdullah and T. Choudhury, "Sensing technologies for monitoring serious mental illnesses," *IEEE MultiMedia*, vol. 25, no. 1, pp. 61–75, 2018.

[9] M. Huang, H. Xie, Y. Rao, J. Feng, and F. L. Wang, "Sentiment strength detection with a context-dependent lexicon-based convolutional neural network," *Information Sciences*, vol. 520, pp. 389–399, 2020.

[10] A. V. Tardelli, A. F. d. S. Dias, and J. B. d. S. França, "Introduction to sentiment analysis with word clouds," *Brazilian computing society*, pp. 38–67, 2019.

[11] F. Benevenuto, F. Ribeiro, and M. Araújo, "Methods for sentiment analysis in social media," *Brazilian computing society*, pp. 31–59, 2015.

[12] D. Sharma, M. Sabharwal, V. Goyal, and M. Vij, "Sentiment analysis techniques for social media data: A review," in *First international conference on sustainable technologies for computational intelligence*. Springer, 2020, pp. 75–90.

[13] T. Beysolow II, *Applied Natural Language Processing with Python: Implementing Machine Learning and Deep Learning Algorithms for Natural Language Processing*. Apress, 2018.

[14] E. D. Liddy, *Natural language processing*. In Encyclopedia of Library and Information Science, 2nd Ed. NY. Marcel Decker, Inc., 2001.

[15] A. Yadollahi, A. G. Shahraki, and O. R. Zaiane, "Current state of text sentiment analysis from opinion to emotion mining," *ACM Computing Surveys (CSUR)*, vol. 50, no. 2, pp. 1–33, 2017.

[16] R. Albalawi, T. H. Yeap, and M. Benyoucef, "Using topic modeling methods for short-text data: A comparative analysis," *Frontiers in Artificial Intelligence*, vol. 3, p. 42, 2020.

[17] D. M. Blei, A. Y. Ng, and M. I. Jordan, "Latent dirichlet allocation," *Journal of machine Learning research*, vol. 3, no. Jan, pp. 993–1022, 2003.

[18] E. Alpaydin, *Introduction to machine learning, 2nd edition*. MIT Press Cambridge, 2010.

[19] P. Harrington, *Machine learning in action*. Simon and Schuster, 2012.

[20] R. Linden, "Clustering techniques," *FSMA Information Systems Magazine*, vol. 4, no. 4, pp. 18–36, 2009.

[21] Y. LeCun, Y. Bengio, and G. Hinton, "Deep learning," *nature*, vol. 521, no. 7553, pp. 436–444, 2015.

[22] F. T. Giuntini *et al.*, "A review on recognizing depression in social networks: challenges and opportunities," *Journal of Ambient Intelligence and Humanized Computing*, vol. 11, no. 11, pp. 4713–4729, 2020.

[23] V. Casani, R. G. Mantovani, A. C. C. Souza, and F. C. M. Souza, "Identification of depressive profiles in social networks using machine learning: a systematic mapping," *Anais do Computer on the Beach*, vol. 11, no. 1, pp. 183–190, 2020.

[24] B. Kitchenham, "Procedures for performing systematic reviews," *Keele, UK, Keele University*, vol. 33, no. 2004, pp. 1–26, 2004.

[25] R. L. Rosa, G. M. Schwartz, W. V. Ruggiero, and D. Z. Rodríguez, "A knowledge-based recommendation system that includes sentiment analysis and deep learning," *IEEE Transactions on Industrial Informatics*, vol. 15, no. 4, pp. 2124–2135, 2018.

[26] A.-S. Uban, B. Chulvi, and P. Rosso, "An emotion and cognitive based analysis of mental health disorders from social media data," *Future Generation Computer Systems*, vol. 124, pp. 480–494, 2021.

[27] D. P. Kansaon, M. A. Brandão, and S. A. de Paula Pinto, "Sentiment analysis in brazilian portuguese tweets," in *Anais do VII Brazilian Workshop on Social Network Analysis and Mining*. Porto Alegre, RS, Brasil: SBC, 2018, pp. 37–48. [Online]. Available: https://sol.sbc.org.br/index.php/brasnam/article/view/3578

[28] V. B. Souza, J. Nobre, and K. Becker, "Characterization of anxiety, depression, and their comorbidity from texts of social networks," *Anais do XXXV Simpósio Brasileiro de Banco de Dados. SBC, Porto Alegre, RS, Brasil*, pp. 121–132, 2020.

[29] K. A. Govindasamy and N. Palanichamy, "Depression detection using machine learning techniques on twitter data," in *2021 5th international conference on intelligent computing and control systems (ICICCS)*. IEEE, 2021, pp. 960–966.

[30] H. Zogan, I. Razzak, S. Jameel, and G. Xu, "Depressionnet: learning multi-modalities with user post summarization for depression detection on social media," in *proceedings of the 44th international ACM SIGIR conference on research and development in information retrieval*, 2021, pp. 133–142.

[31] H. Lin *et al.*, "Detecting stress based on social interactions in social networks," *IEEE Transactions on Knowledge and Data Engineering*, vol. 29, no. 9, pp. 1820–1833, 2017.

[32] F. Cacheda, D. Fernandez, F. J. Novoa, and V. Carneiro, "Early detection of depression: social network analysis and random forest techniques," *Journal of medical Internet research*, vol. 21, no. 6, p. e12554, 2019.

[33] N. Vedula and S. Parthasarathy, "Emotional and linguistic cues of depression from social media," in *Proceedings of the 2017 International Conference on Digital Health*, 2017, pp. 127–136.

[34] F. Azam, M. Agro, M. Sami, M. H. Abro, and A. Dewani, "Identifying depression among twitter users using sentiment analysis," in *2021 International Conference on Artificial Intelligence (ICAI)*. IEEE, 2021, pp. 44–49.

[35] D. J. Joshi, N. Supekar, R. Chauhan, and M. S. Patwardhan, "Modeling and detecting change in user behavior through his social media posting using cluster analysis," in *Proceedings of the Fourth ACM IKDD Conferences on Data Sciences*, 2017, pp. 1–9.

[36] B. Silveira, A. P. C. da Silva, and F. Murai, "Models for predicting the emotional tone of users in mental health communities on reddit," in *Anais do IX Brazilian Workshop on Social Network Analysis and Mining*. SBC, 2020, pp. 13–24.

[37] A. Hu and S. Flaxman, "Multimodal sentiment analysis to explore the structure of emotions," in *proceedings of the 24th ACM SIGKDD international conference on Knowledge Discovery & Data Mining*, 2018, pp. 350–358.

[38] A. H. Yazdavar *et al.*, "Semi-supervised approach to monitoring clinical depressive symptoms in social media," in *Proceedings of the 2017 IEEE/ACM International Conference on Advances in Social Networks Analysis and Mining 2017*, 2017, pp. 1191–1198.

[39] C.-H. Chang, E. Saravia, and Y.-S. Chen, "Subconscious crowdsourcing: A feasible data collection mechanism for mental disorder detection on social media," in *2016 IEEE/ACM International Conference on Advances in Social Networks Analysis and Mining (ASONAM)*. IEEE, 2016, pp. 374–379.

[40] F. T. Giuntini *et al.*, "Tracing the emotional roadmap of depressive users on social media through sequential pattern mining," *IEEE Access*, vol. 9, pp. 97 621–97 635, 2021.

[41] R. Skaik and D. Inkpen, "Using twitter social media for depression detection in the canadian population," in *2020 3rd Artificial Intelligence and Cloud Computing Conference*, 2020, pp. 109–114.

[42] X. Chen, M. D. Sykora, T. W. Jackson, and S. Elayan, "What about mood swings: Identifying depression on twitter with temporal measures of emotions," in *Companion Proceedings of the The Web Conference 2018*, 2018, pp. 1653–1660.

Privacy Protected Identification of User Clusters in Large Organizations based on Anonymized Mattermost User and Channel Information

Igor Jakovljevic
ISDS
Graz University of Technology
Graz, Austria
e-mail: igor.jakovljevic@cern.ch

Martin Pobaschnig
ISDS
Graz University of Technology
Graz, Austria
e-mail: martin.pobaschnig@student.tugraz.at

Christian Gütl
ISDS
Graz University of Technology
Graz, Austria
e-mail: c.guetl@tugraz.at

Andreas Wagner
IT Department
CERN
Geneva, Switzerland
e-mail: andreas.wagner@cern.ch

***Abstract*—Oversharing exposes risks such as improved targeted advertising and sensitive information leakage. Requiring only the bare minimum of data diminishes these risk factors while simultaneously increasing the privacy of each individual user. Using anonymized data for finding communities enables new possibilities for large organizations under strong data protection regulations. While related work often focuses on privacy-preserving community detection algorithms including differential privacy, in this paper, the focus was set on the anonymized data itself. Channel membership information was used to build a weighted social graph, and groups of interest were identified using popular community detection algorithms. Graphs based on channel membership data satisfactorily resembled interest groups within the network but failed to capture the organizational structure.**

Keywords—Data Privacy. Open Data. Large Organizations. Clustering.

I. Introduction

It is estimated that a median of 300 terabytes (TB) of data is generated by large organizations on a weekly basis [1]. The data is generated from the use of various methods of communication (chat, email, face-to-face, phone, short message service, social media) between organization members, data sharing tools, internal processes, different hardware units (mobile phones, tablets, laptops, etc.), and more [1]. Publishing this data to be used for analysis and research has been a excellent source of information for researchers, promoting innovation and advancements in various areas while facilitating cooperation between diverse groups [2][3]. In this context, the term used to describe data available freely for anyone to use for analysis and research is open data [4]. There have been different initiatives for collaboration based on open data, such as the Netflix Prize, OpenStreetMap, CERN (Conseil européen pour la recherche nucléaire) Open Science Initiative, Open City Initiatives, and more [2][4][5]. The purpose of these projects has been to improve existing technologies and algorithms and facilitate innovation and collaboration [2]. Besides these projects, organizations internally analyze user behavior and user data and create new or improve existing services, usually relying on continuous user surveying and behavior tracking while invading their privacy [6].

Sharing of personal data that contains identifiers, quasi-identifiers, and sensitive attributes has been identified as a common issue with similar projects [2]. Sensitive and personal data should not be accessed freely; organizations have to protect and secure it. To achieve this, organizations usually secure and do not release this type of data. By doing so, possible benefits available from private data are not explored. To avoid privacy breaches and to publish organizational data, multiple privacy-preserving techniques for data were developed. Most of them are based on pseudo-anonymization or full anonymization of data [7]. Utilization of anonymized private data gave rise to privacy-preserving data analytics methods. These methods offer a way to utilize private data safely, by considering privacy requirements [8].

CERN always stood for principles of open data and open science, facilitating research and development that is collaborative, transparent and reproducible and whose outputs are publicly available [5]. One such initative is the CERN anonymized Mattermost data set, which contains anonymized user data, relationships between users, organizations, building, teams and channels. The goal of this data set is to facilitate innovation for channel recommendations, user clustering, feature extractions, and others [9].

This research aims to analyze the provided CERN data set and determine privacy aspects and attributes that can be used for privacy aware clustering methods. Based on the observations stated above, more specifically, the main research questions are:

- **RQ1:** Which user information can be extracted from the anonymized Mattermost organizational open data?
- **RQ2:** Is it possible to detect user groups without invading user privacy?

The remainder of this paper is organized as follows: Section II covers the literature overview and discusses current topics in privacy-preserving data mining, open data, and clustering methodologies. In Section III, we discuss and describe the CERN Mattermost data set. Section IV focuses on the findings from the data set and explains the usage of clustering methodologies on the previously mentioned data. We conclude the work in Section V with the discussion of the research questions and future works.

II. Background and Related Work

A. Networks and Graphs

Networks are defined as interconnected or interrelated chains, groups, or systems and can be found in a variety of areas, such as the World Wide Web, connections of friends, connections between cities, connections in our brain, power line links, and citation links. In essence, a network is a set of interconnected entities, which we call nodes, and their connections, which we call links. Nodes describe all types of entities, such as people, cities, computers, Web sites, and so on. Links define relationships or interactions between these entities, such as connections among people, flights between airports, links between Web pages, connections between neurons, and more. A special type of network is a social network. It is a group of people connected by a type of relationship (friendship, collaboration, or acquaintance) [10].

The data structure commonly used for the representation of networks is called a graph. A graph is defined as a set of connected points, called vertices (or nodes) that are connected via edges also called links. The set of vertices is denoted as $V = \{v_1, v_2, v_3, \dots\}$, while the set of edges is denoted as $E = \{e_1, e_2, e_3, \dots\}$. The resulting graph G consists of a set of vertices V and a set of edges E that connect them and can be written as $G = (V, E)$. Two vertices that are connected by an edge are called adjacent or neighbors and all vertices that are connected to a vertex are called neighborhood [11].

Graphs have a variety of measures associated with them. These measures can be classified as global measures and nodal measures. Global measures refer to the global properties of a graph, while nodal measures refer to the properties of nodes. The most important measures are degree measures, strength measures, modularity measures, and clustering coefficient measures. The degree measure is a nodal. It is the sum of edges connected to a node. The sum of the weights of all edges connected to a node is defined as the strength measure, while the extent to which a graph divides into clearly separated communities (i.e., subgraphs or modules) is described by modularity measures [12].

B. Clustering Methods

Fundamental tasks in data mining are clustering and classifications, among others. Clustering is applied mostly for unsupervised learning problems, while classification is used as a supervised learning method. The goal of clustering is descriptive, and that of classification is predictive [13].

Clustering is used to discover new sets of groups from samples. It groups instances into subsets using different measures. Measures used to determine similar or dissimilar instances are classified into distance measures and similarity measures. Different clustering methods have been developed, each of them using different principles. Based on research clustering can be divided into five different methods: hierarchical, partitioning, density-based, model-based clustering, and grid-based methods [13][14].

Hierarchical Methods - Clusters are constructed by recursively partitioning items in a top-down or bottom-up fashion. For example, each item is initially a cluster of its own, then clusters are merged based on a measure until desired clusters are formed [14].

Partitioning Methods - These methods typically require a pre-determined number of clusters. Items are moved between different pre-determined clusters based on different metrics (error-based metrics, similarity metrics, distance metrics) until desired clusters are formed. To achieve the optimal cluster distribution extensive computation of all possible partitions is required. Greedy heuristics are used for this computation because it is not feasible to calculate all possible partitions under time constraints [13].

Density-Based Methods - These methods are based on the assumption that clusters are formed according to a specific probability distribution. The aim is to identify clusters and their distribution parameters. The distribution is assumed to be a combination of several distributions [15].

Model-based Clustering methods - Unlike the previously mentioned methods, which cluster items based on similarity and distance metrics, these methods attempt to optimize the fit between the input data and a given mathematical model [16].

Grid-based methods - The previous clustering methods were data-driven, while grid-based methods are space-driven approaches. They partition the item space into cells disconnected from the distribution of the input. The grid-based clustering approach uses a multi-resolution grid data structure. It groups items into a finite number of cells that form a grid structure on which all of the operations for clustering are performed. The main advantage of the approach is its faster processing time [17].

C. Open Data and Privacy-aware Data Analysis

Open Data describes data available without restrictions for anyone to use for analysis and research [4]. Open innovation is defined as the use of purposive inflows and outflows of knowledge to stimulate internal innovation, while increasing the demands for external use of innovation, respectively. The goal of open innovation and open data is to increase accountability and transparency while providing new and efficient services [18].

Privacy-friendly analytics is a set of methods for collecting, measuring, and analyzing data respecting individual privacy rights. These methods allow for data-driven decisions while still giving individuals control over personal data. Restricting access to the data could be found to restrict to support of various kinds of data analysis. Adopting approaches of restricting information in the data so that they are free of identifiers and free of content with a high risk of individual identification. Techniques for releasing data without disclosing sensitive information have been proposed for various applications. Interest in developing data mining algorithms that are privacy-preserving has been growing over the years [19].

III. DATASET

The Mattermost data set was extracted from an internal Postgre SQL (Structured Query Language) database and is accessible as JSON (JavaScript Object Notation) formatted file [9]. It includes data from January 2018 to November 2021 with 21231 CERN users, 2367 Mattermost teams, 12773 Mattermost channels, 151 CERN buildings, and 163 CERN organizational units. The data set states the relationships between Mattermost teams, Mattermost channels, and CERN users, and holds various pieces of information, such as channel creation, channel deletion times, user channel joining, and leave times. It also includes user-specific information, such as building and organizational units, messages and mention count. To hide identifiable information (e.g., Team Name, User Name, Channel Name, etc.) the data set was anonymized. The anonymization was done by omitting attributes, hashing string values, and removing connections between users/teams/channels.

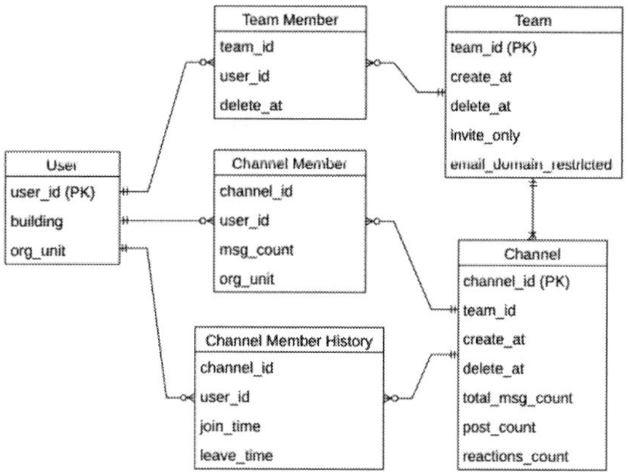

Fig. 1. CERN Mattermost data set Entity Relation Diagram

The entity relationship diagram shown in Figure 1 describes the entities with data attributes and relationships between the entities.

A. Data Transformation

The data set was analyzed and prepared to filter out superfluous teams, channels, and users. Based on the analysis, approximately 22.6% teams consist of only one person and can be removed as they form isolated nodes that do not contribute to the community structure.

Table I shows the five-number summary of the count of members within teams with more than one member. The five-number summary consists of three quartiles, Q_1, Q_2 or median, and Q_3, that divide the data set into two parts with the lower part having 25%, 50% and 75% of the data set's values, respectively. The other two values of the five-number summary consist of the minimum and the maximum value of the data set.

Using the quartiles from the five-number summary, the lower and upper team size fences can be calculated, which act as a boundaries above or below which teams are considered outliers. The upper fence can be calculated by $UpperFence = Q_3 + 1.5 * IQR$, where IQR stands for interquartile range. IQR is defined as $IQR = Q_3 - Q_1$. This results in an upper bound of 51.5.

TABLE I
FIVE-NUMBER SUMMARY OF TEAMS WITH MORE THAN ONE MEMBER.

	Minimum	Q_1	Median	Q_3	Maximum
Team Members	2	4	10	23	4512

When counting the number of teams above that threshold, approximately 87.7% of teams have less than 52 members. The lower fence is calculated by $LowerFence = Q_1 - 1.5 * IQR$ and yields -24.5. Since we do not have negative team sizes, we can limit the lower bound to 2, as team sizes of 1 are isolated nodes.

B. Graph Creation

Channel membership relations were used to generate graphs that act as a basis for community detection and user group analysis. A weighted edge between two users is added if they share the same channel, and the weight of the edge is increased for each additional channel they share. The idea behind channel membership for the graph creation is that team members within CERN join channels related to their organization and work interest. Consequently, the more channels members have in common, the more likely they belong to the same organizational structure. The goal is to find the best communities that resemble CERN's organizational structure and communities.

IV. FINDINGS AND DISCUSSION

Following the procedure described in Section III-B with an upper team threshold of 52, a weighted graph was produced. The igraph's implementation of the Large Graph Layout (LGL) with 2000 iterations was used to visualize it [20]. LGL was used as it creates good layouts for large number of vertices and edges and produces well-observable clusters. The produced graph is displayed in Figure 2.

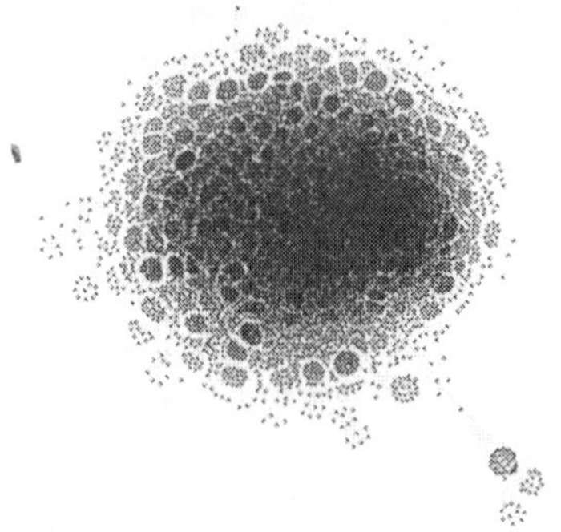

Fig. 2. Graph based on channel membership relationship.

TABLE II

RESULTS INCLUDING FIVE-NUMBER SUMMARY OF SIMILARITIES BETWEEN MATTERMOST TEAMS AND FOUND COMMUNITY WITH DIFFERENT ALGORITHMS. VALUES WITHIN COLUMNS REPRESENT MEAN AND STANDARD DEVIATION OVER 25 ITERATIONS.

Algorithm	Communities	Modularity	Minimum [%]	Q_1 [%]	Median [%]	Q_3 [%]	Maximum [%]
1. Community structure via greedy optimization of modularity [21]	41 ± 0	0.75 ± 0.00	7.85 ± 0.00	23.43 ± 0.00	45.24 ± 0.00	66.67 ± 0.00	100 ± 0.00
2. Infomap community finding [22]	414 ± 3	0.71 ± 0.00	18.13 ± 1.18	46.52 ± 0.19	61.75 ± 0.68	75.97 ± 0.61	100.00 ± 0.00
3. Finding communities based on propagating labels [23]	463 ± 8	0.70 ± 0.00	15.68 ± 2.23	48.18 ± 1.07	61.25 ± 0.81	75.08 ± 0.28	100.00 ± 0.00
4. Community structure detecting based on the leading eigenvector of the community matrix [24]	43 ± 0.00	0.67 ± 0.00	5.85 ± 0.00	15.17 ± 0.00	26.92 ± 0.00	52.48 ± 0.00	95.65 ± 0.00
5. Finding community structure of a graph using the Leiden algorithm [25]	1290 ± 3	0.64 ± 0.00	2.04 ± 0.00	20.00 ± 0.00	42.86 ± 0.00	66.67 ± 0.00	100.00 ± 0.00
6. Finding community structure by multi-level optimization of modularity [26]	40 ± 2	0.78 ± 0.00	8.80 ± 0.77	14.79 ± 1.12	21.75 ± 1.64	50.87 ± 6.80	86.51 ± 6.57
7. Computing communities using random walks [27]	344 ± 0	0.72 ± 0.00	8.33 ± 0.00	55.56 ± 0.00	66.67 ± 0.00	80.00 ± 0.00	100.00 ± 0.00
8. Community detection based on statistical mechanics [28]	25 ± 0	0.77 ± 0.00	8.10 ± 0.71	11.23 ± 0.79	14.06 ± 1.05	17.700 ± 1.39	31 ± 8.51

To evaluate community detection algorithms and their effect on different modularity scores, the following ones were assessed:

Fig. 3. Communities detected by using the label propagation algorithm. A clear separation between individual cluster in the outer part of the graph can be observed.

Out of all available algorithms, algorithms 2, 3, and 7 delivered the best performances concerning modularity, similarity, and communities, as shown in Table II. Calculating the community structure with the highest modularity value (community_optimal_modularity) and community structure detection based on edge betweenness (community_edge_betweenness) were not feasible in practice, since the runtime was too long. Figure 3 displays the result of the label propagation algorithm applied to the previously created graph. Each community gets assigned a unique color, so the separation of individual clusters can be observed. The label propagation algorithm finds communities with slightly less similarity than the infomap algorithm, which performs best concerning similarity measurement. However, it finds many and much more detailed communities.

Figure 4 represents the similarities of users between found communities and the Mattermost teams and Figure 5 illustrates the results of 10 iterations as violin plots. An upper threshold of 52 for the teams was used for this figure, as described later in this section. Of all detected communities, 75% have similarities above 47.79%, 50% have similarities above 61.18%, and 25% have similarities above 74.99%. Similarities are measured by comparing the discovered community with all Mattermost teams and counting the common members in both sets. The percentage value of the Mattermost team with the most common members is used.

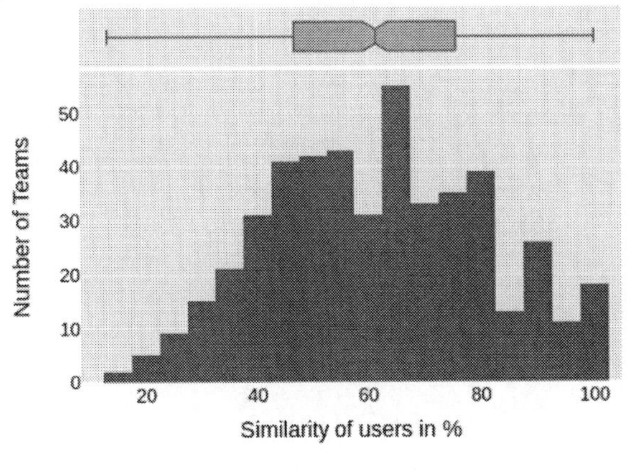

Fig. 4. Sample run showing similarities of users between found communities and Mattermost teams.

Depending on the number of communities found, there might be overlaps, such that one team fits multiple communities as the best match. This might be the case where the size of communities is smaller than the size of teams, such that communities form subgroups of the teams. However, less than 0.01% of discovered communities are matched against the same Mattermost team. The average size of discovered communities is 20 ± 23, the minimum is 2, the first quartile Q_1 is 6, the median is 13, the third quartile Q_3 is 26, and the maximum is 421. Figure 6 shows the similarities of users

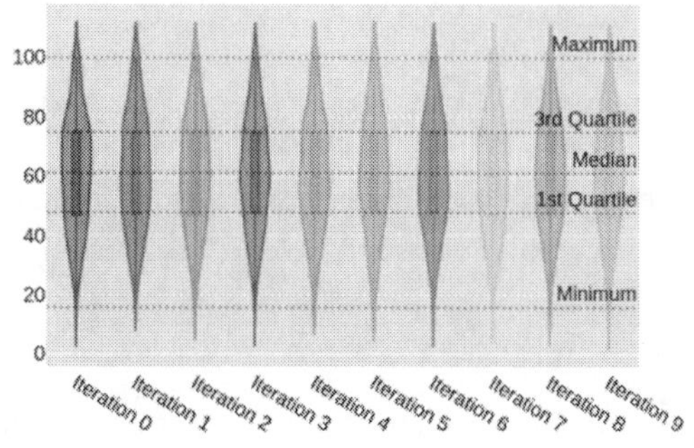

Fig. 5. Similarities between discovered communities and Mattermost teams over iterations with threshold 52.

between detected communities and the organizational units with a threshold of 52, and Table III states the parameters of this figure in detail. We can observe that the similarities are relatively low, with 75% of communities having at most 5.07% similarity. This indicates that the discovered communities generally do not resemble organizational units very well. The main reason is that Mattermost teams often consist of members of different organizational units. This is especially the case where users form groups of interest that are not related to work. This results in discovered communities capturing the teams and structure within Mattermost instead of the organizational structure of CERN.

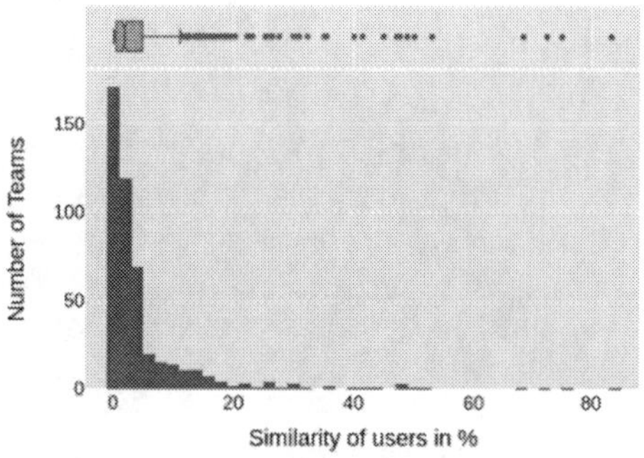

Fig. 6. Sample run showing similarities of users between found communities and organizational units.

When creating the graph, two different methods were used and compared for filtering teams and channels. With the first method, the threshold was used as an upper limit for team members, i.e. only the channels of the teams below the threshold are considered for creating the graph.

TABLE III
FIVE-NUMBER SUMMARY OF SIMILARITIES BETWEEN ORGANIZATIONAL UNITS AND DISCOVERED COMMUNITIES USING LABEL PROPAGATION ALGORITHM. VALUES WITHIN COLUMNS REPRESENT MEAN AND STANDARD DEVIATION OVER 25 ITERATIONS IN PERCENT.

Minimum	Q_1	Median	Q_3	Maximum
0.0 ± 0.0	0.42 ± 0.04	1.77 ± 0.04	5.07 ± 0.29	74.68 ± 4.55

Because of the random nature of the label propagation algorithm, the results of each run slightly differ. The mean and standard derivation over 25 runs were calculated to get more precise results. With the second method, the threshold was used as an upper limit for channel members, i.e. all channels below the threshold are considered for creating the graph. The second method yields more nodes but fewer communities and slightly less similarity than the first. Because of this, the first method was preferred.

TABLE IV
NUMBER OF NODES, EDGES, AND AVERAGE AND STANDARD DEVIATION OF EDGE WEIGHTS OVER DIFFERENT THRESHOLDS.

Threshold	Nodes	Edges	Weight
52	9520	151501	2.94 ± 2.35
200	14906	809012	2.82 ± 2.25
500	17124	1909964	2.65 ± 1.88
1000	17948	3104814	2.53 ± 1.66
1500	18721	5000668	2.34 ± 1.58
None	19682	15194697	2.44 ± 1.62

With a higher threshold, more users are within teams and channels, increasing edge weight between many different users. Because of this, the weight difference of the edges within and outside communities gets smaller, resulting in fewer communities. Table IV shows the number of users, edges, and the average and standard deviation of edge weights over different thresholds. Higher thresholds result in more nodes and edges, but the average weight decreases, as many users are only part of a few channels and teams. With no threshold, the average weight increases due to channels increasing the weight for numerous users. Higher thresholds do not improve community discovery, as the typical size of teams is up to 52, as stated previously. Based on our experiments, the clustering tendency depicted by the modularity value decreased with higher thresholds, with fewer communities found.

V. CONCLUSION AND FUTURE WORK

In conclusion, this research investigates which user information can be extracted from anonymized open data [7]. Information such as user group matching has been the focus of this research. Different clustering algorithms were used for user group detection, without invading user privacy. To achieve this, only communication and interaction user data was used for cluster formation. It was expected to rediscover organizational structure that closely matches the organizational hierarchical structures (organizational Units, Departments, Groups, Sections, etc.). Our research shows that fitting detected clusters to existing organizational structures was not successful and yielded poor results. Matching detected clusters with interest groups, such as Mattermost teams produced satisfactory results. The main reason for this finding is that users interact and communicate with individuals that share their interests (same channels or Mattermost teams). These individuals might not be in the same organizational units, or users from different organizational units might be in the same channel, introducing noise to the data.

Future work might include the usage of novel clustering algorithms that are based on neural networks. Additionally, new metrics for weighting user-to-user connections could be used to identify not only interest groups but also organizational connections between users. Besides these improvements, the data could be brought into connection with external data to identify certain teams, users, or organizational structures and the level of communication between them.

REFERENCES

[1] I. Jakovljevic, A. Wagner, and C. Gütl, "Open search use cases for improving information discovery and information retrieval in large and highly connected organizations," 2020. doi: 10.5281/zenodo.4592449. [Online]. Available: https://doi.org/10.5281/zenodo.4592449.

[2] J. Zhang, Y. Wang, Z. Yuan, and Q. Jin, "Personalized real-time movie recommendation system: Practical prototype and evaluation," *Tsinghua Science and Technology*, vol. 25, pp. 180–191, Apr. 2020. doi: 10.26599/TST.2018.9010118.

[3] G. Navarro-Arribas, V. Torra, A. Erola, and J. Castellà-Roca, "User k-anonymity for privacy preserving data mining of query logs," *Inf. Process. Manag.*, vol. 48, no. 3, pp. 476–487, 2012. doi: 10.1016/j.ipm.2011.01.004. [Online]. Available: https://doi.org/10.1016/j.ipm.2011.01.004.

[4] S. Antony and D. Salian, "Usability of open data datasets," in Oct. 2021, pp. 410–422, isbn: 978-3-030-89021-6. doi: 10.1007/978-3-030-89022-3_32.

[5] K. Naim *et al.*, "Pushing the Boundaries of Open Science at CERN: Submission to the UNESCO Open Science Consultation," Jul. 2020. doi: 10.17181/CERN.1SYT.9RGJ. [Online]. Available: http://cds.cern.ch/record/2723849.

[6] P. Rao, S. Krishna, and A. Kumar, "Privacy preservation techniques in big data analytics: A survey," *Journal of Big Data*, vol. 5, pp. 1–12, Sep. 2018. doi: 10.1186/s40537-018-0141-8.

[7] I. Jakovljevic, C. Gütl, A. Wagner, and A. Nussbaumer, "Compiling open datasets in context of large organizations while protecting user privacy and guaranteeing plausible deniability," *In Proceedings of the 11th International Conference on Data Science, Technology and Applications (DATA 2022)*, pp. 301–311, 2022, issn: 2184-285X. doi: 10.5220/0011265700003269.

[8] S. R. M. Oliveira and O. R. Zaiane, "A privacy-preserving clustering approach toward secure and effective data analysis for business collaboration," *Comput. Secur.*, vol. 26, no. 1, pp. 81–93, Feb. 2007, issn: 0167-4048. doi: 10.1016/j.cose.2006.08.003. [Online]. Available: https://doi.org/10.1016/j.cose.2006.08.003.

[9] I. Jakovljevic, C. Gütl, A. Wagner, M. Pobaschnig, and A. Mönnich, "Cern anonymized mattermost data," version 1, Mar. 2022. doi: 10.5281/zenodo.6319684. [Online]. Available: https://doi.org/10.5281/zenodo.6319684 (visited on 06/27/2022).

[10] F. Menczer, S. Fortunato, and C. A. Davis, *A first course in network science*. Cambridge University Press, 2020, isbn: 9781108471138.

[11] V. Voloshin, *Introduction to graph theory*. 2009, isbn: 9781606923740.

[12] L. Tang and H. Liu, *Community Detection and Mining in Social Media*, 1. Jan. 2010, vol. 2, Publisher: Morgan & Claypool Publishers. doi: 10.2200/S00298ED1V01Y201009DMK003. [Online]. Available: https://www.morganclaypool.com/doi/abs/10.2200/S00298ED1V01Y201009DMK003 (visited on 08/14/2022).

[13] L. Rokach and O. Maimon, "Clustering methods," in Jan. 2005, pp. 321–352. doi: 10.1007/0-387-25465-X_15.

[14] C. Hennig, "An empirical comparison and characterisation of nine popular clustering methods," *Advances in Data Analysis and Classification*, vol. 16, no. 1, pp. 201–229, Mar. 2022, issn: 1862-5355. doi: 10.1007/s11634-021-00478-z. [Online]. Available: https://doi.org/10.1007/s11634-021-00478-z (visited on 06/27/2022).

[15] J. D. Banfield and A. E. Raftery, "Model-based gaussian and non-gaussian clustering," *Biometrics*, vol. 49, no. 3, pp. 803–821, 1993, issn: 0006341X, 15410420. [Online]. Available: http://www.jstor.org/stable/2532201 (visited on 06/27/2022).

[16] P. D. McNicholas, "Model-based clustering," *Journal of Classification*, vol. 33, no. 3, pp. 331–373, Oct. 2016, issn: 1432-1343. doi: 10.1007/s00357-016-9211-9. [Online]. Available: https://doi.org/10.1007/s00357-016-9211-9 (visited on 06/27/2022).

[17] J. Han, M. Kamber, and J. Pei, *Data Mining: Concepts and Techniques*. Morgan Kaufmann Publishers, 2012, isbn: 0123814790. [Online]. Available: http://www.amazon.de/Data-Mining-Concepts-Techniques-Management/dp/0123814790/ref=tmm_hrd_title_0?ie=UTF8&qid=1366039033&sr=1-1.

[18] J. West, A. Salter, W. Vanhaverbeke, and H. Chesbrough, "Open innovation: The next decade," *Research Policy*, vol. 43, no. 5, pp. 805–811, Jun. 2014, issn: 0048-7333. [Online]. Available: https://www.sciencedirect.com/science/article/pii/S0048733314000407.

[19] I. Pramanik *et al.*, "Privacy preserving big data analytics: A critical analysis of state-of-the-art," *Wiley Interdisciplinary Reviews: Data Mining and Knowledge Discovery*, vol. 11, pp. 207–218, Jan. 2021. doi: https://doi.org/10.1002/widm.1387. [Online]. Available: https://wires.onlinelibrary.wiley.com/doi/abs/10.1002/widm.1387 (visited on 08/14/2022).

[20] A. Adai, S. Date, S. Wieland, and E. Marcotte, "Lgl: Creating a map of protein function with an algorithm for visualizing very large biological networks," *Journal of molecular biology*, vol. 340, pp. 179–90, Jul. 2004. doi: 10.1016/j.jmb.2004.04.047.

[21] M. E. J. Newman and M. Girvan, "Finding and evaluating community structure in networks," *Physical Review E*, vol. 69, no. 2, p. 026 113, Feb. 2004, arXiv: cond-mat/0308217, issn: 1539-3755, 1550-2376. doi: 10.1103/PhysRevE.69.026113. [Online]. Available: http://arxiv.org/abs/cond-mat/0308217.

[22] M. Rosvall and C. T. Bergstrom, "Maps of random walks on complex networks reveal community structure," *Proceedings of the National Academy of Sciences*, vol. 105, no. 4, pp. 1118–1123, Jan. 29, 2008, issn: 0027-8424, 1091-6490. doi: 10.1073/pnas.0706851105. arXiv: 0707.0609. [Online]. Available: http://arxiv.org/abs/0707.0609.

[23] A. Rezaei, S. M. Far, and M. Soleymani, "Near linear-time community detection in networks with hardly detectable community structure," ASONAM '15, pp. 65–72, 2015. doi: 10.1145/2808797.2808903. [Online]. Available: https://doi.org/10.1145/2808797.2808903.

[24] M. E. J. Newman, "Modularity and community structure in networks," *Proceedings of the National Academy of Sciences of the United States of America*, vol. 103, no. 23, pp. 8577–8582, Jun. 2006, issn: 0027-8424. doi: 10.1073/pnas.0601602103. [Online]. Available: https://www.ncbi.nlm.nih.gov/pmc/articles/PMC1482622/.

[25] V. Traag, L. Waltman, and N. J. van Eck, "From louvain to leiden: Guaranteeing well-connected communities," *Scientific Reports*, vol. 9, no. 1, pp. 5233–5233, Dec. 2019, arXiv: 1810.08473, issn: 2045-2322. doi: 10.1038/s41598-019-41695-z. [Online]. Available: http://arxiv.org/abs/1810.08473.

[26] V. D. Blondel, J.-L. Guillaume, R. Lambiotte, and E. Lefebvre, "Fast unfolding of communities in large networks," *Journal of Statistical Mechanics: Theory and Experiment*, vol. 2008, no. 10, P10008–P10020, Oct. 2008, arXiv: 0803.0476 version: 2, issn: 1742-5468. doi: 10.1088/1742-5468/2008/10/P10008. [Online]. Available: http://arxiv.org/abs/0803.0476.

[27] P. Pons and M. Latapy, "Computing communities in large networks using random walks," ISCIS'05, pp. 284–293, 2005. doi: 10.1007/11569596_31. [Online]. Available: https://doi.org/10.1007/11569596_31.

[28] J. Reichardt and S. Bornholdt, "Statistical Mechanics of Community Detection," *Physical Review E*, vol. 74, no. 1, p. 016 110, Jul. 2006, arXiv: cond-mat/0603718, issn: 1539-3755, 1550-2376. doi: 10.1103/PhysRevE.74.016110. [Online]. Available: http://arxiv.org/abs/cond-mat/0603718.

Twitter Sentiment Analysis: A Survey in Cricket and Bollywood

Nayantara Kotoky*, Smiti Singhal†, Anushka Sharma‡ and Dhara Ajudia§
*Applied Neurocognitive Systems, Fraunhofer Institute for Industrial Engineering, Germany
†‡§Department of Computer Engineering, Pandit Deendayal Energy University
Gandhinagar, India
Email: *nayantara.kotoky@gmail.com, †smitis2000@gmail.com, ‡anushkas0706@gmail.com, §dhara.ajudia1108@gmail.com

***Abstract*—Twitter has been the voice of the public for a long time now. With the rise in the usage of Twitter, the active participation of its users in expressing their views across all domains has significantly increased. This paper aims to perform sentiment analysis and study the influence of Bollywood and Cricket celebrities on Twitter users. Three different types of information are extracted from the tweets using sentiment analysis, namely, (1) sentiments of people towards cricket, cinema (Bollywood), and gender, (2) identifying the highly discussed individuals and events for each category, and (3) co-occurrence analysis for identifying closely discussed celebrities belonging to different categories. Our analysis identifies that females in the cricket sport are not as popular as compared to their male counterparts whereas females in the entertainment industry (Bollywood) are equally popular as the males. We also identify current trends that are the target of discussion in Twitter using Network of Words analysis. In addition, the co-occurrence analysis shows very high association between Male Cricketers and female Bollywood stars. In essence, we try to determine the emotional tone of people to gain an insight of the hidden attitudes and opinions expressed in a tweet regarding cricket and Bollywood.**

Keywords*—*Twitter; Sentiment analysis; Text mining; Co-occurrence Network.

I. Introduction

Twitter is a micro-blogging site that has become a public forum for anyone who wants their voice to be heard. People post their views in the form of short messages consisting of words, images, or videos, up to 280 words, and these posts are famously known as tweets. The recent numbers suggest that over the years, the Twitter market has seen notable growth in its number of users in all major developing or already developed countries. Hence, big companies and brands try to understand the sentiments of people through the variety of views from a plethora of tweets. These sentiments are studied in order to get meaningful results that help them understand the collective opinion on their services.

Twitter has been widely used for performing sentiment analysis on various topics like politics [1] [10], entertainment [11], etc. A large number of researchers have studied Twitter sentiment analysis on the basis of a number of factors such as polarity, or sentiments like anxiety, anger, etc. Several tools have been created for identifying various sentiments, some of which include Linguistic Inquiry and Word Count (LIWC) [1], TextBlob [8], Valence Aware Dictionary for Sentiment Reasoning (VADER) [5] [10], and Orange [2].

In this paper, we have collected data from Twitter for two categories - Entertainment and Cricket, to perform sentiment analysis and classify them on the basis of the emotions attached to those tweets. The objective of this research is to understand the influence of cricket sport and Bollywood cinema, two very popular sources of entertainment in India, and understand how they can be utilized as media to influence the masses and bring societal changes. Our work analyzes public sentiments associated with individuals in these two groups as well as a collective outlook into cricket and Bollywood. With the insights drawn from several analyses on tweets regarding these topics, we identify a few ways in which people's emotions are impacted.

We have collected a total of 6000 tweets using Tweepy which included 20 hashtags for every category. The collected tweets are tagged as Cricket, Bollywood, male and female depending on the subject of the tweet. Using the tweets, we have identified the sentiments of people regarding the four categories *cricket-male, cricket-female, bollywood-male, bollywood-female* and then recognized the celebrities in Cricket and Bollywood which are two groups that are very influential among the people in India. Furthermore, an in-depth analysis of co-occurrence in the four different categories was performed to determine the association between these categories and to investigate which categories are mentioned together and why.

The main contributions of this research work are:

- Sentiment analysis is performed on the tweets using VADER and Tweet Profiler. The results show that the tweets consisting of the happiest emotion of the people are shown for the category of women actresses and women cricketers.
- KH Coder [16] (named after the developer Koichi Higuchi) is used to carry out performance analysis of the celebrities in the four categories using their corresponding tweets where they are mentioned. The analysis uncovers tweets in support and criticism of certain people showing close correspondence to real-life phenomena.
- Co-occurrence analysis of the four categories of tweets is performed using Jaccard Coefficient. The results show that *bollywood-male* and *bollywood-female* are the two categories that are highly associated with Twitter discussions.

Outline: The paper is structured as follows. Section 2 gives insights into the research done in this domain and the various papers published in this area. Section 3 briefly describes the objective and implementation details and guides through the approach. Next, Section 4 covers in detail the results obtained and the interpretations of the analysis. Section 5 concludes the paper.

II. Related Work

In this section, we mention specific articles which are used for this research purpose. The literature contains twitter analysis performed for understanding people's emotions for various domains and their use. This section also discusses certain tools and their utility in performing sentiment analysis.

A. Predicting Elections with Twitter: What 140 Characters Reveal about Political Sentiment

Tumasjan et al. [1] determine whether Twitter can be used to predict the result of the federal election of the national parliament in Germany. 104300 political tweets were first translated from German to English and the text analysis software "Linguistic Inquiry and Word Count (LIWC)" was used to get the results. In conclusion, the results depicted that Twitter can be undoubtedly regarded as a plausible indicator of political opinion.

B. Content Analysis of Dark Net

Nattuthurai and Aryal [9] used KH Coder to analyze the data from the darknet using Co-occurrence network analysis. The data collected was categorized into business-related and non-business-related data. Multi-Dimensional Scaling and Co-occurrence network analysis were performed on the dataset to uncover a higher frequency of negative words associated with both categories.

C. Analysis of Data Using Data Mining tool Orange

Kukasvadiya et al. [2] discuss the concept of data mining and how the Data Mining tool Orange performs when subjected to any kind of data. The paper provides a practical implementation of Orange. It concludes how Orange is easier than others and can perform a wide range of data analysis using its widgets such as sentiment analysis, visualizing Time series data and plotting heatmaps.

Marcu et al. [12] analyzed data related to educational aspects collected from various high schools using Orange and classified them according to Ekman and Plutchik models of emotions. Tweet Profiler, a feature provided by Orange, classified the data based on these models and both the results were compared to find the best solution for sentiment analysis.

Thange et al. [13] have worked upon a COVID-19 dataset of India and have visually represented the relationships in the dataset using Orange. As a result of their analysis, it has been found that there have been more cases of infection in men compared to women and maximum number of infected patients are in the 30 years age-group.

D. KH Coder: An exploratory analysis of the text mining of news articles about "water and society"

Hori [3] aims to discover social interest in the issues of water and society from media reports and to compare it in Japanese and international media. This research uses the online databases of two newspapers: the Japan News and the International New York Times. The social interest is discovered by cluster analysis, that is, to derive clusters that have value with respect to the problem being addressed. The articles extracted from those databases are analyzed using KH Coder and the generated co-occurrence network.

E. Twitter Sentiment Analysis Using Natural Language Toolkit (NLTK) and VADER

Elbagir et al. [10] aim to compare two powerful sentiment analysis tools - NLTK and VADER on the data collected for the 2016 US presidential elections from the microblogging service Twitter. The analysis concludes how VADER was an effective and better choice for sentiment analysis classification.

III. Proposed Work and Implementation Details

The purpose of the paper is to analyze the tweets and compare the influence, joint mentions, and other different aspects of the text to get meaningful results. The three main experimental analysis are as follows:

1) Classification of sentiments
2) Twitter as a reflection of performance
3) Relative frequency of joint mentions inter-category and intra-category

A. Data Collection

Around 6000 tweets were collected as part of the dataset. The time span considered is January 2021 to November 2021. It is to be noted that the collected tweets span for the specific time frame and for the specific categories of interest, that is, Indian cricket and Bollywood (Indian cinema). The methodology used for data collection is as follows [4]:

- Importing Tweepy - an easy-to-use Python library for accessing the Twitter API
- Authentication for Twitter Developer account
- Defining list of hashtags for every category
- Defining the *date_since* date as a variable
- Filtering retweets
- Output data as .csv file

With the use of Twitter API, recent tweets for most popular persons of all 4 categories were collected and merged together. For instance, #ViratKohli, #RohitSharma for *cricket-male*, #SmritiMandhana, #HarmanpreetKaur for *cricket-female*, #RanbirKapoor, #KartikAaryan for *bollywood-male*, #AliaBhatt, #DeepikaPadukone for *bollywood-female*, to name a few hashtags considered. The distribution of the data for each category can be seen in Figure 2.

In order to verify the actuality of the data collected, document map was used. Document map, a feature in the Orange Tool for text mining, shows geolocation from the textual data (here, tweets). It finds the mentions of countries/capitals (whenever it is present in a tweet) and displays the frequency of occurrence in the world map. Around 125 tweets mentioned the name of a country/capital which is used to create the document map.

In Figure 1, we can see that the number of mentions of India (red) is considerably higher than the other countries and these countries have been accurately displayed because of the 2021 T20 World Cup (T20 is an international cricket world cup tournament which consists of 16 teams competing with each other in a twenty-over cricket match. India was one of the top 12 teams to play in the 2021 T20 world cup and thus was vigorously discussed on Twitter). The participants in the T20 World cup were Namibia, Pakistan, Afghanistan, England, Bangladesh, Australia, etc. which are highlighted on the world map too.

B. Classification of sentiments

The tools we used for sentiment analysis were TextBlob [8], Empath, Pattern, Sentiwordnet and VADER. The most precise results were shown by VADER [5], which accurately categorized the sentiments into positive and negative.

C. Twitter as a reflection of performance

Orange tool [6] was used for the sentiment analysis of tweets based on the seven basic emotions proposed by Ekman [14]: fear, anger, joy, sadness, disgust, appreciation, and surprise.

D. Relative frequency of joint mentions inter-category and intra-category

KH Coder is a text mining tool which is typically used for finding the potential relationships between entities represented within a document [7]. Here, we first load the required file as the data and then pre-process it as a necessity for analysis. The tool is implemented to obtain co-occurrence matrices and networks to get insights into major themes from the text and analyze the associations between the text that appear together.

IV. Results and Interpretations

A. Classification of sentiments

1) Visualizations between categories: Figure 2 shows the amount of positive and negative emotions for all the four categories. From the figure, we observe that:

- The positive sentiments for the almost same amount of tweets are the highest for Female Bollywood Stars.
- The negative sentiments reflected through the tweets are the highest for Male Cricketers.

This suggests that people publicly post their opinion about celebrities and, even though Male Cricketers are the most famous personalities, as we see them more frequently in other social media discussions and advertisements, it does not discourage people from openly sharing negative views about them.

B. Twitter as a reflection of performance

1) Results for Male Cricketers: Figure 3 shows the polarity of sentiments of the tweets for individual Male Cricketers. We observe the following:

Highly Appreciated: MS Dhoni

In light of the 2021 T20 World Cup, people were excited and happy because of Dhoni's presence as the mentor for Team India.

Involved in Negative Discussion: Axar Patel and Krunal Pandya

Board of Control for Cricket in India (BCCI) [15] had announced through their social media handles that Axar Patel would be replaced by Shardul Thakur in the T20 matches. This did not go well with a lot of people and hence people shared their disappointment through Twitter. Negative emotions were shared using Axar Patel as the topic, although the negativity was not necessarily targeted toward him. On the other hand, the negative emotion towards Krunal Pandya is due to his poor performance in the Indian Premier League (IPL) matches that made the Twitterati furious. Here, we see negative emotions being expressed but under two different circumstances, the first one supporting the player and the second one being targeted toward the player.

2) Results for Male Bollywood Stars: Figure 4, visualization for Male Bollywood Stars, shows the following results:

Highly Appreciated : Ranbir Kapoor

Despite any recent project announcements or any other controversies, Ranbir Kapoor still remains the most highly appreciated actor because of his huge fan following.

Involved in Negative Discussion: Nawazuddin Siddiqui

Nawazuddin Siddiqui's statement garnered attention due to its critical comment on racism being a bigger issue in the Bollywood Industry as compared to nepotism. People supported him and highly criticized the Bollywood Industry.

3) Results for Female Celebrities (Cricketers and Bollywood Stars): On a similar pattern, the other 2 categories showed the following results.

As shown in Figure 5, Yastika Bhatia, under Female Cricketers category, received huge appreciation for her brilliant innings in one of the league matches. Also, it can be clearly seen that no female cricketer received harsh criticism.

Among female Bollywood Stars, as per Figure 6, Ananya Pandey being highly active on social media was amongst the favourites while news of Nora Fatehi being involved in money laundering led to unfavourable discussions.

4) Sentiment Analysis using TweetProfiler: Tweet Profiler, a widget provided by orange, retrieves information about the emotions attached to the sentiment by sending data to the server where a model calculates the emotion scores/probabilities according to the text. This is then plotted with the help of a Box Plot. This analysis provides seven different sentiments in comparison to only positive and negative sentiments.

Sentiment Analysis of Female Cricketers using Tweet Profiler is shown in Figure 7. The figure clearly explains that Yastika Bhatia and Priya Punia have the highest percentage

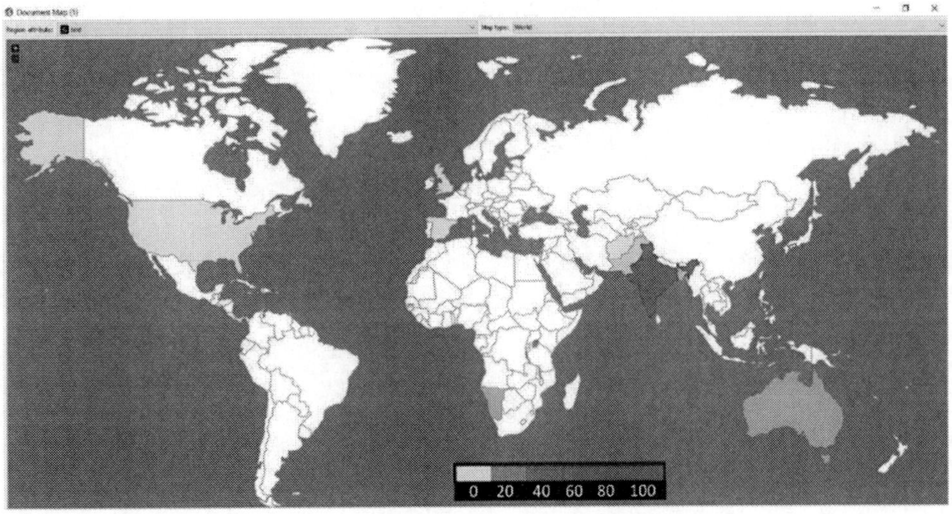

Fig. 1. Document Map for Male Cricketers.

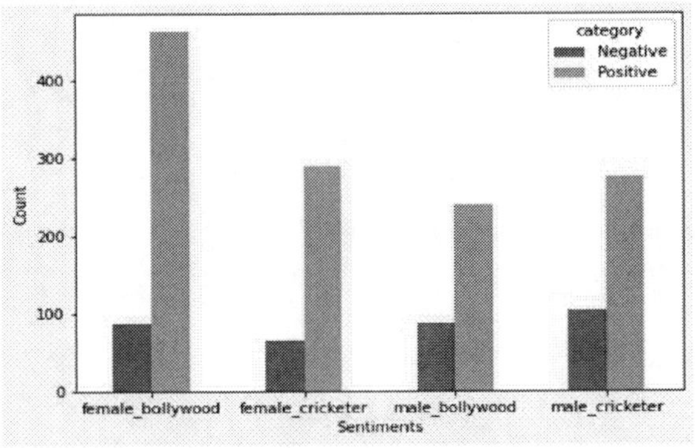

Fig. 2. Visualizations between categories.

of joyful tweets while the tweets mentioning Shikha Pandey depicted highest percentage of surprise emotion.

Yastika Bhatia and Priya Punia are indicated as having the highest positive sentiments using VADER (Result IV-B3, Figure 5) as well as the most joyful emotions using Orange (Figure 7).

C. Relative frequency of joint mentions inter-category and intra-category

This analysis clusters the nodes that have similar occurrence. In this work, it means that nodes which are often mentioned together by people's tweets are clustered, where nodes represent individuals from the four categories. The representation shows the words with similar appearance patterns, that is, with high degrees of co-occurrence, connected by lines. To determine edge strength, Jaccard coefficients are calculated for all possible combinations of target words. It was carried out on a combined document for all categories. Figure 8 shows the network of words showing clusters of closely discussed individuals. From these clusters, we can identify real-life events that led to the discussion. The following are the interpretations for Figure 8:

1) Network of Words:

- Green (03) - Shows the discussions regarding the announcement of the film "Vikram Vedha" starring Hrithik Roshan and Saif Ali Khan.
- Light Orange (12) - This cluster depicts the discussions on the recent film Sooryavanshi, and it can be concluded that through these tweets we can correctly make out the major cast and director of this film.
- Blue (01) - Talks on the T20 World Cup 2021.
- Orange (02) - This cluster comprises the tweets related to KKR Vs DC semi-finals and KKR vs CSK finals having the common factor, KKR in IPL.

2) Network of Codes: This analysis plots a network diagram to explore the association of people of different categories.

Male and Female Cricketers: Figure 9 shows the association between male and Female Cricketers. The network shows how rarely the Female Cricketers are mentioned along with the Male Cricketers. There is a clear separation of categories of Female Cricketers yellow (02) and orange (06) and the link with the Male Cricketers green (01) and blue (05) is extremely weak. Additionally, the size of the circles also shows that the frequency with which the Male Cricketers are discussed with each other within the category is much greater than when they are mentioned with the Female Cricketers. Also, the frequency with which the Female Cricketers are mentioned together within their category is much lower in frequency (which can be deduced by the size of the circle), indicating that Female Cricketers do not receive as much popularity among the Twitter people as Male Cricketers.

Male and Female Bollywood stars: Figure 10 shows the network of codes for the Bollywood fraternity. This analysis shows an intricate connection between the males and the females which brings us to the conclusion that these categories

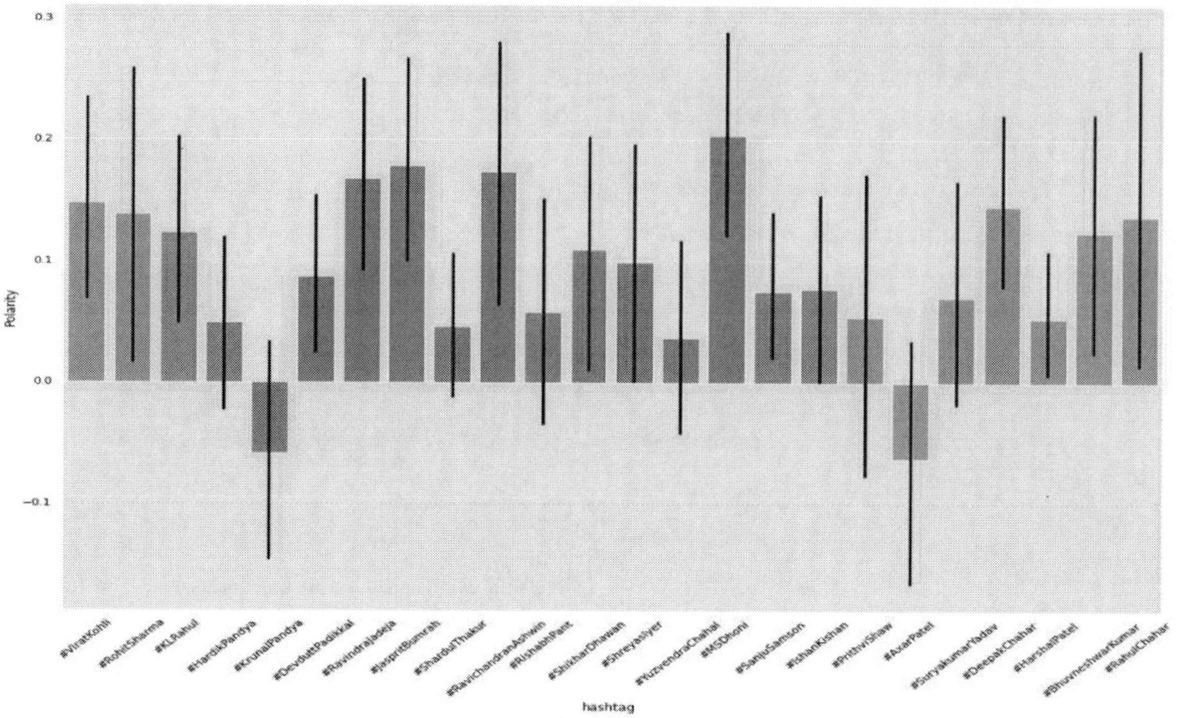

Fig. 3. Visualization of positive and negative sentiments for Male Cricketers using VADER.

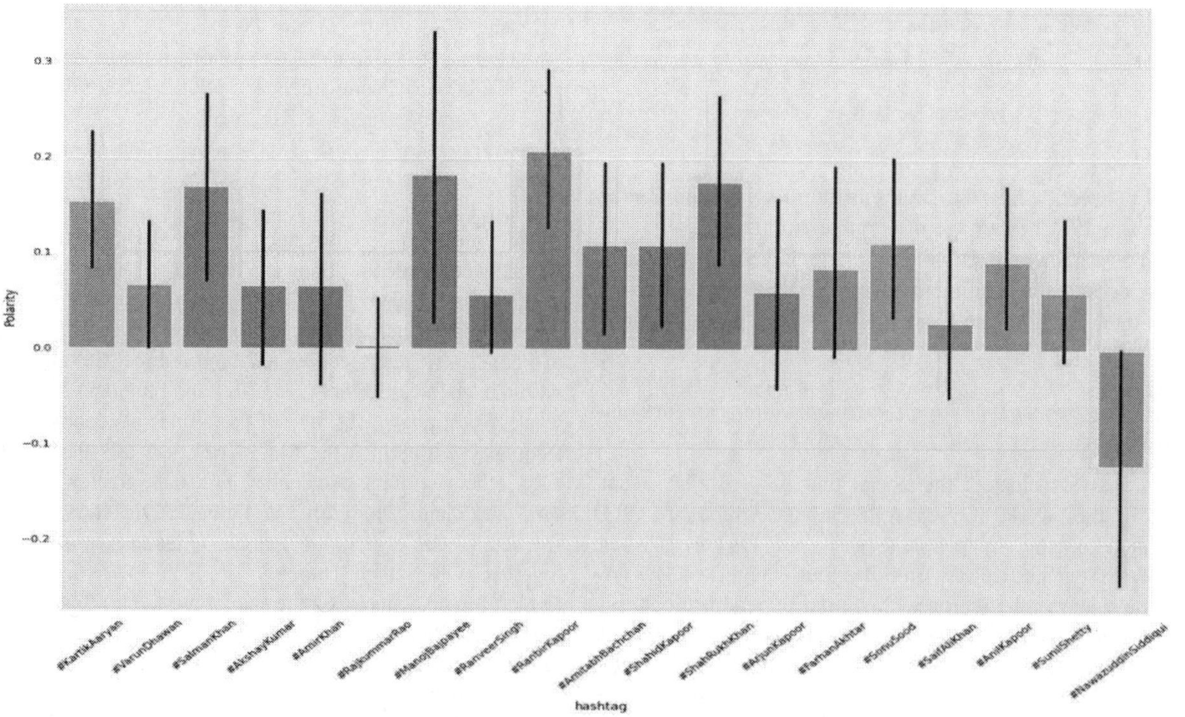

Fig. 4. Visualization of positive and negative sentiments for Male Bollywood stars using VADER.

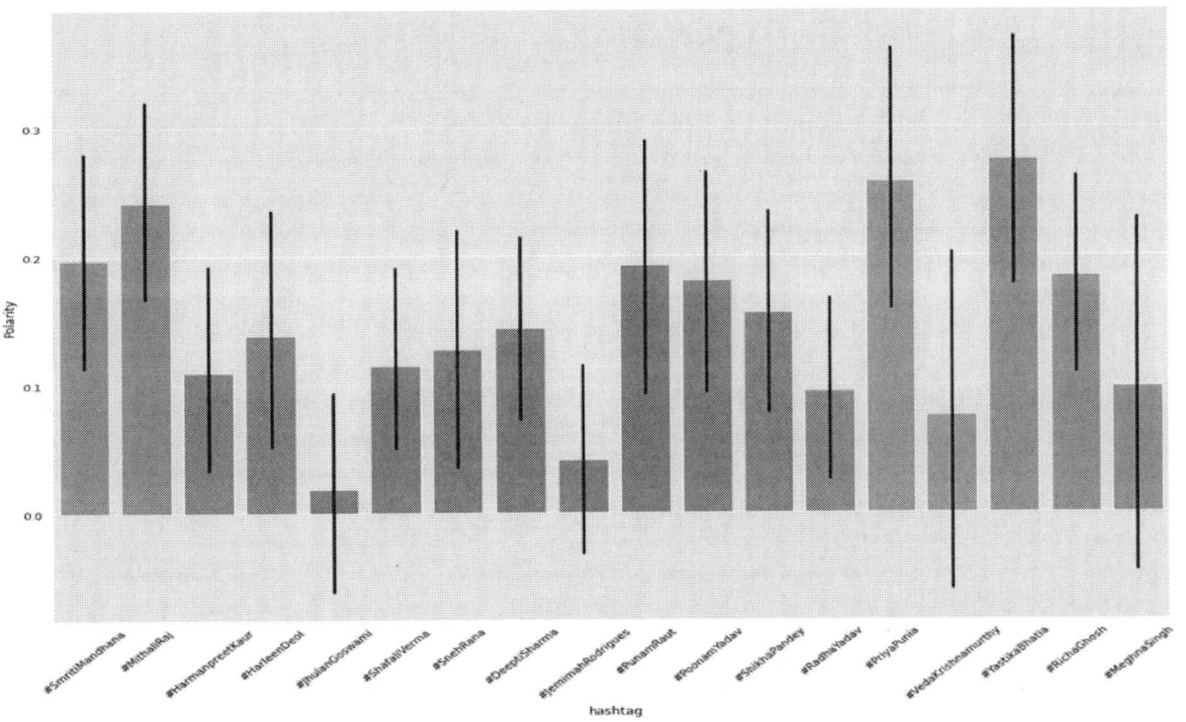

Fig. 5. Visualization of positive and negative sentiments for Female Cricketers using VADER.

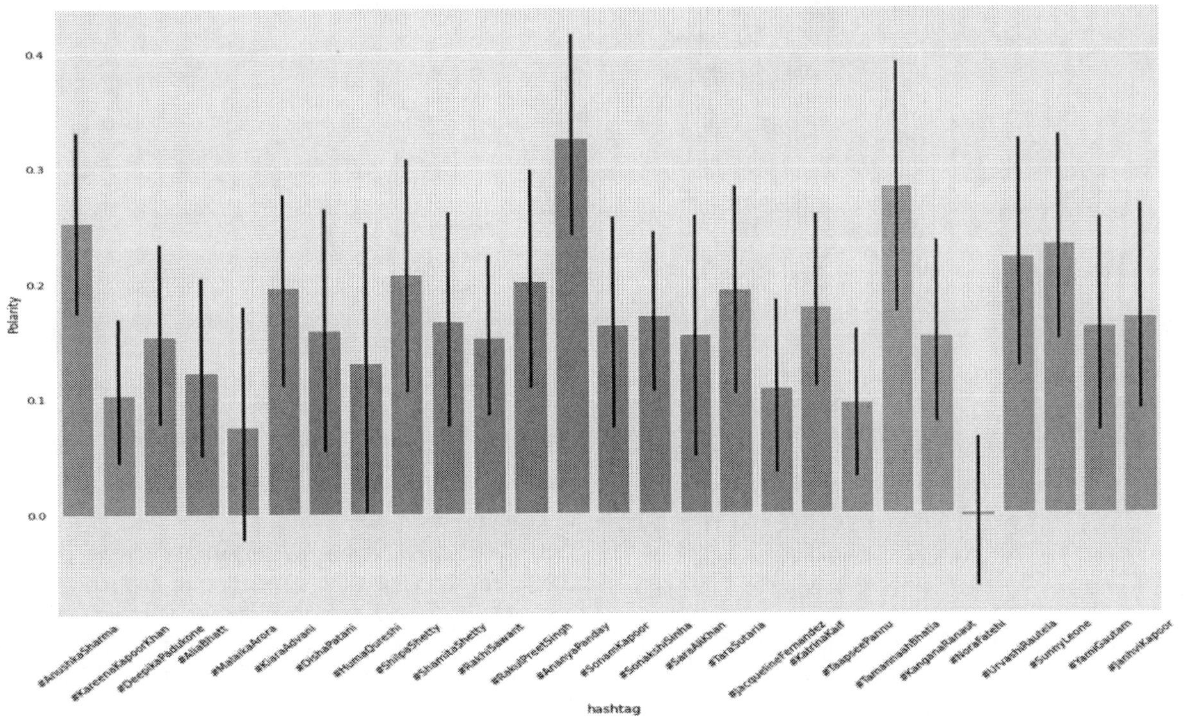

Fig. 6. Visualization of positive and negative sentiments for Female Bollywood Stars using VADER.

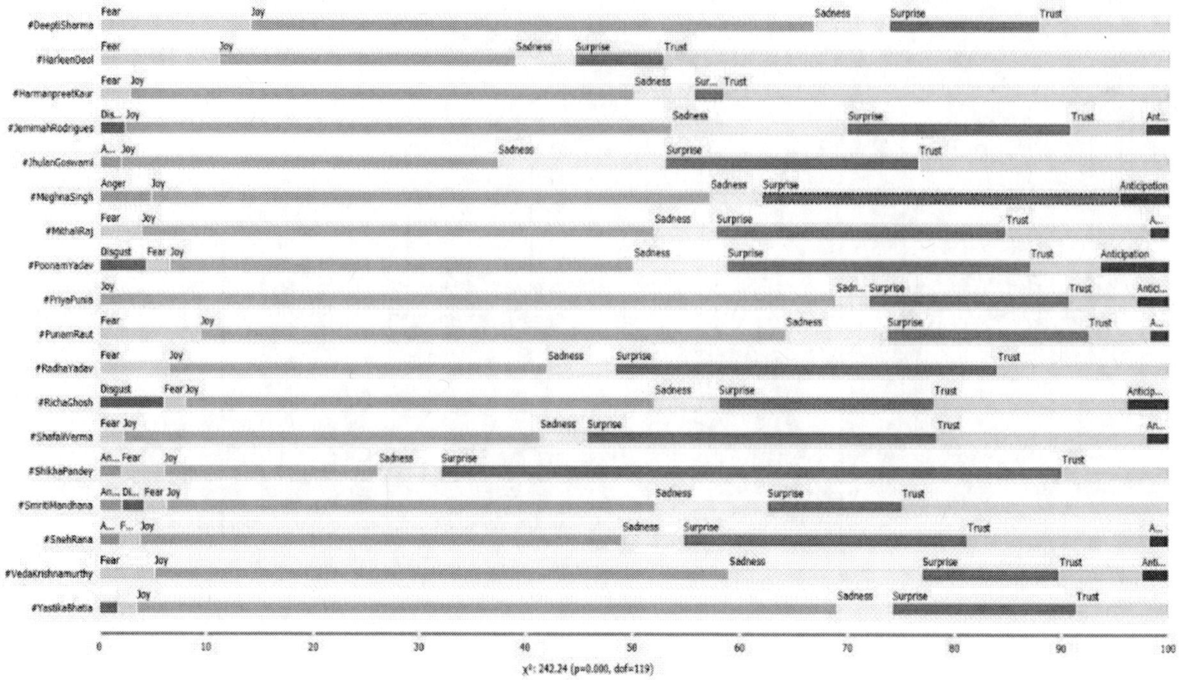

Fig. 7. Sentiment Analysis of Female Cricketers using Tweet Profiler.

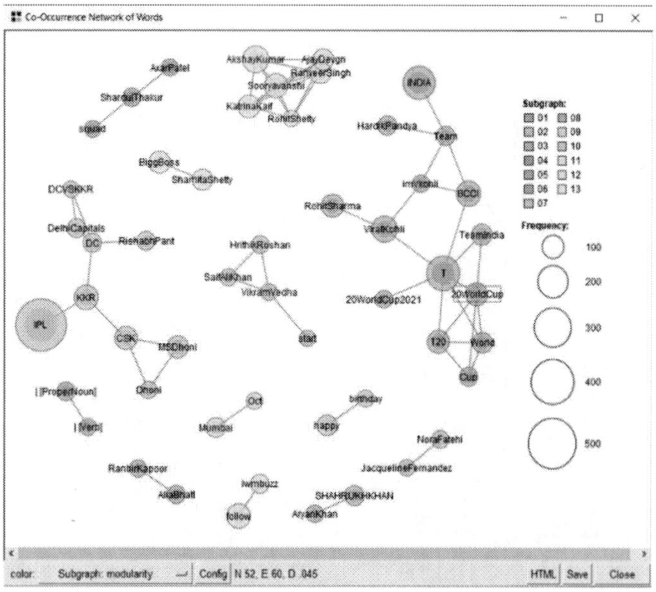

Fig. 8. Network of Words for all categories combined.

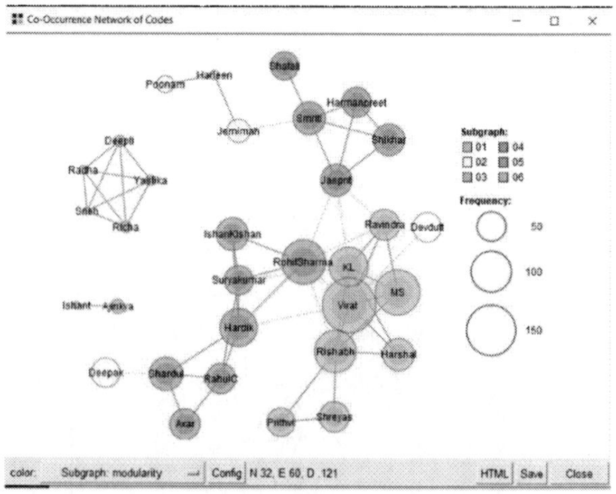

Fig. 9. Network of Codes for Male and Female Cricketers.

are often mentioned together and are not under-shadowed by each other. Unlike the case of the cricket sport, the entertainment industry enjoys similar popularity and discussion among the Twitter people for both males and females. For example, the green cluster (01) consists of the cast of Sooryavanshi, and Ranbir (male) and Alia (female) are mentioned together in many tweets.

3) Co-occurrence Matrix: Figure 11 shows the Jaccard coefficient that shows the association of two individuals with respect to how much they are discussed together in the tweets. In Figure 11, the red circle depicts the Jaccard coefficient for Virat Kohli (male cricketer) and Smriti Mandhana (female cricketer).

The co-efficient is calculated as follows:

$$\frac{|Virat \bigcap Smriti|}{|Virat \bigcup Smriti|} = 0.004$$

(The number of times both were mentioned together divided

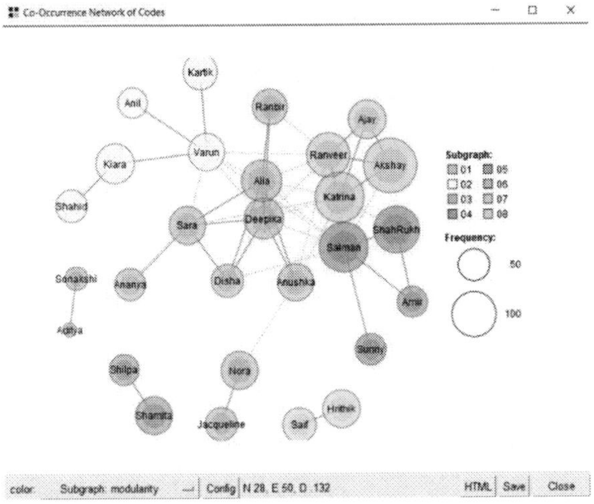

Fig. 10. Network of Codes for Male and Female Bollywood stars.

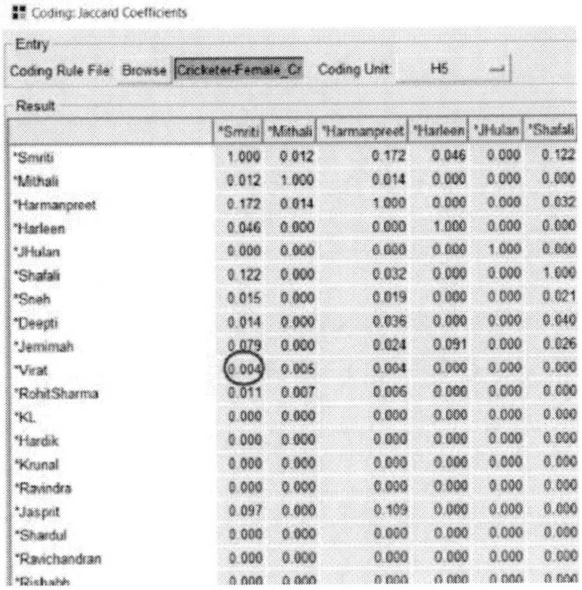

Coding: Jaccard Coefficients

Entry

Coding Rule File: Browse | Cricketer-Female_Cr | Coding Unit: H5

Result

	*Smriti	*Mithali	*Harmanpreet	*Harleen	*JHulan	*Shafali
*Smriti	1.000	0.012	0.172	0.046	0.000	0.122
*Mithali	0.012	1.000	0.014	0.000	0.000	0.000
*Harmanpreet	0.172	0.014	1.000	0.000	0.000	0.032
*Harleen	0.046	0.000	0.000	1.000	0.000	0.000
*JHulan	0.000	0.000	0.000	0.000	1.000	0.000
*Shafali	0.122	0.000	0.032	0.000	0.000	1.000
*Sneh	0.015	0.000	0.019	0.000	0.000	0.021
*Deepti	0.014	0.000	0.036	0.000	0.000	0.040
*Jemimah	0.079	0.000	0.024	0.091	0.000	0.026
*Virat	0.004	0.005	0.004	0.000	0.000	0.000
*RohitSharma	0.011	0.007	0.006	0.000	0.000	0.000
*KL	0.000	0.000	0.000	0.000	0.000	0.000
*Hardik	0.000	0.000	0.000	0.000	0.000	0.000
*Krunal	0.000	0.000	0.000	0.000	0.000	0.000
*Ravindra	0.000	0.000	0.000	0.000	0.000	0.000
*Jasprit	0.097	0.000	0.109	0.000	0.000	0.000
*Shardul	0.000	0.000	0.000	0.000	0.000	0.000
*Ravichandran	0.000	0.000	0.000	0.000	0.000	0.000
*Rishabh	0.000	0.000	0.000	0.000	0.000	0.000

Fig. 11. Co-Occurence Matrix.

by the number of times either of them was mentioned)

We counted the results, which lie between 0 and 1 (exclusive), to get the count of the number of cases where the celebrities were mentioned together for all cases and they were combined to get the final results. The final count for the co-occurrence matrix is shown in Figure 12. We observe:

- While the maximum joint mentions are of Male Cricketers with fellow Male Cricketers (count=233), the joint mentions of Female Cricketers with female actors (1) and male actors (2) are negligible.
- It can be concluded that Female Cricketers, in general, were tweeted much less with other men as well as women compared to Male Cricketers. The popularity of Female Cricketers is less among the Indian Twitter people.

	Actor Female	Actor Male	Cricketer Female	Cricketer Male
Actor Female	163	176	1	17
Actor Male	176	136	2	18
Cricketer Female	1	2	54	15
Cricketer Male	17	18	15	233

Fig. 12. Co-Occurrence Matrix Result.

- It is observed that there are quite a high number of tweets mentioning male and female actors together (count=176). This analysis shows resonance to the real-life phenomenon where movies include both genders (unlike cricket teams), and hence their count of joint mentions is much higher than the other category.

V. Conclusion

In this paper, we present three different analyses on how discussions are held regarding Indian actors and cricketers using Twitter as a platform of expressing opinions. Here, Sentiment Analysis was performed mainly using 3 tools - VADER, Orange, and KH Coder on a dataset of around 6000 tweets, collected with the help of Twitter API Tweepy. With three distinct analysis methods, we have identified several interpretations of how the Twitter people view the four categories, that is, Male Cricketers, Female Cricketers, male actors and female actors.

Interpretations were drawn based on the outputs obtained from the experiments. Some significant observations were the less mention of women cricketers compared to other categories (Section IV-C2) and the noteworthy association between Bollywood (Females and Males) and Cricket (Males) Figure 12. Also, analyzing the most appreciated and criticized celebrities helps the brands publicize their products to customers by connecting with those celebrities for marketing purposes. This eventually helps the brands in making their product famous by attracting customers. Furthermore, we also observed that a well-balanced overview of current affairs can be acquired by looking at the significant amount of tweets in light of the latest happenings. This leads us to believe that Twitter can be seen as a reliable platform to view the actual sentiments of the people given our current analysis and context.

The findings of this study strengthen the fact that Twitter is an effective platform for resonating with the audience. Twitter Sentiment Analysis lets users ascertain the vibe of a conversation and gives leverage to users as they are able to delve deeper into the emotions involved in interactions. Although the analysis is performed at the Indian context, the methodology is generic and can be extended to other countries or world-wide topics. In addition, the analysis techniques can be used for identifying people's emotions on various other topics like war, usage of specific technology, natural phenomenon like climate change, etc.

REFERENCES

[1] A. Tumasjan, T. Sprenger, P. Sandner, and I. Welpe, "Predicting Elections with Twitter: What 140 Characters Reveal about Political Sentiment," The International AAAI Conference on Web and Social Media 16 vol.4, No.1, May 2010, pp. 178-185, doi:10.1609/icwsm.v4i1.14009.

[2] M. Kukasvadiya and N. Divecha, "Analysis of data using data mining tool orange," International Journal of Engineering Development and Research 5.2, June 2017, pp. 1836-1840, ISSN - 2321-9939.

[3] S. Hori, "An exploratory analysis of the text mining of news articles about water and society," WIT Transactions on The Built Environment, 168, 2015, pp. 501-508, doi:10.2495/SD150441.

[4] Automate Getting Twitter Data in Python Using Tweepy and API Access [Online], Available from: https://www.earthdatascience.org/courses/use-data-open-source-python/intro-to-apis/twitter-data-in-python/

[5] A. Beri, "Sentimental Analysis Using Vader, interpretation and classification of emotions". [Online] Available from: Aditya Beri, https://towardsdatascience.com/sentimental-analysis-using-vader-a3415fef7664 [retrieved: November, 2022].

[6] Orange widget catalog, https://orangedatamining.com/widget-catalog/text-mining/twitter-widget/ [retrieved: November, 2022].

[7] KH Coder 3 Reference Manual, Available from: https://khcoder.net/en/manual_en_v3.pdf[retrieved: November, 2022].

[8] Sentiment Analysis using TextBlob. Parthvi Shah. Available From: https://towardsdatascience.com/my-absolute-go-to-for-sentiment-analysis-textblob-3ac3a11d524.

[9] P. Nattuthurai, and A. Aryal, "Content Analysis of Dark Net: Academic Journals from 2010-2017 Using KH Coder," ACET Journal of Computer Education and Research 11, 2018, pp. 25-35.

[10] S. Elbagir and J. Yang, "Twitter sentiment analysis using natural language toolkit and VADER sentiment." Proceedings of the international multiconference of engineers and computer scientists. Vol. 122, 2019, pp. 16.

[11] Y. Yu and X. Wang, "World Cup 2014 in the Twitter World: A big data analysis of sentiments in U.S. sports fans' tweets, Computers in Human Behavior", Volume 48, 2015, pp. 392-400, ISSN 0747-5632, doi:https://doi.org/10.1016/j.chb.2015.01.075.

[12] D. Marcu and M. Danubianu, "Sentiment Analysis from Students' Feedback : A Romanian High School Case Study," 2020 International Conference on Development and Application Systems (DAS), 2020, pp. 204-209, doi:10.1109/DAS49615.2020.9108927.

[13] U. Thange, V. Shukla, R. Punhani and W. Grobbelaar, "Analyzing COVID-19 Dataset through Data Mining Tool Orange," 2021 2nd International Conference on Computation, Automation and Knowledge Management (ICCAKM), 2021, pp. 198-203, doi:10.1109/ICCAKM50778.2021.9357754.

[14] P. Ekman, Basic emotions Handbook of cognition and emotion, 1999, pp. 16.

[15] BCCI Official Website. [Online]. Available from: https://www.bcci.tv/

[16] KH Coder. [Online]. Available from: http://khcoder.net/en/